BLUE COLLAR BAYOU

BLUE COLLAR BAYOU

Louisiana Cajuns in the New Economy of Ethnicity

Jacques M. Henry and
Carl L. Bankston, III

PRAEGER

Westport, Connecticut
London

Library of Congress Cataloging-in-Publication Data

Henry, Jacques M., 1955–
Blue collar Bayou : Louisiana Cajuns in the new economy of ethnicity / Jacques M. Henry and Carl Leon Bankston III.
p. cm.
Includes bibliographical references and index.
ISBN 0–275–97817–6 (alk. paper)
1. Cajuns—Ethnic identity. 2. Cajuns—Economic conditions. 3. Cajuns—Social conditions. 4. Louisiana—Ethnic relations. 5. Louisiana—Economic conditions. 6. Louisiana—Social conditions. 7. Ethnicity—Economic aspects—Louisiana. I. Bankston, Carl L. (Carl Leon), 1952– II. Title.
F380.A2 H46 2002
305.84'10763—dc21 2002021574

British Library Cataloguing in Publication Data is available.

Library of Congress Catalog Card Number: 2002021574
ISBN: 0–275–97817–6

First published in 2002

Praeger Publishers, 88 Post Road West, Westport, CT 06881
An imprint of Greenwood Publishing Group, Inc.
www.praeger.com

Printed in the United States of America

The paper used in this book complies with the Permanent Paper Standard issued by the National Information Standards Organization (Z39.48–1984).

10 9 8 7 6 5 4 3 2 1

Copyright Acknowledgments

The authors and publisher gratefully acknowledge permission for the use of the following material:

From interviews with the persons known as Sue Arceneaux, Blaine Landry, Dwayne Meaux, Robert Prejean, Suzie Quebodeaux, and Sallie Prejean in February and March 2001. Used by permission of the interviewees.

Carl Bankston and Jacques Henry, "Endogamy among Louisiana Cajuns: A Social Class Explanation," *Social Forces* 77(4) (1999): 1317–1338. Used by permission of Forces, University of North Carolina.

Carl Bankston and Jacques Henry, "The Silence of the Gators: Cajun Ethnicity and Intergenerational Transmission of Louisiana French," *Journal of Multilingual and Multicultural Development* 19(1) (1998): 1–23. Used by permission of Multilingual Matters Ltd.

Jacques Henry, "From *Acadien* to *Cajun* to *Cadien*: Ethnic Labelization and Construction of Identity," *Journal of American Ethnic History* 17(4) (Summer 1998): 29–62. Used by permission of the *Journal of American Ethnic History.*

Carl Bankston and Jacques Henry, "Ethnic Self-Identification and Symbolic Stereotyping: The Portrayal of Louisiana Cajuns," *Ethnic and Racial Studies* 24(6) (2001): 1020–1045. Used by permission of Taylor & Francis Ltd, http://www.tandf.co.uk.

Copyright 1999 From "Louisiana Cajun Ethnicity: Symbolic or Structural?" by Jacques Henry and Carl Bankston. Reproduced by permission of Taylor & Francis, Inc., http://www.routledge-ny.com.

Copyright 2000 From "Spectacles of Ethnicity: Festivals and the Commodification of Ethnic Culture Among Louisiana Cajuns" by Jacques Henry and Carl Bankston. Reproduced by permission of Taylor & Francis, Inc., http://www.routledge-ny.com.

BLUE COLLAR BAYOU

Contents

Illustrations

TABLES

FIGURES

Acknowledgments

The result of a twenty-plus-year endeavor, this book owes its existence to the cooperation of more people than can be acknowledged here, especially the innumerable Cajuns, Creoles, and other Louisiana residents and visitors whose paths we have crossed. Be they thanked here for their willing or anonymous assistance, insights, and hospitality. For their direct and invaluable contributions, we particularly want to thank Barry Ancelet, Rita Babineaux, David Barry, John Bertrand, Randy Broussard, Vickie Cappel, Wayne Comeaux, Christine Crittenden, James Domengeaux (in memoriam), Michael Doucet, Ken Douet, Tara Duhon, Lelia and Francis Dupre, Carolyn Dural, James Fontenot, Jules Guidry, Richard Guidry, Shane Guilbeau, Philippe Gustin, Bruno Haroche, Claire Hernandez, Amanda Lafleur, A. J. Leblanc, France Lemay, David Marcantel, Paul Martin, C. Eddie Palmer, Lois Petitjean, Sadie and Rodney Quibodeaux, Marc Savoy, Floyd Sonnier (in memoriam), Adam Steg, and the Sullivan brothers. Finally, I (Henry) would not have been able to work without the unwavering support of my parents and my wife. I (Bankston) add my thanks to my wife and other members of my family. Merci, y'all.

Introduction: The Paradox of Cajun Ethnicity

Imagine a solitary house with a bayou running beside it on the right. The house is wood, with a high peaked roof that has brick chimneys protruding from each side. A square porch, a covered platform with four vertical wood planks for columns, extends from the front of the house. A dirt path, shaded by an oak tree draped with moss, leads away from the porch. A mustachioed man in a broad-brimmed hat stands by the path. He holds the reins of a mule harnessed to a small buggy, and his posture and expression are those of one calmly posing for a portrait.[1]

Imagine another house in the suburbs of a small town. This one is a box-shaped, one-story brick house, with a low ceiling for efficient cooling by central air-conditioning. It is not an expensive home, but it is well kept and the lawn is well trimmed. In the driveway, there is a polished, recent-model Chevrolet pickup truck and a Hyundai automobile. An aluminum flat-bottom boat rests beside the vehicles by a hedge that separates the yard surrounding this house from the neighbor's yard. Behind the home, just outside a sliding glass door, a wife, a husband, and two teen-aged children sit in lawn chairs peeling and eating crawfish, dropping the shells onto old newspapers. Inside, in the living room on the wall above a couch facing a color television, hangs a framed drawing of a mustachioed man with a mule buggy standing in front of a solitary wooden house beside a bayou.

When people think of Louisiana, the word "Cajun" almost always comes to mind. In the state, the term is well known to farmers in the rice country, to deckhands on oil platforms in the Gulf of Mexico, to salesclerks in Lafayette or Lake Charles, to administrators in the state capital in Baton

Rouge, and to tourists landing at New Orleans' Louis Armstrong airport. In the privacy of their homes, Louisianians refer to some people as Cajuns and they hear about Cajuns from the radio and television. They see the word written on billboards, in newspaper articles, on the labels of commercial products, and on Web sites. Even outside of Louisiana, throughout the United States, people are likely to have come across something described as Cajun if they are interested in American folk music, colorful politicians, or spicy foods.

The longtime Louisiana resident, the occasional visitor, and the armchair traveler may well share similar understandings of what the word "Cajun" means. Many of these understandings have some basis in fact. There is a particular group of people known to themselves and to others as Cajuns. There are products, notably foods, that are seen as Cajun. There is a region within the state of Louisiana called Cajun country. There is, arguably, a Cajun way of life, although this may be harder to define than the region.

The term "Cajun," in the present day, carries mostly positive connotations. Those who claim the Cajun label, and many who do not, connect the word with sentimental, aesthetic, and even moral values. The difference that the term suggests—Cajunness as a discrete quality not shared by everybody or everything—is a plus. Being Cajun has not always been a virtue, though, and even today, for some people and in certain situations, "Cajun" remains a bad word and a condition to be avoided. But overwhelmingly, the contemporary Cajun's image is a positive one in Louisiana and elsewhere.

But what exactly does the term mean today? What makes someone a Cajun? The label refers to a combination of Acadian heritage, residence in Southwestern Louisiana, and a general sense of difference from neighboring groups such as white Anglos, Hispanics, African Americans, and Native Americans. Acadia, once a province in Colonial Canada on the Atlantic shore between Maine and Newfoundland, no longer exists outside of historical memory. The Acadian peninsula is now occupied by the Canadian provinces of New Brunswick, Nova Scotia, and Prince Edward Island. The presence of Acadian descendants in the subtropical climate of Louisiana is due to the deportation of approximately 8,000 French-speaking Catholic Acadian settlers by the British administration in 1755. After an exile that lasted up to thirty years for some refugees, a contingent of 3,000 Acadians eventually made their way to Louisiana and opted to settle there with the assistance of the French and Spanish colonial administrations.

In French, the exile was called *le grand dérangement*, which can be translated as "the great displacement" or "the great disturbance," since it was and remains both a displacement and a disturbance. We do not intend to retell here the dramatic history of the Acadians, the topic of celebrated works by historians and poets from Henry Wadsworth Longfellow's *Evangeline* to Antonine Maillet's *Pélagie la Charrette*. We are interested in the Louisiana experience of those who see themselves as descendants of the Acadian ref-

Figure I.1
Percentages of the White Population in Louisiana Parishes Claiming Acadian Ancestry, 1990

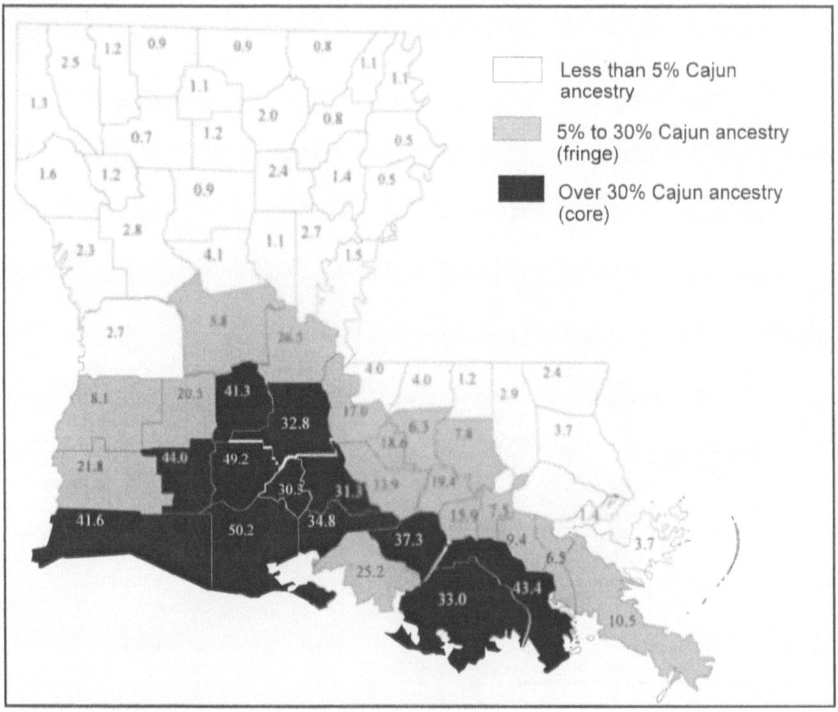

Source: U.S. Bureau of the Census, *1990 Census of Population. General Population Characteristics* (Washington, DC: Bureau of the Census, 1992).

ugees. Instead of investigating how they got to Louisiana, we want to look at what has become of the group since its settlement and at what continues to make it a distinctive group of people in the eyes of its members and in the eyes of others. In doing so, we also want to consider the broader issue of what constitutes "ethnicity," an issue of central importance for the social sciences.

Nowhere are the signs of an enduring Cajun identity more apparent than in Southwestern Louisiana, in an area composed of twenty-two parishes (the equivalent of counties in other states) that was informally (1964) then officially (1971) labeled "Acadiana," a combination of Acadia and Louisiana (see Figures I.1 and I.2). This is where most of the self-defined Cajuns can be found: in 1990, of the 668,000 Americans who claimed Cajun ancestry, more than 432,000 (65%) were Louisianians and 88% of the Cajuns in Louisiana were living in Acadiana. Road signs let drivers know when they are entering Cajun Country or the Cajun Heartland. Local media outlets report

Figure I.2
Percentages of French-Speakers in Louisiana Parishes, 1990

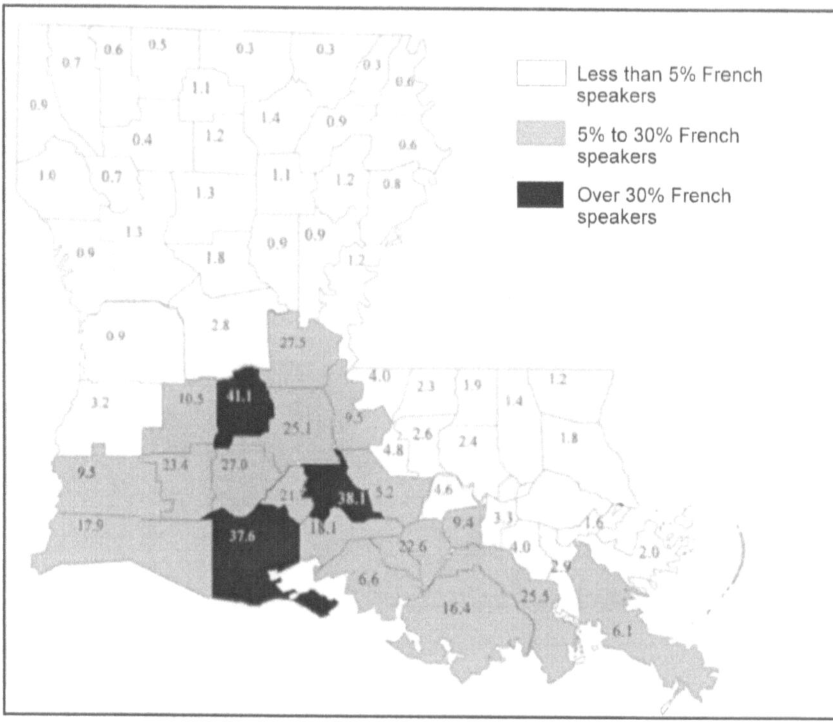

Source: U.S. Bureau of the Census, *1990 Census of Population. General Population Characteristics* (Washington, DC: Bureau of the Census, 1992).

on, celebrate, and advertise endeavors related to Cajun ethnicity on a daily basis and have been doing so for the past thirty years. Media recognition of the ethnic identity takes the form of a newspaper column titled "*Savez-vous?*" (Do you know?) that collects tidbits of local lore; of an early morning television show titled "*Passe-Partout*" that offers news and weather in Cajun French; of local humorists taking advantage of an exaggerated Cajun accent to advertise cars, banks, or spices. Businesses from the Texas border to the French Quarter capitalize on the Cajun label to sell lawn mowers, computers, police supplies, motorcycles, real estate, and, of course, a wide array of food items.

French, spoken as a native language, can still be heard in Acadiana. Languages other than English are a staple of American culture, but French is rarely one of them. One can hear Spanish spoken in many places in the United States. Asian languages are now common in California, New York, and other sites of settlement of new immigrants. Still, Southwestern Louisiana is about the only locale in the United States where you are likely to hear people speaking French at the grocery store, the post office, the racetrack, or in people's homes.

Conversations with longtime residents of Acadiana in English are also likely to include Cajunisms. French words and phrases continually slip into English speech. Local colloquialisms dance through the language (to "pass by" somebody's house means "to stop and visit," motorists "get down" from a car). A distinctive accent can be detected in the nasalization of vowels and in the occasional shifting of the "th" sound to "d." Responses to inquiries about the local culture will certainly include remarks about a past when shame and segregation were rampant, mentions of an ongoing movement promoting Louisiana's French heritage and Cajun culture, and vague but adamant assertions that there is a "Cajun way."

The impression of a flourishing Cajun culture can be misleading, though. Both immediate appearances and careful examinations of the objective basis of the Cajun experience reveal some degree of superficiality in ethnic claims. For example, the city of Lafayette, the biggest regional urban center and self-proclaimed Cajun capital, is notable mostly for its Americanness, its renovated downtown district, and its recent and unplanned suburban sprawl. Lafayette's proliferation of shopping outlets and billboards makes it resemble other midsize American urban areas more than an ethnic enclave. The residential blocks of this regional retail center show little "Cajunness."

If a sense of Cajun ethnicity is to be found, it is in the countryside surrounding Lafayette, where the lingering influence of the past (or its careful reconstruction) conveys a touch of cultural distinction and exoticism. Small towns such as Saint Martinville or Abbeville remain huddled around central squares where balconied bourgeois houses circle the Catholic church and city hall. In these small towns, though, boarded windows, disjointed sidewalks, and the absence of pedestrian traffic undermine the impression of idyllic, thriving traditional communities. Casual contacts with residents reveal the depth of their integration into mainstream American culture. French phrases give way to English. Local politics, family affairs, and syndicated television talk shows are the common topics of conversation. Parents' claims of ethnic pride seem strangely inconsistent with the bits and pieces of cultural heritage that they pass on to their children. Cajun parents, like other parents, frequently seem more concerned with improving their children's chances for upward mobility in American society than with preserving a unique subculture. Observation of social life suggests that the elderly are the most culturally aware and endowed. Although it is easy to find a French-speaking grandmother, Francophone teenagers are rare individuals.

Beyond superficial appearances or anecdotal evidence, data on one of the strongest indicators of ethnic vitality among Cajuns, use of French, suggest a weakening of Cajunism. According to the 1990 census, 261,678 Louisianians (6.7% of the population 5 years old and over) declared that they spoke

French at home. That is 30,000 fewer people than in 1980 and far fewer than the 572,264 people who listed French as their mother tongue in 1970. The steep statistical decline of the French-speaking population is because of the fact that French speakers are aging and are not being replaced by young ones: Whereas 72% of Cajuns 50 years of age and over in Southwestern Louisiana speak French, only 8% of those under 30 years of age do. We are thus faced with a puzzling situation. Claims of ethnicity are widespread and increasing, but objective ethnic characteristics seem to be declining. We must, then, address the central and paradoxical question: How can a people and a culture continue to claim a distinctive existence when there are fewer objective reasons to do so? In other words, how does Cajun ethnicity endure when its ancestral roots are becoming more distant and its core cultural components are apparently waning?

THEORIES OF ETHNICITY: WHAT IT MEANS TO BE AN ETHNIC IN CONTEMPORARY AMERICA

Today's Cajuns are not alone in their celebration of ethnic identity. Indeed, the celebration of cultural particularism within nation-states appears to have been a major characteristic of the second part of the twentieth century. Often expressed violently, claims of ethnicity have been instrumental in nation-building, as seen in the partition of India and the creation of Israel in the years following World War II, and lately in the establishment of independent republics following the disintegration of the Soviet Union. They have also torn societies apart as present-day intergroup conflicts in equatorial Africa, the Balkans, and Melanesia illustrate. These recent internal dissensions join long-standing struggles by the Irish, the Kurds, and the Basques. In fact, most major armed conflicts can plausibly be characterized as having some ethnic dimension, although the strong association between violence and ethnicity does not preclude peaceful arrangements.[2] In Europe and North America, indigenous and immigrant populations have achieved various levels of political recognition, territorial entitlements, and cultural autonomy within larger states and without generalized violence. Canadian Inuits, Australian Aborigines, Bretons in France, Saami in Finland, and Catalans in Spain are cases in point. Intense and vibrant ethnic identification movements in the United States have provoked little open conflict in recent years.

Yet, even when expressed nonviolently, ethnicity is problematic because it is a complex and confusing concept, and it plays a paradoxical role in social reality. The paradox of Cajun ethnicity, in our view, is part of a wider paradox of ethnicity in American society. Subjective identification with ancestral groups that have historically been culturally distinctive minorities is flourishing. At the same time, the cultural practices that define these groups in the eyes of both members and nonmembers seem to be steadily disappearing. How did this happen? Why is there so much attachment to Cajun ethnicity and to other American ethnicities when ethnic traits seem to be declining? In a serious article with a humorous title, researchers at the University of California in Berkeley wondered how "4.5 million Irish immigrants became 40 million Irish Americans." They estimated that demographic processes alone such as marriage, fertility, and mortality trends could not substantiate current figures on ethnic claims. Whereas there were more Irish and Germans than objectively possible, identification with the British and Italian seemed to be deficient. They concluded that individual preference, a subjective component, was obviously at play. Joane Nagel has analyzed the same phenomenon among Native Americans. According to Nagel, the number of Americans reporting American Indian as their race more than tripled from 1960 to 1990. Their numbers jumped from 523,000 to 1,878,000, she maintains, as a result of an increase in claims, not as a result of a natural increase in the Native American population.[3] We hope that our sociological and anthropological examination of contemporary Louisiana Cajuns can not only help us understand this fascinating corner of the American social landscape, but also provide some insight into the role and nature of ethnicity in the modern world.

Ethnicity is such a commonly accepted part of our society that we often take it for granted. It is actually a complicated social arrangement that deserves careful scientific attention. One begins to do social science when one looks at social groups, relations, and practices as problems to be solved and as questions to be answered. The social scientist needs to apply critical judgment to the instruments used in examination, and to the concepts, methods, data, and theories involved.

A cursory examination of the development of the idea of ethnicity in Western thought uncovers a surprisingly brief history. Admittedly, the root adjective "ethnic" is old: it has been recorded in the English language as early as 1470 and 1541 in French. In the following centuries, along with versions in German, Spanish, and Italian, various derivatives appear:"ethnicism" in 1613, "ethnographie" in 1819, "ethnographer" in 1854, "ethnocentrism" in 1908. Still, it was only in 1922 that Max Weber inaugurated a sociological treatment of "ethnic groups" and in 1941 that W. Lloyd Warner and his colleagues at Columbia University introduced "ethnicity" as a significant characteristic to be considered alongside "age, sex and religion."[4] By the 1970s, the Civil Rights Movement, the Native American Movement, and other cultural claims that flourished in American society brought about a flowering of "ethnic"-based concepts among social scientists. It quickly became apparent that the "ethnic" field needed some formalization if these concepts were to be useful in explaining what was going on between all these different social groups.[5] Ethnic phenomena have now been studied worldwide by all branches of behavioral sciences, including sociobiologists, psychologists, archeologists, and political scientists. Theories of ethnicity have been advanced, modified, and refuted, leaving the conceptual field very much fragmented. The concept of ethnicity itself has been probed to the point that its usefulness and validity as a scientific tool have been doubted, especially by European scholars, on the basis that it is opaque and ethnocentrist, a modern version of the discarded concept of race.[6]

The term "ethnic" can be confusing because it involves dimensions of ancestry, religion, race, language, geography, economic interests, and political power. Ethnicity elicits strong emotions of attachment and hate. It is a component of individual and collective identities. We can start to think about ethnicity by asking the question: What is an ethnic group? The Greek word εθνος, from which we derive our words "ethnic" and "ethnicity," is often translated as "nation" in the older and etymological sense, a set of people who share a common peoplehood by virtue of birth and ancestry. Claims of descent, from Aeneas or African captives or the Acadian exiles, give ethnicity much of its emotional force and sacred character. A number of anthropologists and other social scientists have therefore emphasized the "primordial" character of ethnicity.[7] The need for belonging causes individuals to identify strongly with the particular groups into which they are born and with the cultural expressions of those groups. Typical of this approach is the view of ethnicity as a form of extended kinship.[8] Co-ethnics are viewed as relatives with the social obligations and the sentiments such a conception entails.

Although beliefs in a shared heritage do seem to be a fundamental characteristic of ethnic groups, however, the objective reality of a heritage passed from generation to generation is open to question. In short, the association between culture and ethnicity is problematic. Claims of ethnic tradition can often be traced to actual historical events, but these are generally matters of people in the present interpreting history, and interpretation is of necessity selective. The past is a ground that can be mined for many different metals. Because ethnicity is a matter of interpreting and reinterpreting a putatively primordial collective past, the nature of ethnicity changes and specific ethnicities change in character as the social influences on interpretations change. New ethnic groups come into existence, a process referred to as "ethnogenesis." Some ethnic groups assimilate. They disappear or merge with others. Ethnic identities may wax and wane in popular appeal, so that some periods may be times of ethnic renaissance or ethnic revival.[9] Ethnicity is no longer seen by most social scientists as something that people and groups are born with, or into, a culture. The "social construction" of ethnicity is now widely accepted among theorists.[10] Social constructionist theories maintain that ethnic groups are not products of the order of nature but are ways that people understand their own places and the places of others in the world.

Anthropologist Fredrick Barth was a pioneer of the constructionist perspective. He proposed that what people produced, wore, or spoke, or how they married or organized power were not the principal criteria that distinguished them from their neighbors. He dismissed such "cultural stuff" as insufficient for defining ethnic groups because groups of people are not discrete or stable "culture-bearing units." Cultural traits are borrowed, created, transformed, or shared by people as they interact with others and move between groups. Barth convincingly argued that ethnicity is chiefly defined by the conceptual "boundary" that marks the difference between "us" and "them," the idea, not the reality, that "they" are different from "us."[11] Ethnicity was to be viewed as a process of interaction rather than as a state of being. Barth's insight allowed for a dynamic and conceptual approach of ethnicity by integrating the other major sense of "ethnic" as "different" and expanding the understanding of ethnic relations.

The other major etymological sense of εθνος is that of "gentile," "heathen," a meaning that expanded to include all the groups and people that are not like "us," those who are different by religion, race, language, the "others."[12] Thus ethnicity defines others, as well as the self. From this perspective, to be ethnic is to be different from some standard. Much of the literature on ethnicity in American society concerns itself with immigrant ethnic groups, that is, with groups that owe their distinctiveness to migration into an Anglo-dominated society. Yet many ancestral groups in the United States are not generally seen as "ethnic groups." Americans of English ancestry frequently maintain that they have no ethnicity. Languages and cultures of politically and economically dominant groups and areas became identified with the nation itself, and those who participated in these languages and cultures developed myths of common heritage and descent. Other languages and cultures could continue to exist, but they would be identified with people who became "ethnic minorities." Nevertheless, being "ethnic" meant being part of a group that defined itself and was defined by others by contrast to a central national community. As Conzen and Gerber have observed, "in the second quarter of the nineteenth century, Americans themselves were engaged in a self-conscious project of inventing a national identity, and in the process found themselves also inventing the category of ethnicity—'nationality' was the term they actually used—to account for the culturally distinctive groups in their midst. These two inventions were closely intertwined with one another and indeed with the invention of particular immigrant ethnicities in ways that historians have only recently begun to uncover."[13]

The realization that ethnicity was a phenomenon more complex than the simple sum of objective cultural traits has greatly complicated the understanding of the processes at play when different ethnic groups are in contact. Ethnic relations vary from peaceful coexistence to extermination, and world history provides ample examples of all types in between. These relations can also change, quite drastically and suddenly, for the best or the worst as European Jews, Japanese Americans, African Americans, and refugees around the world can attest. The challenge for social scientists is to integrate all this variety and change into a coherent model. Because it has brought together so many different groups of people, American society offers a unique setting for the study of ethnic relations, a topic that has been dominated by American scholarship over the past century.

Assimilationist theory remains influential in explaining how interethnic relations work and change. Building on the work by Robert E. Park and his colleagues at the University of Chicago in the 1920s on the integration of immigrant groups to American society, assimilationist views of ethnicity, expressed most notably in the work of Milton Gordon, tend to look at ethnicity as a matter of contact of cultures. When Eastern Europeans or Italians or Irish arrived in the United States, they came from different cultural heritages and had social relations with each other, rather than with other Americans. As members of the immigrant groups increased their contact with other Americans, their cultures became more similar to the dominant culture (cultural assimilation), and they formed social ties with people who were not Eastern European or Italian or Irish (structural assimilation). Typically, as immigrants and their children learned English and shed their ancestral ways and values, they were able to gain better employment and marry out of their group. Gordon expected that as objective ethnic traits declined, subjective ethnic traits (such as ethnic self-definition) would dissipate. This scientific account of the "melting pot" also applied to those who trace their ancestral presence in North America back to the days before European, English-speaking Americans attempted to establish squatting rights. Gordon maintained that nonimmigrant groups, such as African Americans and Native Americans, who had assimilated culturally but not structurally, were exceptions to be explained by special barriers, such as racial prejudice and discrimination.[14] Although Gordon recognized the theoretical possibility of cultural pluralism, he believed that assimilation to the social structures and cultural forms of the dominant society was much more likely.

It seems fairly evident that there has been a good deal of assimilation in American life and that it remains an ongoing process. If we consider language as an indicator of cultural adaptation, studies of the most recent Hispanic and Asian immigrants show a second-generation shift toward English. The ultimate form of structural assimilation, marriage out of the ethnic group, has become common in American society. Analyses of nationwide samples of ethnic groups have consistently shown that the majority of ethnic minority marriages are exogamous with rates of in-marriage among the major ethnic groups typically varying from 15% for spouses declaring multiple ancestries to a range of 30 to 40% for spouses of unmixed ancestry. The majority of Japanese American marriages are to non-Japanese, and out-marriages of other Asians increase steadily with each generation in the United States. This apparent trend toward assimilation has led a number of influential observers to maintain that minority ethnicity in the United States is declining.[15]

Although objective ethnic traits do seem to be in decline, even among the Hispanic and Asian groups who have arrived in the post-1965 immigration wave, it might be difficult to conclude that ethnic identification is disappearing. As early as 1938, Marcus Lee Hansen had warned about the "problem of the third generation immigrants" and the "almost universal phenomenon that what the son wishes to forget the grandson wishes to remember." Indeed, by the 1970s, scholars noted that even third- and fourth-generation descendants of many groups continued to identify strongly with their ancestries and that this identification had become a basis of political mobilization. Others noted an "ethnic resurgence" as Native Americans, African Americans, Italian Americans, Irish Americans, and other "hyphenated Americans" seemed to be eagerly embracing the identities of their putative forebears. Theorists of ethnicity in American life, then, have to struggle with the same paradox we have identified in the situation of the Louisiana Cajuns. Contrary to the expectations of assimilationist theory, cultural and structural assimilation had been accompanied by intensifying, not declining, subjective identifications. Instead of ethnics becoming Americans, it seemed that all Americans were becoming ethnics, including many who could be seen as "Wasps," or White Anglo-Saxon Protestants.[16]

Social theorists have struggled to account for these interpretations of social existence apparently becoming detached from the objective bases of cultural practices and social relations. Assimilation obviously works in some ways, since immigrants do become Americans, but many Americans still see themselves as something other than simply American. Scholars often point out that ethnicity is socially constructed and contextual, not a product of culture. Nevertheless, ethnicity is expressed by ethnics and nonethnics alike in cultural terms such as historical heritage, language, and religion, and these perceived differences serve as the basis for the organization of relationships between groups. There is a sense that ethnic matters are both cultural and political, although theories differ on the relative importance of culture and politics in shaping ethnicity. The discussion of two contrasting positions on ethnicity in American society can illustrate the debate.

The concept of "symbolic ethnicity" proposed by Herbert Gans is a plausible response to the growing claims of ethnicity in the face of fading ethnic traits. Gans describes this kind of ethnicity as "a nostalgic allegiance to the culture of the immigrant generation, or that of the old country; a love for and pride in a tradition that can be felt without having to be incorporated in everyday behavior".[17] He argues that objective ethnic characteristics have largely disappeared: ancestral languages have been forgotten and ancestry is mixed or unknown; intermarriage across ethnic lines and a lack of ethnic socialization by parents have resulted in the loss of most ethnic traits. The structural basis has also subsided: ethnic enclaves have melted in suburbanization and gentrification; marriage choices respond more to socioeconomic considerations than to ethnic endogamy. From this perspective, change in American society has emptied ethnicity of any real significance as members of ethnic groups have become assimilated into the dominant culture. Ethnic labels have become matters of pride as a result of nostalgic attachment to the past.

Symbolic ethnicity is less a matter of contemporary ties to co-ethnics than it is a matter of perceived historical bonds. The new ethnics that Gans describes are categories of individuals who have similar views on their descent. They do not make up social groups because they do not interact with one another on the basis of a common bond, in this case a similar origin. American ethnic groups have reached a stage of acculturation in which membership is chiefly a matter of consumption of ethnic symbols detached from their roots in social reality. Yet ethnicity remains a powerful source of identification for individuals and a criterion of distinction for groups. It appears to be more deeply felt than other forms of group membership, such as class, church, or profession. Its resilience is explained by personal choices and strategies. Members of American ethnic groups may eat an occasional ethnic meal, show a general but distant interest in the country of their forebears, sprinkle a few foreign words in their English speech, and participate in heavily commercialized ethnic events, but they display no consistently distinctive behavior. A matter of self-ascription framed by individual representations and feelings, disconnected from its objective social basis, ethnicity has become symbolic and functionally expressive rather than instrumental.

Another perspective on the paradox of modern ethnicity comes from Joane Nagel. In an insightful article on the construction of ethnicity, Nagel describes how ethnic groups and ethnic boundaries constantly undergo redefinition and transformation as a consequence of "the interplay between ethnic group actions and the larger social structures with which they interact."[18] Both the groups themselves and their cultural contents shift as members negotiate with the society surrounding them. She reviews the techniques that groups utilize to both reconstruct historical culture and construct new culture such as language revitalization campaigns, the revival of forgotten cultural practices (ceremonies, dances, music), and the establishment of ethnic organizations.

Nagel's approach is promising for several reasons. Building on Barth's constructionist argument and emphasis on group boundaries, it reintroduces culture—whose importance Barth dismissed—into the mix. Cultural symbols and institutions, "shared meanings," are vitally important to the construction of community and ethnic mobilization. Building on Gans's thesis, she moves the focus of analysis from feelings of nostalgia and everyday behavior by individuals to collective strategies. "The notion that ethnicity is simply a matter of personal choice runs the risks of emphasizing agency at the expense of structure," she writes. Individuals can choose their identities but only from a set of "socially and politically defined ethnic categories with varying degrees of stigma or advantage attached to them." Finally, Nagel calls attention to the combined effect of "internal and external pressures" on the construction of ethnic boundaries and meanings. Ethnic identity varies in response to changes internal to the group (such as ecological adaptation or demographic movement), changes in the larger social structures (such as economic and political change in the surrounding or neighboring society), and changes in the relations between groups (for instance, a shift from tolerance to discrimination). Such a proposition has the advantage of removing assimilationist determinism from the understanding of modern ethnicity—present in Gans's argument where the "symbolic" stage appears as a vacuous period preceding total integration. Ethnicity is an ongoing process, both "a saga of structure and external forces shaping ethnic options, . . . [and] a tale of human agency and internal group processes of cultural preservation, renewal and innovation."[19]

These approaches may seem a little abstract, but we think they raise a number of points that can help our investigation of the paradox of Cajun ethnicity. Ethnicity is constructed; it is a process involving internal and external social structures; it involves contemporary social life, culture, structural forces, subjective identification, and interpretations of history. Nevertheless, these theories leave some important questions unanswered. Gans' view raises one of these questions. The symbolic ethnicity perspective tends to overlook the fact that symbols, ethnic or not, must have referents to be meaningful. The question, then, is What do symbols of ethnicity stand for? Ethnic words, icons, artifacts, and ritual behavior get their meaning from history, but, as we have seen, the past is in part created in the present and new symbols appear. Do ethnic symbols also stand for the present, and if they do, what is it about the present that they symbolize? Although culture is not concomitant with ethnicity, it still provides the guidelines to construct it (seeking the heritage) and express it (acting ethnic).[20]

Another question, raised by Nagel's work, deals with the structures and social forces at play in shaping ethnic boundaries and identities. What are they and how do they work? In particular, she describes many of the major social pressures that can lead to the construction of ethnicity, but she does not consider how fundamental changes in the framework of modern society can affect how people understand and express themselves and their connection to the world around them.

We see the central problem in explaining contemporary American ethnicity as one of integrating all the dimensions of these two theoretical frameworks and answering the questions they suggest. In contrast to the theorists of symbolic ethnicity, we argue that ethnicity is "grounded in real life context and social experience."[21] If the objective bases of an ethnic group seem to be disappearing, it may simply be that we are looking for the wrong sorts of social experience. Contemporary Cajun ethnicity may be based less and less on speaking French, but this does not mean that Cajunness is becoming baseless. Ideas about the world use emotionally moving images from the past, but these ideas are shaped by the present. Although historians and anthropologists have exposed the "invention of traditions," to borrow a term from Eric Hobsbawm, recent scholarship investigating the social construction of the past has established that historical processes and present ideologies play a combined role. Therefore, if we want to know what gives rise to the selective interpretation of ancestries, we must look at the contemporary social position of those who claim these ancestries.[22]

Expanding on Nagel's views, we believe that the forces shaping groups' identity and culture are primarily socioeconomic. In the industrial market economies that fostered the development of modern nation-states, the groups that were defined by contrast to the central national community often shared a common class or socioeconomic position. In taking this view, we join a long list of social scientists who have examined the connections between economic and ethnic forces and processes. Drawing from the macro-theories by Karl Marx, Georg Simmel, and Max Weber, contemporary theorists of society offer different possible combinations and diverging explanations of class and ethnic affiliations. Some such as Immanuel Wallerstein and Michael Hechter have pointed to socioeconomic differences on a worldwide scale as bases of ethnicity. In these views, ethnic identification emerges as a result of unequal economic development, a product of a capitalist world economy that leaves haves and have-nots, or the massive immigration of citizens of developing nations to Western nations.[23] Within his ambitious wide-ranging theory of society and action, Pierre Bourdieu ascribes a pivotal role to different forms of capital—economic, social, and cultural. His central concepts of "distinction," "reproduction," and "symbolic power," articulate social class with the other dimensions of social life as illustrated by his definition of "habitus": "the structures constitutive of a particular type of environment (e.g., the material conditions of existence characteristics of a class condition) produce habitus, systems of durable, transposable dispositions."[24]

The interplay of ethnicity and race with economic position and social mobility within American society has been the subject of a wide array of analyses. To synthesize a complex debate, most theorists agreed that racial and ethnic stratification was a matter of both cultural factors and structural conditions. The influential authors Nathan Glazer and Daniel P. Moynihan saw ethnicity as arising from the solidarity created by a common socioeconomic position among people who could see themselves as sharing ancestry and historical experience. Although mixed with primordial emotion, social class remained meaningful. Gordon's concept of ethclass describes a subsociety "created by the intersection of the vertical stratifications of ethnicity with the horizontal stratifications of social class."

Analysts continue to disagree on how ethnicity, culture, and socioeconomic position are related. Some, such as Thomas Sowell, have maintained that the cultural heritage of a group greatly determines its economic success. Others, such as Stephen Steinberg examining the success of Jews in American society, have denounced the "ethnic myth" and argued for the primacy of occupational skills, thus minimizing the role of cultural traits. During most of the 1960s and 1970s, a vigorous debate on ethnicity and socioeconomic status yielded the now-classic concepts of split labor market, internal colonialism, middleman minorities, and immigrant enclaves. Sometimes the argument reached acrimonious levels, as in the disagreement of William Julius Wilson and Charles Willie about the primacy of race or social class in understanding race relations in the American society.[25]

From our perspective, socioeconomic position can be a structural influence on the shaping of ethnicity in modern America because the industrial market economy and social classes continue to provide the foundations of American social structure. We will argue in this book that socioeconomic position is a major factor in the continued existence of Louisiana Cajuns. We will present evidence that there is a strong statistical association between claims of Cajun ethnicity and relatively low-income, working-class positions in Southwestern Louisiana society. In addition, being concentrated in a particular geographic region helps maintain personal and familial ties between Cajuns. We will introduce evidence on the high rate of endogamy among Cajuns and demonstrate how socioeconomic status influences marriage in or out of the group. These dimensions, we propose, constitute the structural basis of Cajun ethnicity.

Although the status of a regional working class is important in sustaining ethnicity, this is not the only factor. Cajunness can no more be reduced to a class position than it can be understood as a culture. As we will point out, Cajuns do not see themselves as members of a particular economic or social class. In fact, as we will see, some of those who identify most strongly with Cajun ethnicity work in professional and managerial occupations. We will introduce evidence on how Cajuns in different socioeconomic positions transmit French to their children and participate in ethnic manifestations at different rates. What unites both blue-collar and white-collar members of the group is the "shared meaning" of cultural symbols. Being ethnic is not the same as feeling ethnic, and cultural symbols are key to ethnic identity, a subjective dimension. In fact, as traditional cultural practices are declining, their idealized versions are becoming even more prominent in stereotypes and self-images of the group. New versions of traditional foods, electronically amplified Cajun music, and emphases on hunting and fishing are now critical to the group's self-representation.

We argue that understanding the consequences of social change can enable us to resolve the paradox of Cajun ethnicity, less lived but more felt, traditional and modern at the same time, structurally situated, yet reconstructed by human agency. Social position helps to give coherence to the group, but it is a changing social position. Contemporary Cajun ethnicity, then, is about socioeconomic position, but it is also about socioeconomic change. A common life situation among individuals helps to maintain a group. A changing situation creates collective self-awareness by members of the group. Today's Cajuns are living lives that are quite different from those of their parents and grandparents. Being disconnected from a tradition fosters a new self-consciousness of that tradition and an eagerness to embellish on it. But the symbols of "symbolic ethnicity" are not matters of empty nostalgia for an imagined past. Instead, making sense out of the present is what elicits a need for a new collective identity, often drawn from historical sources.

The view of ethnicity as a function of modernization is admittedly at the core of all treatments of things ethnic by social scientists. The emergence of ethnicity in nation-states, its connection with social class, and its usefulness to identity construction by disconnected individuals all point to the crucial role of rationalization, industrialization, and individualization in the modern world. Certainly, views diverge on whether ethnic organization is a "tribal" resistance to modernity, an adaptive reaction to its homogenizing impact, or a dysfunctional consequence of Western expansionism; whether ethnic identification is sociobiologically "primordial," a misbegotten prop in a scheme of generalized self-deception, or the ultimate relief to postmodern angst gnawing at alienated selves.[26] Although we will not discuss in detail the premises of these competing theories, we aim at expanding the examination of the relationship between ethnicity and modernization. We believe that contemporary social changes help explain Cajun ethnicity in two ways. One is the differential impact that modern processes of industrialization and formal education have had on the descendants of Acadian exiles in Louisiana. Changes in American and Louisiana society have played a dual role: instrumental in the formation of Cajun ethnicity, and influential in the placement of Cajuns in diverse socioeconomic positions and espousal of different lifestyles and attitudes. Modernity has had both integrating and disintegrating effects on Cajun ethnicity. This proposition departs from most paradigms, which tend to focus on one kind of consequence of modernization on ethnic groups seen as consolidated entities. Further, consistent with emerging theories of modernity, we argue that social change has resulted in social organization, behavior, and attitudes becoming increasingly based on the consumption of mass-produced commodities. Whereas production was the cornerstone of industrial societies, consumption has emerged as the pivotal characteristic of postindustrial societies.[27] We propose that Cajuns, as other participants in today's economies, are in part defined by what they consume. Ethnic commodities, be they festivals, food items, or mementos, draw from a shared historical past and create a new collective bond. Cajuns, though, are not passive consumers of an ethnicity manufactured by others. They are deeply involved in the production of their ethnic symbols, artifacts, and situations. The combination of these two developments—the differential adaptation to modernization and the commodification of ethnicity—constitute the new economy of ethnicity.

THE NEED FOR A SOCIAL SCIENTIFIC STUDY OF CAJUNS

Although contributing to a theoretical understanding of ethnicity is one of our goals in writing this book, our priority is to provide an account of a neglected dimension of this group. We attempt to provide a more comprehensive treatment of the Louisiana Cajun situation than is currently available in the literature on the subject. A brief review of articles, books, and dissertations in the social sciences published in the past decade shows that research has been limited, mostly descriptive of cultural dimensions, and historically nostalgic in nature. A small group of social scientists affiliated with Louisiana State University pioneered research on Cajuns in the 1930s by briefly describing some social dimensions (the family, rurality) and examining the effect of acculturation. Close to forty years elapsed before more research was conducted, this time mostly by anthropologists. These later researchers produced monographs—detailed descriptions—of communities around the Atchafalaya Basin, in the prairies, and along the Gulf Coast, highlighting the residual communal and ethnic characteristics. In many anthropological studies, the process of acculturation continued to receive much attention because of its increasingly obvious and feared consequences.

The limited scope of recent socio-anthropological research appears to be, paradoxically, a consequence of the newly found popularity of Cajunism. Numerous publications by historians, folklorists, and cultural activists may contribute to the illusion that the phenomenon is well described. Although this scholarship undoubtedly addresses some social aspects, it deals only superficially with the analysis of sociological dimensions such as stratification, social institutions, and social change. In addition, if Louisiana's exotic difference attracts many domestic and foreign tourists, it seems to leave scholars rather cold. Much of the research has been conducted by native scholars or academics with a particular Louisiana connection. The bulk of the work is sound and valid, but a lack of distance and an ethnocentric regionalism have been identified as obstacles to more fruitful research. Both scholarly and nonscholarly writers often seem more concerned with the celebration of the culture than with its analysis. As both insiders and outsiders, we have been particularly conscious of this situation and have strived to come up with remedies (explained in the section called "A Combination of Methods"). There is nothing wrong with regional cheerleading. Local pride can be a valuable emotion. Our goal, though, is to turn away from the prevailing "local color" approach to Louisiana Cajuns and to approach them as an American ethnic group, to situate them in American society.

The second dimension of existing scholarship is its heavy concentration on describing cultural aspects rather than on explaining the whole ethnic context. The situation of the French language (threatened yet revalued), the issue of Cajun identity (stigmatized then reconstructed), and folk practices are by and large the topics most approached. Foodways and celebrations appear to be as interesting to scholars as they are popular with consumers. In the literature, we learn that the specificity of Cajun cuisine lies in the ingredients, the local origin, and preparation according to a "Cajun style and esthetic"; that consumption of emblematic products such as game and seafood "expresses and validates the ecological competence of Cajuns." Authors agree on the sociability function of foodways, which appears to establish boundaries between Cajuns and non-Cajuns, although commercialization of Cajun products and Americanization of the Cajun diet render the distinction less concise.

Thirdly, a sense of historical nostalgia pervades the literature overall. It takes the form of documentation of surviving folk practices, retracing of Acadian roots, or extolling of flimsy global connections. Some, most notably historian Carl Brasseaux, have been up to the task of documenting the Acadian past on the basis of empirical evidence. As a result, it is now clear that in the beginning the Acadian exiles were not the homogeneous flock of grateful settlers seen in popular portrayals. United by language and purpose, they were, nevertheless, a diverse community marked by differences in religion, in dealings with colonial authority, and in economic success. Later, accounts of participation in slavery, vigilante groups during Reconstruction, and lynching and violence in the 1920s dispute the picturesque representation of Cajuns as gentle folks safely isolated from a brutal outside world. Yet, despite indisputable records, images of a pastoral, cohesive past linger on in evocations of today's Cajuns.

Finally, there is the issue of race. Our major focus is on Cajuns, who happened to be labeled as white. It is not on Creoles, members of another Louisiana ethnic group with French connection, who are mostly labeled as black, although this racial identification has experienced much historical variation. There were and there are many examples of interaction and similarities between Cajuns and Creoles. Both groups settled in Louisiana during the Colonial period, used a French-based idiom, were stigmatized and suffered discrimination by English-speaking whites, inhabit the southwestern region of the state, long shared an agricultural existence, and now occupy a relatively low socioeconomic position while experiencing a cultural renaissance. Past and present relations between Cajuns and Creoles are abundantly documented by indications of miscegenation (hard to prove given the racial divide, but likely), sharing of cultural items in foodways, music, architecture, or storytelling, and recent cooperation in ethnic activism, for instance. There is also significant evidence of racist attitude and behavior by Cajuns toward their African American neighbors, even though the scholarship on this phenomenon is all but nonexistent. Still, despite a recent trend in scholarship and business that tends to highlight the Cajun-Creole connection,[28] we do not believe that ethnic awareness among Cajuns can be reduced to a racial phenomenon. We are well aware of the role of race in Cajuns' past and present situation. We are also familiar with the past and recent scholarship on Louisiana's white, colored, and black Creoles, and have contributed to it.[29] Indeed, the Acadians' settlement in Louisiana took place alongside slavery, Cajuns' emergence as a group accelerated after the Civil War, and the late-twentieth-century Cajun cultural revival owes much to the Civil Rights Movement, as most other American white ethnic movements do. Relationship and coincidence do not equate with causality. Little in our quantitative and qualitative data suggests that race is a primary factor in Cajuns' ethnic identification. Is it a subterranean subtext? It may well be, given the complex and profound grip racial issues have on American society. But overreliance on race-based explanations is risky. Our analysis does not support the view that Cajuns emerged as a group or experienced a cultural revival in an attempt to differentiate themselves from Creoles or African Americans.[30]

HOW THIS BOOK CAME TO BE

This book is the product of a rather long quest started by one author (Henry) as a student some twenty-five years ago. An initial interest in the dynamics and meaning of the French renaissance movement for a degree in cultural anthropology led to residence in Lafayette and subsequent involvement in the actions to promote Louisiana French culture. He was hired to be the spokesman for the Council for the Development of French in Louisiana (CODOFIL), a state agency created in 1968 to promote Louisiana's French heritage; he later became its executive director. The transition from fieldwork in an academic setting to cultural activism in Louisiana politics and bureaucracy was an enlightening journey by itself. In addition it yielded several lessons whose usefulness has endured. The stint with CODOFIL—an almost obligatory rite of passage for those interested in Louisiana French in the 1970s and 1980s—revealed the centrality and complexity of the language issue, the importance of class division and cultural allegiance among Cajuns, and the indomitable belief that they had not endured centuries of discrimination just to melt away. The experience led to an effort to flesh out theoretical views of society as dialectical processes and of ethnicity as interactive construction. It also led to some insight into the paradoxical nature of the whole Cajun French phenomenon. The agency's founder and longtime chairman, Lafayette attorney James Domengeaux, himself a bilingual patrician, liked to proclaim, *"Sans la langue, on est foutu"* (Without the language, we're done) to foreign dignitaries more than to working-class Cajuns. A mural in downtown Lafayette clamored *"Trois cent ans et on a juste commencé"* (Three hundred years and we are just starting), provokingly oblivious to the fact that most potential readers could not decipher it. The CODOFIL experience suggested that something was happening with Louisiana Cajun French, but it was something complex and self-contradictory in many ways. It was something that needed to be explored and explained.

The other author (Bankston) came to this study primarily as a sociologist with an interest in ethnicity, but also found the subject appealing as a Louisiana native. Ironically, he developed his specialization in ethnicity by leaving his home state since he worked in Southeast Asia during almost all of the 1980s. From 1985 through the end of 1989, he served as a supervisor in a refugee camp in the Philippines, preparing refugees from Vietnam, Laos, and Cambodia for resettlement in the United States. On returning to the United States, he entered a doctoral program in sociology to find out what he had been doing in helping to send tens of thousands of people around the globe to create new American minority groups. His dissertation looked at a Louisiana Vietnamese community. Although the interest in ethnicity may have arisen overseas, many of the topics covered in this book came close to Bankston's own experience. He remembered his French-speaking grandmother visiting older people who had lived in the United States all of their lives and spoke no English. He recalled driving around Cajun country with his grandfather, who sold adding machines to banks in the southwestern Louisiana region. Seeing the vast changes in Louisiana life over the past three decades pushed him to look again at his native state as a place that was at once familiar and strange. Trips around the globe, if completed, always lead home, although neither the home nor the traveler is the same as before.

A COMBINATION OF METHODS

To answer our central question on the apparently paradoxical maintenance of Cajun ethnicity, we rely on several sources of data and a combination of quantitative and qualitative methods. This sort of multipronged approach is, we believe, one of the advantages of collaboration between two scholars from somewhat different backgrounds, enabling each to contribute his own strengths. Data from censuses of the American population were used to obtain a measurement of the objectified dimensions of the phenomenon and to analyze the correlations between variables. The Public Use Microdata Samples (PUMS) were particularly useful since they make it possible to establish these correlations at the individual and household levels, a step that aggregate data do not permit. Other available statistical data were used as needed, particularly results from a survey conducted by CODOFIL in 1990. We have strived to present only the relevant data and analysis as needed to support our argument, and to provide the necessary information to explain their meaning. Throughout, we have tried to follow the principle that even readers who are unfamiliar with quantitative analysis or averse to it should be able to follow our argument.

We have relied on many of the categories used by census takers and analysts to give an extensive portrait of a population. Throughout the book, we present figures on number of people, age, level of education, ability to speak English, occupation, income, and others. The reader will notice that we particularly emphasize two dimensions of ethnicity: ancestry and language. Because these concepts lie at the core of our argument and are among our most used tools, a word about their meaning and our choice is in order. "What is this person's ancestry or ethnic origin?" and "Do you speak a language other than English at home?" were questions asked of 15% samples of the population, which received, at random, longer forms of the decennial U.S. Census in several years. The answers to these questions were largely left to the respondents. Examples of some categories of ancestral origin were offered as examples. In the 1990 questionaire, Cajun was for the first time offered as an example alongside German, Mexican, Croatian, Thai, and others. However, respondents were asked to write their own answers. These self-reports yielded an astonishing variety of answers: more than 300 racial categories, 600 Native American categories, and 400 ancestry categories were recorded in 1990! To make the data fit for analysis and publication, then, census administrators coded the various answers and organized them into larger categories; for example, "Acadian," "Cajun," and its varying spellings were collapsed into one ancestry category, "Acadian." Similarly, "Cajun French," "Louisiana French," or French were categorized as "French." Arguably, the phrasing of questions, the sampling and codification procedures, all methodological issues, have a bearing on the quality of the data and thus on the basis of our analysis. We address these issues as needed, but it is safe to say that although not perfect—who and what is?—data by the Bureau of the Census constitute an overall reliable and unequaled tool to conduct social research.

Of all the dimensions recorded by the census, ancestry and language are the most closely related to ethnicity (Cajuns being white and of French origin, neither race nor Hispanic origin are relevant in this case). Although they do not encompass the whole feeling of belonging to a particular cultural heritage or to a unique set of roots, and yield little information on ethnic behavior, these variables are still valuable because they record what people think and do on at least two facets of the phenomenon. They do not provide a full assessment of one person's ethnic sentiment, but they open a window on a person's ethnic situation. However, we have not chosen these dimensions only because they are related to our topic and because they happen to be available. Both Acadian ancestry and French language were and still are at the core of what Cajuns, and non-Cajuns alike, for that matter, think they are. We will document how, from their arrival in Louisiana, descendants of the Acadian exiles have been largely defined in terms of their origin and their language. That pattern has remained valid to this day; other researchers interested in exploring contemporary Cajun identity from the perspective of Cajuns have concurred on the centrality of ancestry and language.[31] There are undoubtedly other traits of Cajunism mentioned by Cajuns; religion, family traditions, foodways, a particular worldview, a way of life, and a general disposition are among those often mentioned when the issue of identity is addressed. But ultimately the fact that Cajuns' ethnicity is multifaceted does not detract from the pivotal importance of ancestry and language.

Although quantitative analysis is an invaluable tool for social scientists, and indeed the closest to the approach of physical science, its limitations are well known. They are most obvious when the task is to assess social dimensions involving interpretation by individuals; for instance, it has been argued that self-reports of ancestry to the U.S. Bureau of the Census are in part unreliable because they are unstable, inconsistent, and simplistic.[32] Depending on their perceptions of an origin, individuals may choose to identify themselves as French in 1980 and Cajun in 1990, just as head of households may apply an inadequate label to their spouses and children. There are also methodological problems with census data because some dimensions are not measured (because of the constitutional separation of powers, information about religion may not be gathered by a governmental agency) and because design and codification procedures used by the Census Bureau can sometimes distort the data. Notwithstanding these reservations, it is widely acknowledged that census data is highly reliable if not perfect. Still, once figures have been compiled and correlations determined, what do they mean?

Qualitative evidence gathered from interviews, written sources, observation, and participation can help uncover the meaning of the events and situations under study. It is one thing to know that a person speaks French; it is another to know when and with whom, what topics are discussed, what kind of language is used, and what feelings are associated by the speaker and the audience with the use of the language in a particular situation. We have drawn primarily from the extensive data gathered over the years through our combined and diversified fieldwork in Southwestern Louisiana and in smaller measure from qualitative evidence collected by other researchers.[33]

Qualitative analysis is helpful in uncovering cultural meaning but it requires the negotiation of several obstacles to be valid. Involvement of real people in research necessarily means that the perspective is limited (one cannot see and hear everything in a single situation much less in a territory as large as Acadiana), likely to be skewed by preconceptions, feelings and emotions, and subject to questionable interpretations. Diaries by noted anthropologists (Malinowski, Evans-Pritchard, Chagnon), as well as our own experience, have revealed how the demeanor of informants, the feelings inherent to a situation (say, a funeral or Mardi Gras celebration), or the plain physiological and psychological condition of the investigator can affect the collection of information. Finally, the generalization of findings based on partial and limited data is always problematic.

In accordance with the current trend of sociologists and anthropologists to utilize all available means and tools to make sense of social behavior, we have relied on varied data and methods to achieve a comprehensive and multileveled look at the contemporary Cajun experience. We begin by charting in Chapter 1 the history of the "Cajun" label, its emergence in the nineteenth century, and the evolution of its meaning from an ethnic slur to a badge of pride. In Chapter 2, we outline the evolution of the content of Cajuns' stereotyped image and discuss how the Cajuns have become participants in the construction of their self-image. In chapters 3 and 4 we describe the structural basis of Cajun ethnicity. We survey the changing socioeconomic situation of Southwestern Louisiana and the movement of Cajuns between 1930 and the end of the twentieth century from a predominantly agricultural economy to a blue-collar existence in an industrialized context. Then we analyze how family processes and especially marital strategy affect the transmission of Cajunism. We then present a synthetic view of the structural bases of Cajun ethnicity in Chapter 5. Finally, the new economy of ethnicity is presented in chapters 6 and 7 with a discussion of the interrupted transmission of French and of the growing centrality of the consumption of ethnic goods as conspicuous display of ethnicity.

NOTES

1. This is a description of the pen-and-ink drawing *Ti Jules and His Friend* by artist Floyd Sonnier.

2. Thomas H. Eriksen, *Ethnicity and Nationalism* (London: Pluto Press, 1993). For more on ethnic conflict see Donald Horowitz, *Ethnic Groups in Conflict* (Berkeley: University of California Press, 1985); Ted Robert Gurr, *Minorities at Risk* (Washington, DC: United States Institute of Peace, 1993); Rajat Ganguly & Ray Taras, *Understanding Ethnic Conflict: The International Dimension* (New York: Longman, 1998).

3. Michael Hout and Joshua R. Goldstein, "How 4.5 Million Irish Immigrants Became 40 Million Irish Americans: Demographic and Subjective Aspects of the Ethnic Composition of White America," *American Sociological Review* 59(1) (1994): 64–82; Joane Nagel, "Constructing Ethnicity: Recreating Ethnic Identity and Culture," *Social Problems* 41(1) (1994):152–176.

4. Werner Sollors (ed.), *Theories of Ethnicity: A Classical Reader* (New York: New York University Press, 1996).

5. Wsevolod Isajiw, "Definitions of Ethnicity: New Approaches," *Ethnic Forum* 13(2)–14(1):(1993) 9–16; Milton J. Yinger, *Ethnicity: Source of Strength? Source of Conflict?* (Albany: State University of New York Press, 1994).

6. Dominique Schnapper, *La France de l'intégration. Sociologie de la nation en*

1990 (Paris: Gallimard, 1991). Philippe Poutignat & Jocelyne Streiff-Fenart, *Théories de l'ethnicité* (Paris: PUF, 1995). Interestingly, calls to jettison "ethnicity" as an explanatory concept echo the early warning in Max Weber, *Economy and Society*, vol. 1 (New York: Bedminster Press, 1968), that "the collective term 'ethnic' would be abandoned for it is unsuitable for a rigorous analysis . . . [for it] dissolves if we define our terms exactly."

7. Clifford Geertz, *The Interpretation of Cultures* (New York: Basic Books, 1973); H.R. Isaacs, "Basic Group Identity: The Idols of the Tribe" in Nathan Glazer & Daniel Moynihan, (eds.), *Ethnicity, Theory and Experience*, (Cambridge: Harvard University Press, 1975), 29–52.

8. Pierre van den Berghe, *The Ethnic Phenomenon* (New York: Elsevier, 1981); Horowitz, *Ethnic Groups in Conflict.*

9. Eugeen Roosens, *Creating Ethnicity: The Process of Ethnogenesis* (Newbury Park, CA: Sage Publications, 1989); Milton Gordon, *Assimilation in American Life* (New York: Oxford University Press, 1964); Anya P. Royce, *Ethnic Identity, Strategies of Diversity* (Bloomington Indiana University Press, 1982); Richard H. Thompson, *Theories of Ethnicity: A Critical Appraisal* (Westport, CT: Greenwood Press, 1989).

10. Joane Nagel, "The Political Construction of Ethnicity" in Susan Olzak & Joane Nagel (eds.), *Competitive Ethnic Relations* (New York: Academic Press, 1986); Nagel, "Constructing Ethnicity: Recreating Ethnic Identity and Culture," *Social Problems* 41(1); Anton Allahar, "More Than an Oxymoron: Ethnicity and the Social Construction of Primordial Attachment," *Canadian Ethnic Studies* 26 (1994), 18–34.

11. Fredrick Barth, *Ethnic Groups and Boundaries: The Social Organization of Culture Difference.* (Boston: Little, Brown & Co., 1969), 15.

12. Sollors (ed.), *Theories of Ethnicity: A Classical Reader.*

13. Kathleen Conzen, David Gerber, Ewa Morawaska, George Pozzetta & Rudolph Vecoli, "The Invention of Ethnicity: A Perspective from the U.S.A," *Journal of American Ethnic History* 12(1) (1992):3–41; see also Benedict Anderson, *Imagined Communities: Reflections on the Origin and Spread of Nationalism* (London: Verso, 1983).

14. See also Gunnar Myrdal, Richard Sterner & Arnold Rose, *An American Dilemma: The Negro Problem and Modern Democracy* (New York: Harper, 1944) on the blocked assimilation of African Americans.

15. On Hispanic immigrants see Alejandro Portes & Rubén Rumbaut, *Immigrant America: A Portrait* (Berkeley: University of California Press, 1990); on Asian immigrants see Min Zhou & Carl Bankston III, *Growing Up American: How Vietnamese Children Adapt to Life in the United States* (New York: Russell Sage Foundation, 1998); on increasing exogamy see Richard Alba & Reid M. Golden, "Patterns of Intermarriage in the United States," *Social Forces* 65(1) (1986):206–208; Herbert Barringer, Robert W. Gardner & Michael J. Levin, *Asian and Pacific Islanders in the United States* (New York: Russell Sage Foundation, 1993); Harry H. Kitano, "The Japanese American Family" in Charles H. Mindell, Robert W. Habenstein & Roosevelt Wright, Jr. (eds.), *Ethnic Families in America: Patterns and Variations*, (New York: Elsevier, 1988), 258–275; Harry H. Kitano, Wai-Tsang Yeung, Lynn Chai & Harry Hatanaka, "Asian American Interracial Marriage," *Journal of Marriage and the Family* 46 (1984):179–190; on declining ethnicity see Stanley Lieberson &

Mary Waters, *From Many Strands: Ethnic and Racial Groups in Contemporary America* (New York: Russell Sage Foundation, 1988); Richard Alba, *Ethnic Identity: The Transformation of White America* (New Haven, CT: Yale University Press, 1990).

16. Michael Novak, *The Rise of Unmeltable Ethnics* (New York: Macmillan, 1971); Peter Kivisto, "The Attenuated Ethnicity of Contemporary Finnish-Americans" in Peter Kivisto (ed.), *The Ethnic Enigma: The Salience of Ethnicity for European-Origin Groups* (Philadelphia: Balch Institute, 1989), 67–88; Mary Waters, *Ethnic Options: Choosing Identities in America* (Berkeley: University of California Press, 1990); Anny Bakalian, *Armenian-Americans: From Being to Feeling Armenian* (New Brunswick, NJ: Transaction Publishers, 1993).

17. Herbert Gans, "Symbolic Ethnicity: The Future of Ethnic Groups and Cultures in America," *Ethnic and Racial Studies* 2(1) (1979):1–20.

18. Nagel, "Constructing Ethnicity: Recreating Ethnic Identity and Culture," 167.

19. Nagel, "Constructing Ethnicity: Recreating Ethnic Identity and Culture," 156, 161, 167.

20. For more on the ongoing debate on the connections between culture and ethnicity see John R. Hall, "The Capital(s) of Culture: a Nonholistic Approach to Status Situations, Class, Gender, and Ethnicity" in Michèle Lamont & Marcel Fournier (eds.), *Cultivating Differences: Symbolic Boundaries and the Making of Inequality* (Chicago: University of Chicago Press, 1992), 257–288; Luc de Heusch, "*L'ethnie.* The Vicissitudes of a concept," *Social Anthropology* 8(2) (2000):99–116.

21. Conzen et al., "The Invention of Ethnicity: A Perspective from the U.S.A," 5.

22. Eric Hobsbawm & T. Rager (eds.), *The Invention of Tradition* (Cambridge: Cambridge University Press, 1983); George C. Bond & Angela Gilliam (eds.), *Social Construction of the Past: Representations as Power* (New York: Routledge, 1997); David Lorenzen, "Who Invented Hinduism?" *Comparative Studies in Society and History* 41(4) (1999):630–659.

23. Michael Hechter, *Internal Colonialism: The Celtic Fringe in British National Development, 1536–1966* (London: Routledge and Kegan Paul, 1975); Ernest Balibar & Immanuel Wallerstein, *Race, nation, classe, les identités ambiguës* (Paris: La Découverte, 1988); see also Nathan Glazer & Daniel Moynihan (eds.), *Ethnicity, Theory and Experience* (Cambridge: Harvard University Press, 1975).

24. Pierre Bourdieu, *Outline of a Theory of Practice* (Cambridge: Cambridge University Press, 1977), 72.

25. Gordon, *Assimilation in American Life*; Hubert Blalock, *Toward a Theory of Minority Group Relations* (New York: Wiley, 1967); Edna Bonacich, "A Theory of Ethnic Antagonism: The Split Labor Market," *American Sociological Review* 37 (1992):547–559; Hechter, *Internal Colonialism: The Celtic Fringe in British National Development, 1536–1966*; William Julius Wilson, *The Declining Significance of Race: Blacks and Changing American Institutions* (Chicago: University of Chicago Press, 1978); Charles V. Willie, *The Caste and Class Controversy* (Bayside, NY: General Hall, 1979); Thomas Sowell, *Ethnic America: A History* (New York: Basic Books, 1981); Stephen Steinberg, *The Ethnic Myth: Race, Ethnicity and Class in America* (New York: Atheneum, 1981); Alejandro Portes & Ruben Rumbaut, *Immigrant America: A Portrait* (Berkeley: University of California Press, 1990).

26. For views on the relationship between ethnicity and modernization, see

George De Vos & Lola Romanucci-Ross (eds.), *Ethnic Identity: Continuities and Change* (Palo Alto, CA: Mayfield, 1975); A.D. Smith, *The Ethnic Revival in the Modern World* (Cambridge: Cambridge University Press, 1981); Stephen Steinberg, *The Ethnic Myth: Race, Ethnicity and Class in America*; M. Featherstone (ed.), *Global Culture* (London: Sage, 1990); Eriksen, *Ethnicity and Nationalism*; Gheorghita Geana, "Ethnicity and Globalisation: Outline of a Complementarist Conceptualisation," *Social Anthropology* 5(2) (1997):197–210.

27. See Chapter 7 for references on theories of modernity and commodification of ethnicity.

28. Cajuns and Creoles are united in the title of books by Patrick Griolet, *Cadjins et Créoles en Louisiane* (Paris: Payot, 1986); Barry J. Ancelet, *Cajun and Creole Folktales: The French Oral Tradition of South Louisiana* (New York: Garland, 1994); Shane Bernard, *Swamp Pop: Cajun and Creole Rhythm and Blues* (Jackson: University Press of Mississippi, 1996); Albert Valdman (ed.), *French and Creole in Louisiana* (New York and London: Plenum Press, 1997). Creoles are also given important treatment in works on Cajun identity and culture by Barry J. Ancelet & Elemore Morgan, *The Makers of Cajun Music* (Austin: University of Texas Press, 1984); and Sara LeMenestrel, *La voie des Cadiens: Tourisme et identité en Louisiane* (Paris: Belin, 1999).

29. Among the major works are Virginia Dominguez, *White by Definition: Social Classification in Creole Louisiana* (New Brunswick, NJ: Rutgers University Press, 1986); Gwendolyn Midlo Hall, *Africans in Colonial Louisiana: The Development of Afro-Creole Culture in Louisiana in the Eighteenth Century* (Baton Rouge: Louisiana State University Press, 1992); Arnold Hirsch & Joseph Logsdon (eds.), *Creole New Orleans: Race and Americanization* (Baton Rouge: Louisiana State University Press, 1992); Carl Brasseaux, Keith Fontenot & Claude Oubre, *Creoles of Color in the Bayou Country* (Jackson: University Press of Mississippi, 1994); James Dormon (ed.), *Creoles of Color of the Gulf South* (Knoxville, TN: University of Tennessee Press, 1996); Valdman (ed.), *French and Creole in Louisiana*; Sybil Kein (ed.), *Creole: The History and Legacy of Louisiana's Free People of Color* (Baton Rouge: Louisiana State University Press, 2000). Our contribution consists of Carl L. Bankston III & Jacques Henry, "The Socioeconomic Position of the Louisiana Creoles: An Examination of Racial and Ethnic Stratification," *Social Thought and Research* 21 (1998):253–277; Jacques Henry & Carl Bankston, "Propositions for a Structuralist Analysis of Creolism," *Current Anthropology* 39(4) (1998):558–566.

30. Although we have no evidence of a strong correlation between emergence of modern Cajunness and race, the issue warrants attention. A comparable connection is hypothesized in Richard Alba's *Ethnic Identity: The Transformation of White America*, in the conclusion to his examination of white ethnics in the northeast United States, and fieldwork on that issue is reportedly being conducted in Louisiana as of this writing.

31. See Marjorie Esman, *The Celebration of Cajun Identity: Ethnic Unity and the Crawfish Festival* (Ph.D. dissertation, Tulane University, 1981); Cécyle Trépanier, *French Louisiana at the Threshold of the 21st Century*, Projet Louisiane, Monograph 2 (Québec: Laval University, 1989); Cécyle Trépanier, "The Cajunization of French Louisiana: Forging a Regional Identity," *Geographical Journal* 157(2) (1991):161–171. The utilization of operational definitions and criteria is concomitant with the likely and simplistic objectification of Cajuns as French-speakers of Acadian descent

residing in Louisiana. Our data and analysis demonstrate that we do not espouse such a limited view of this ethnic group. To the extent that such "objective" criteria are used, and are useful to understand the situation, it should be noted as we show that they are categories claimed by Cajuns themselves and not solely imposed by others.

32. Stanley Lieberson & Mary Waters, "The Ethnic Responses of Whites: What Causes Their Instability, Simplification, and Inconsistency?" *Social Forces* 72(2) (1993):421–450.

33. The qualitative data were gathered over twenty years in a variety of settings. Original fieldwork was conducted by Henry in 1981–82 as a participant observer of the formal actions taken to promote Louisiana's French heritage and Cajun culture. Operations of the Council for the Development of French in Louisiana (CODOFIL) were actively observed during an eighteen-month period along with educational endeavors, ethnic festivals, French media productions, and various touristic business ventures (museums, restaurants, tours). Semistructured interviews were conducted with approximately thirty key informants selected on the basis of their direct involvement in the ethnic movement as educators, CODOFIL board members and personnel, foreign representatives, artists and musicians, activists, event organizers, and radio and television announcers. Additional and invaluable data were collected, as an unobtrusive observer, in the course of repeated informal contacts with CODOFIL personnel, educators, festival organizers and participants, and Cajun women and men met on a daily basis. Involvement with CODOFIL, ethnic festivals, and the tourism business between 1984 and 1992, this time as a complete participant, yielded more data; structured and semistructured interviews again were conducted with about two dozen informants (including some already on record). Finally, both authors collected life histories and recent data on economic processes for this particular project through structured and ethnographic interviews with a dozen Cajun women and men, employers and employees.

CHAPTER 1

The Emergence of the Cajun Label and Identity

If one were to take the superficial indicators at face value, evidence of a profusion of Cajun ethnicity in Southwestern Louisiana is overwhelming. Signs and advertisements proudly proclaim Cajun identity, musicians play Cajun music, restaurants cook and sell Cajun food products, and visitors flock to tour Cajun country. Still, the answer to the question "What is a Cajun?" remains elusive. Operational and anecdotal definitions abound: individual Cajuns, scholars, legislators, and writers of all kinds from poets to humorists offer their views of Cajun identity, but these definitions fail to provide a clear consensus. On one hand, views of Cajun ethnicity by Cajuns vary according to situational and referential contexts. The views expressed depend on who is asking, and who is around, on what the person knows and how much he or she feels about the cultural heritage. Claims of Cajun identity can range from "I'm proud to be Cajun" to "Here, it's all Cajun" to the derogative "Me, I'm a coonass." These claims involve references, made or implied, to a Nova Scotian ancestry, to an area of residence, or to a working-class existence.

Sociologists, anthropologists, linguists, and folklorists have attempted their own definitions of "Cajun" from a variety of theoretical perspectives. These scholarly definitions have been directed by goals as diverse as providing an official definition, delineating a territory, finding informants, or analyzing Cajun ethnic identity. As often happens with efforts to define things in the complicated world of human relations, the academic definitions frequently fall short of perfect clarity and precision. Two of our colleagues have for example offered the following statement:

A Cajun is most emphatically identifiable as an individual who is Roman Catholic, is rural or of rural extraction, emphasizes kinship relations over those of nonkin-based associations, and who speaks or understands both English and Louisiana French languages or has relatives who do so.[1]

Although factually correct, this definition is vague and overlooks some critical dimensions, such as the Acadian origin or the self-identification as a Cajun. Definitions typically focus on or refer in some way to a limited set of characteristics: the Acadian ancestry, French language, ecological and cultural adaptation to Southwestern Louisiana, Catholicism, agriculturalism, and a particular folk culture. The location and size of the original Acadian settlements, common surnames, French as mother tongue, or a combination of racial, religious, and residential criteria have all been used to characterize if not define Cajuns. Over the years, varied definitions have produced shifting geographical boundaries and widely different demographic estimates.[2]

Most efforts at saying what a Cajun is or who the Cajuns are have been inadequate for several reasons. Reliance on French surnames or on the proportion of Catholics in a population rests on vague assumptions (all Cajuns are Catholic and vice versa) and debatable criteria (what about Anglo Martins and Cajun Smithes? Or the numerous Romeros and Schexnayders who consider themselves Cajuns?). The fast-evolving, multidimensional, and sometimes paradoxical nature of the phenomenon at hand is another significant obstacle in pinning down the size and location of Cajun country. Considering that two characteristics considered pivotal by Cajuns, ancestry and language, are recorded by the U.S. Bureau of the Census, it would seem simple enough to compute those individuals claiming Acadian descent and use of French. The problem is that prior to the 1970s Cajuns tended not to claim a stigmatized Acadian ancestry, choosing French instead, a trend that continues, although on a lesser scale. In addition, the measure of linguistic abilities is more complex than a yes or no answer to a census question: What does it mean to "speak" a language other than English? Does it mean to have learned it at school or home, and be able to use it? Or does it mean to actually use it regularly? Moreover, should a person claiming French descent and no use of French be counted as Cajun or not? Short of interviewing every subject, much has to be left to interpretations both by respondents and census tabulators. Thus, the Council on the Development of French in Louisiana (CODOFIL) at one point managed to employ data from the 1970 census to come up with extremely generous estimates of the number of French Louisianians (1.4 million) and the number of French-speakers in Louisiana (750,000). Changes in methodology by the U.S. Bureau of the Census add another level of difficulty. Redefinitions of categories (before 1960, only the ancestry of whites was recorded), shifts in the wordings of questions, and changes in coding procedures all limit comparisons across different census years. Finally, beyond these methodological issues, ethnic identity cannot be reduced to such a simple set of objective criteria.

In this chapter, we take another, more historical approach to the problem of "what is a Cajun?" We ask how the ethnic label came into existence and what it has represented. To answer this question, we analyze written occurrences of the labels, especially the English-French pair *Cajun/cadien*,[3] used to describe the descendants of the Acadian exiles in Louisiana. The ethnohistorical exploration of the creation, use, and meaning of these terms reveals the dialectical process at play in the construction of Cajun ethnicity. It confirms the early realization of *cadien* in Louisiana Acadian speech and the coining of *Cajun* by outsiders who popularized the word in the late nineteenth century. This approach presents the variations in patterns of utilization of *Cajun/cadien* from its emergence as a derogative term used by outsiders to its current positive but divergent realizations in English and French. The analysis of the evolution through changing social contexts and from in-group and out-group perspectives shows that the use and meaning of *Cajun/cadien* has been closely linked to social and cultural changes. Stable symbol of a changing culture or constant marker of shifting ethnic boundaries, *Cajun/cadien* appears through historical evolution as a reliable indicator of the ongoing construction of Cajun ethnicity.

THE EMERGENCE OF CAJUN ETHNICITY: AN ETHNOHISTORICAL APPROACH

The data for this chapter consist of written occurrences of *Cajun/cadien*, a derivative of *acadien* [akadiɛ], which refers to the people and culture of Acadie, a region on the Canadian Atlantic coast. *Cajun/cadien* is now used to designate the group, language, and culture of people assumed to descend from the Acadian exiles who settled in Louisiana after their deportation from Canada in 1755. A key word here is "assumed" because the definition of *Cajun/cadien* is still a knot of confusion despite a long presence in Louisiana and a surge of commercial and scholarly interest in the past two to three decades. One issue is unanimously agreed upon: there would have been and there would be no Cajuns if Acadians had not settled in Louisiana between 1765 and 1785. The rest is a matter of debate.

Cajun is the written form of the American English pronunciation of [kɛdžʌn]; [kɛdžʌn] is used universally by Cajuns and non-Cajuns as well as by English- and French-speakers. In conformity with English morphology, it is the only form of the adjective and the singular noun both at the masculine and feminine.

Cadien and *cadjin* are the written forms of the Louisiana French pronunciation of [kadžɛ]. [kadžɛ] is used exclusively by French-speakers, mostly by Cajuns but also by non-Cajuns. The feminine form of both terms is respectively *cadienne* [kadiɛn] and *cadjine* [kadžin]. The plural of both the noun and adjective, masculine and feminine, is marked with the *s* ending, which is not realized in speech.

The original oral realization of the term will remain shrouded by the eternal silence of its long-gone unrecorded speakers. Modern oral usage ranges from [ka:džɛ] to [kadiɛ] in French and [kedžʌn] in English. The historical evolution can, however, be reconstructed from written sources that provide diachronic and codified information.

We cannot claim that our data are exhaustive. It would be beyond the scope of this book to track down all of the early and rare occurrences of the words. Current use of the word "Cajun" is so widespread that accounting for all examples of it would be a massive, perhaps impossible, undertaking. Compilations of manuscripts (administrative documents, personal correspondence) were the source of some eighteenth-century uses of the term.[4] Nineteenth- and early twentieth-century material comes from published accounts of contacts with the Louisiana Acadian population and territory.[5] These reports originate from administrators, scholars, travelers, journalists, and fiction writers, and are presented in Tables 1.1[6] and 1.2.[7] Modern material has been collected through observation-participation in books, articles, dictionaries, administrative documents, signs, and lately, in electronic form. Table 1.3 presents the use of ethnic code words in telephone directories of the Lafayette area (1905–2000).

There are methodological questions pertinent to the ethnohistory of a written ethnic label. The evolution, use, and meaning of a name are worthy topics of inquiry. Anthropologists and sociolinguists have studied ethnic labels to identify ethnic groups and analyze ethnicity.[8] As for the ethnic situation in Louisiana, the confusing label *Creole/créole* has been the subject of several studies but *Cajun/cadien* has not received the same amount of scrutiny.[9]

Another issue deals with the use of written data. In Louisiana, writings in French and Creole have long been provided a measure of the cultural vitality of Louisiana French and Creole cultures. The decline of these writings signaled the demise of French among elites, and the literary renaissance of the 1970s is hailed as a manifestation of the resurgence of Cajun ethnicity.[10] The analysis of the written symbols, along with the firsthand information provided by writers, can offer a valuable way of looking at the formal representation of Louisiana Cajuns.

We acknowledge that both *Cajun* and *cadien* were spoken before they were recorded on paper and that their use was wider than the limited view of their existence allowed by a handful of texts. The questions pertaining to the correspondence between oral realization and graphic representation will be addressed; in fact they are at the core of this "ethnography of writing."

Finally, the validity of the written portrayal of a largely illiterate group by erudite outsiders must be assessed. Early accounts of the use of *Cajun/*

cadien originate from non-Acadian sources and are by and large noticeably pejorative. In contrast, publications by Cajun authors, especially in French, are recent and rare, and reflect a renewed ethnic pride. If we keep in mind the distinction between the insiders and the outsiders, though, we can see the portrayals as a kind of historical conversation between Cajuns and non-Cajuns about the images of the group and about the shifting boundaries between members and nonmembers.

CREATION OF THE ETHNIC LABELS

The etymology of *Cajun/cadien* is undisputed; there are Cajuns in Louisiana because Acadians settled there after their deportation from Acadie by the British in 1755. However, the etymology of *Acadie* is not as clear. Historians award the coining of the term to Giovanni Verrazano; in 1524, the Florentine navigator called the upper part of the American Atlantic Coast *Archadia* "for the beauty of its trees" in reference to Arcadia, a rural region of Ancient Greece regarded as a pastoral paradise. Between 1548 and 1575, maps named the area corresponding to Nova Scotia *Larcadia, Larcadie*, or *Arcadia*. Samuel de Champlain, the founder of French Canada, used both *Arcadie* (1603) and *Accadie* (1613). In 1603, the French king Henri IV opened the region of *la Cadie* to settlers. A group of French merchants incorporated a *"Compagnie de l'Acadie"* in 1604, providing the first written record of the term.[11]

A second interpretation proposes a different source. Poirier submitted that "*Cadie* is the primitive name of the territory taken from the natives." According to this interpretation, the word originated from terms used by the Algonquin tribes who resided along the north Atlantic coast. *Acadie* was a variation of the Micmac *algatig*, a camp, as found today in *Tracadie, Subenacadie*, or the Malecite term *quoddy*, a fertile place, as found in *Passamaquoddy* and *Chappaquiddick*.

The scarcity of written records, the early variations in spelling, and the lack of recorded seventeenth-century speech hamper any definite conclusion on the origin of the term and its early oral realization and use. Nevertheless, throughout the eighteenth century, *Acadian/acadien* unequivocally designated the Catholic descendants of French farmers and fishermen settled around the Baie Française. Descendants of English and Scottish settlers who arrived after France ceded Acadie to England in 1713 were not labeled Acadians.

The *grand dérangement* (the great displacement) that followed the deportation resulted in the settlement of approximately 5,000 Acadians in Louisiana. The refugees were labeled *Acadians/acadiens*. In May 1765, Charles Aubry, military commander of New Orleans, noted,

> Lorsque j'ai rendu compte de l'arrivée d'une soixantaine de familles acadiennes venues de Saint Domingue, je ne croyais pas qu'elles seraient suivies de beaucoup

d'autres qui arrivent continuellement et que la Louisiane allait bientôt devenir une nouvelle Acadie.

When I reported the arrival of sixty Acadian families from Saint Domingue, I did not think they would be followed by many others who are arriving continuously and that Louisiana was soon to become a new Acadia.[12]

Their descendants were long referred to as *Acadians/acadiens*; so indicate official correspondence and authors (see Tables 1.1 and 1.2). There is, however, scant evidence that the abbreviated term was in use, and available data suggest an early origination in French. In a 1771 letter, a priest in Louisiana complained that

Il y a pres d'un mois que vers les onze heures du matain quatre Cadiens entrerent ches moy scavoir les nommees Richard pere, Poyri, Bergeron, dit Andre, sous pretexte d'allumer leur pype . . .

About a month ago at around eleven in the morning four Cajuns, the elder Richard, Poyrie, Bergeron known as Andre, came to my house under the pretext to light their pipe . . .

Not much can be deduced from this unique occurrence; the writer was not an Acadian, the tone of the letter conveys a dislike of the behavior of said *Cadiens*, but it cannot be concluded that the abbreviated terms was universally used as a derogative. Historians have recorded the use of this abbreviated form elsewhere; it mostly applied to Acadian settlements in Québec; Poirier claimed that Acadians called themselves *Cadgiens* or more simply French.[13] It can be assumed that a derivative of *Acadien* was used in speech, but it is unclear how it was used by Acadians or outsiders and what meaning it carried.

A century would elapse before *cadien* appeared in print in Louisiana. It is used by Désirée Martin (1877) in an autobiographical essay in which she refers to "*la colonie franco-cadienne*" and the "*francs Cadiens de 1754.*" The term later appears in a novel by Sidonie de la Houssaye (1888) and writings by Creole scholar Alcée Fortier (1894). *Cadien* is the only early French derivative of *Acadien*; later, other abbreviations have been proposed: *Cayens, cajin, Cadgiens, Cajen, Cadjun, Cadjein, Cadjien*, and *cadjin*.[14]

Most sources agree to award the coining of *Cajun* to *Putnam's Magazine* contributor R. L. Daniels in 1879. It was one of many variations of *Acadian*. In 1873, a planter wrote of *Cagians; Cajen* is recorded in 1873, *Cadian* in 1876.[15] Even though *Cajun* would become the standard English spelling, other forms were later proposed by writers: *Cajan, 'Cadian, Cajian*, and *Cajin*,[16] *Kajun* is also currently used by local businesses.

In addition to the parallel variations of both French and English spellings, other clues point to an origination of the abbreviated term in Louisiana Acadian speech. Authors indicated that they were transcribing a term used in speech; Daniels wrote: "Acadian—or rather its corruption 'Cajun' as they pronounce it"; "Presently we saw our first Acadians—nowhere spoken of in their own country otherwise than as 'Cajuns,'" noted Ralph. De la Houssaye wrote,

[Ils] nommèrent ce coin de terre qu'ils venaient d'adopter la Petite Cadie, du nom de la patrie perdue . . . "Maître," répondit l'esclave, "c'est une des Cadiennes du campement."

They named the piece of land they had just adopted the small Cadie, the name of the lost motherland . . . "Master," the slave said, "it's one of the Cadiennes from the camp."[17]

In addition, whether in English or French, authors resorted to different typographical devices to transcribe the word. Noyes used italics, and others used quotation marks; an anonymous 1901 glossary indicated the proper French pronunciation in "cadien (pron. Cadjen)."[18]

Furthermore an analysis of the spelling reveals that

- The dropping of the initial *a* is unanimously noted in both French and English. This consensus supports the assumption that the spelling correctly represented the abbreviated pronunciation of *Acadian/acadien*. However, the continued use of *Acadian/acadien* and the recent creation of *Acadiana* indicate that the aphesis (suppression of an initial sound) is not uniquely the result of internal linguistic pressure; there were nonlinguistic factors at play in the coining and the writing of *Cajun/cadien*.
- The introduction of the letters *j* or *g* accurately symbolizes the oft-noted shift in both Acadian and Cajun French from [d] to [dz] when followed by an open vowel [i]. Such a shift is found in *Dieu* [dioe] pronounced [dzoe], and *diable* [diabl] pronounced [djab]. French spelling has no codified symbol to represent the sound [dz], which is not a French consonant; French writers used two methods to indicate the shift: the use of *j* or *g* in conjunction with the letter *d* as in *cadjin, cadgein*, and an indication of how to pronounce *cadien*. The maintenance of the conventional orthography is most likely because of the etymological pressure of *Acadian/acadien*.

  It is easier to represent the phonetic shift in Acadian French with English spelling: [j] is an English consonant represented by the symbols *j* and *g*; English writers uniformly used *j* or *g* to coin *Cajun, Cajan, Cajen, Cajin, Cagians*. So did some Canadian Acadians: letters by an Acadian housewife in the 1890s give *acajin* and *canajin*.[19]
- The various endings *-ian,-an,-un,-en*, and *-in* used by English writers reflect the difficulty to represent the sound [ɛ], which does not exist in English. It is frequent in French and was originally noted with the *-ien* ending; later, endings in *-in,-en*, and *-ein* were introduced. In conclusion, evidence shows that the abbreviated form

of *Acadian/acadien* was used in Louisiana Acadian speech and that written forms were coined by outsiders in both French and English approximately one century after the arrival of Acadian exiles. The coining of *Cajun/cadien* thus appears to be larger than a mere linguistic event such as a phonetic transcription; its significance lies in the interaction between social groups in nineteenth-century Louisiana. It is to be sought in the use and meaning of the term.

EARLY USAGE AND NEGATIVE ASCRIPTION OF THE ETHNIC LABELS

Tables 1.1 and 1.2 map the use of names in French and English accounts from the eighteenth and nineteenth century to designate the descendants of Acadian exiles in Louisiana. Table 1.1 shows that Acadians were not a topic of great interest for French writers; Bossu, Baudry des Lauzières, Chateaubriand, and Sauvalle do not mention the Acadians despite traveling in the area and showing keen interest in describing the natural environment and local population, especially the *sauvages*, as Native Americans were called.[20] When Acadians are mentioned, mostly by Louisiana-based writers, they are referred to as *acadien* and in a couple of instances as *créole*. The Acadians are never labeled *français*, a term reserved for French citizens or for those claiming direct French descent. Then, toward the end of the century, limited use of the abbreviated term is made or recorded by outsiders; in these instances, *cadien* is clearly used as a derogative or a term indicating rurality, lack of education, and low social status.

Table 1.2 shows a greater interest of Anglo-American writers in the Acadians. Name usage also reveals significant differences in the perspective adopted by these writers. In Colonial Louisiana, authors used only *Acadians*. Then, after the Louisiana Purchase and until the 1880s, Acadians were referred to as *Acadians, Creoles*, and *French*. It is sometimes unclear whether the authors wrote about Acadians, French Canadians, French-born, or native Creoles. For instance, Stoddard's account of the "character of the Louisianians" did not mention *Acadians* but *French, Creoles, Creole French*, or *French Creoles*; it differentiated between "Creoles of Upper-Louisiana" and "those along Red River and the Delta," between Creoles that are "partly the descendants of French Canadians, and partly of those who migrated under some of the first governors of Louisiana"; mentions of settlements on the western side of the Mississippi, of "mixing" with "Spaniards, German and other strangers" as well as with the aborigines, and of "peculiar customs wholly derived from their Canadian ancestors" suggest that the Acadians may have been included in the description.[21] Similarly, memoirs by Flint and Prentiss contain no references to *Acadians* even if their mentions of the *French* are likely to include the Acadians. Nevertheless, in these early accounts, the Acadians did not appear as a discrete group.[22]

Table 1.1
French Names Used for Descendants of Acadian Exiles, Eighteenth and Nineteenth Centuries

Authors	No Mention	Creole	Acadien	Cadien
Aubry (1765) in Arcenault (1965)			X	
Conseil Supérieur (1768) in Historical Records (1940)			accadien	
Valentin (1771) in Archivo General de Indias				X
Champigny (1773)			X	
Bossu (1777)	X			
Favrot (1779) in Historical Survey (1941)			X	
Raynal (1780)			X	
Baudry des Lauzières (1802)	X			
Berquin Duvallon (1802)		X		
Perrin du Lac (1805)			X	
Robin (1807)			X	
Chateaubriand (1827) in (1929-1938)	X			
Tixier (1844) in (1866)*			X	
Barde (1861)		X	X	
Martin (1877)				X
Delahoussaye (1888)			X	X
Sauvalle (1891)	X			
Fortier (1894)			X	X
anonymous (1901) in Ditchy (1932)		X	X	X
Voorhies (1907)			X	

*The author uses the term once in "*Quand nous arrivâmes aux Acadiens,*" referring to the Acadian Coast on the Mississippi.

The use of *French* to refer to the Acadians was unique to the Anglo-American perspective and, as shown, could be problematic. There was more confusion over the use of *Creole*. This was because of the term's multiple meaning and the inconsistent use that writers made of it. The various meanings of *Creole* in Louisiana result from historical evolution and the absence of clear-cut boundaries between the various groups it labeled; from the original sense of "native to the colonies," the meaning was later expanded to refer to cultural differences (Creole versus American) and racial distinctions (black, white, or both); furthermore, the term had both ethnic and linguistic dimensions that did—and still do—not coincide: for instance, a Creole does

Table 1.2
English Names Used for Descendants of Acadian Exiles, Eighteenth and Nineteenth Centuries

Authors	French	Creole	Acadian	Cajun
Gordon (1766) in Mereness (1912)			X	
Pittman (1770)			Accadians	
Hutchins (1784)			X	
Pitot (1802) in (1979)			X	
Stoddard (1812)	X	X		
Cramer (1814)			X	
Darby (1816)	X	X	X	
Flint (1826, 1835)	X			
Prentiss (1829) in (1855)	X			
Sealsfield (1842) in McMillan (1943)			Acajan	
Longfellow (1847)			X	
Lyell (1849)	X	X		
Olmsted (1856)	X	X	X	
Dorr (1860) in Prichard (1938)			X	
Waud (1866)			X	
Noyes (1868)		X	X	Cagians
Lockett (1873)			X	
Rhodes (1873)		X	X	Cajens
De Leon (1875)			X	
King (1875)			X	
Nordhoff (1876)			X	Cadians
Daniels (1879-1880)	Créoles	français	X	X
Finerty (1880)				Cagin
Sparks (1882)			X	
Cable (1886)			X	Cadians
Davis (1887)			X	Cajans
Cable (1888) in (1901)			X	X
Harris in Poole (1889)			X	X
Perrin (1891)			X	Cajan
Ralph (1893)			X	X
Chopin (1894) in (1969)			'Cadian	X

not necessarily speak Creole.[23] Predictably, its use varied greatly according to the social location of users. Anglo-American writers systematically used *Creole* in combination with other labels; the overlap is apparent in this notation by Frederick L. Olmsted: "We were passing a hamlet of cottages, occupied by the Acadians, or what the planters call *habitans*, poor white French Creoles."[24]

Then, by the end of the nineteenth century, writers no longer associated the Acadians with *Creole*; the literary accounts of Louisiana Creole society by George W. Cable make the distinction quite clear: for him, Creoles were the white elite of European descent.[25] Since Acadians were not perceived as belonging to the ruling class, English names used to characterize them were limited to *Acadian* and its abbreviated forms. In parallel with the evolution in French, the Acadians no longer *French* or *Creoles* were exclusively labeled *Acadians* or *Cajuns.*

However, the two terms were by no means synonyms. The distinctiveness of *Cajun/cadien* is clearly marked semantically. The label is presented as a corrupted term, to be used with precaution because it was an insult:

> The name Acadians, by which they were first known, was soon contracted or corrupted into the term 'Cajan,' by which they are frequently known. For some reason unknown to us, these people object to the name Cajan. There is certainly no disgrace in being a descendant of an innocent people who were driven from their homes in Acadia and settled in this country; and we can see no reason for being ashamed of the name or its contracted form, Cajan.[26] Nearly all the white folks who trudged along the highways were Acadians, all but hallowed by the magic of Longfellow, and it was strange indeed to hear that we not call them Cajuns to their faces lest they be offended, that the term is taken as one of reproach[27]

The same meaning was ascribed to the French derivative; this 1901 definition is assumed to have been written by an Acadian scholar:

> CADIEN. [. . .] Ce nom est quelquefois donné dans le sens d'ironie mais le plus souvent de mépris. Il ne semble pas du tout l'abrégé de *Acadien*; car on l'applique indistinctement à tout créole, quelle que soit son origine, qui sent la campagne et qui a l'air d'un paysan. C'est un Cadien!"

> CAJUN. [. . .] This name is sometimes used ironically but most often conveys disdain. It does not at all appear to be the abbreviated form of Acadian; it is applied indiscrimately to any Creole who, whatever its origin, smells like the country and looks like a peasant. That's a Cajun![28]

No longer *French* or *Creole, Cajuns/cadiens* are not either necessarily *Acadians/acadiens.* Separated from their Frenchness, denied the Creole label, Cajuns were being pulled away from their Acadian ancestry; by the turn of the century, *Cajuns/cadiens* are a group symbolically discrete. Their distinctiveness is greater in English than in French. If *cadien* retains the graphic mark of the Acadian origin, the spelling of *Cajun* does not convey it at all; in fact, it follows the pattern employed to coin *Injun*, the spelling used by

American writers to convey scorn and disdain of American Indians. Indeed, Cajuns were constructed as a breed apart.

The symbolic distinction of Cajuns reflected their new position in the social structure of postbellum Louisiana. Recent scholarship has exposed the mechanism that resulted in the stratification of nineteenth-century Acadian society. Historians have identified several factors that led to the breakup of a culturally homogeneous community into different classes. These factors included settlement in natural environments as diverse as levee lands, swamps, prairie, and coastline marshes, the adoption of slavery and the plantation system by second- and third-generation Acadians, unequal access to land and capital, intermarriage with higher-class Creoles or endogamy, the failure of the state and the Catholic church to provide educational opportunities in French, co-optation of the Acadian elite by the Anglo-American system, and the refusal by Cajuns to "make the necessary compromises and concessions to Anglo-American ways."[29] The devastation brought on by the Civil War and the crises of Reconstruction resulted in a greater polarization. Carl Brasseaux noted,

> Before the Civil War, the Acadians constituted a highly stratified and diversified socioeconomic group. The community contained planters, prosperous small slaveholding farmers, ranchers, urban professionals, rural artisans, independent yeomen, and landless day laborers. In the postbellum period, however, Acadian agriculturalists divided into two basic groups: a small upper and upper-middle class that was largely co-opted by the region dominant's Anglo-American culture, and the impoverished, poorly educated, but culturally steadfast masses.[30]

The Acadian upper class remained *Acadian/acadienne* and the lower class became *Cajun/cadienne*. According to Dormon, the process of exclusion that resulted in the distinction between "lowly 'Cajun' and Lordly 'Genteel Acadian' " was achieved by 1865; Brasseaux estimates that the transition from "Acadian to Cajun" was completed by 1877. Objective differences in social class were symbolized by different labels. The systematic use and ascribed meaning of *Cajun/cadien* concur with the time line and analysis proposed by historians.

The use of both terms by nineteenth century writers is exemplary. Davis drew a distinction between the good "Acadian" and the "wretched Cajans": *Acadian* is used when positive qualities are mentioned and *Cajun* is associated with condemnable behaviors:

> "I am Acadian myself on my mother's side. Oh I know my people!"
> "I heard much of them at New Orleans."
> "Then," hastily, "I am glad to have met you to correct your false impressions of the lazy, wretched 'Cajans'!"
> "They do not seem to be a progressive people," ventured Mr. Ely.
> "No, perhaps not. But is progress everything? They are not lazy. The men work

faithfully—when they work at all. . . . It is true that they are separate from the world in that they have no schools, no books, no newspapers [. . .] The Acadian is a moral, sober, honorable man. He is fond of his wife and children."[31]

A similar use is made of the terms by Louisiana novelists; in his Acadian trilogy, *Bonaventure*, Cable exclusively refers to Acadian people, history, and language as *Acadian* and reserved the use of *Cajun* for low-class characters, a Black and a laborer whose discourses are noted in phonetic vernacular. In her writings, Louisiana fiction author Kate Chopin uses mostly *'Cadian* although one of her characters, a black servant, uses *Cajun* to describe "a gentleman of the Bayou Têche."[32]

This pattern organized the usage of both terms in French and English until recently. Little oral and written data were found on the use of *cadien* by the people so labeled at the turn and first decades of the twentieth century. However, written evidence by outsiders provides some indications. The use of *cadien* during this period was very limited. One reason was that French-language print had all but disappeared, ensuring the supremacy of English; besides historical works, there are a handful of travel accounts by French and Canadians scholars in which Louisiana Acadians are referred to as *acadiens.* In his memoir on a trip to Louisiana, Robert made a rare mention of *cadien*:

Un chauffeur d'auto à qui je demande s'il parle le français répond: Non, je parle le cadien. Et comme la conversation se continue, il se rend compte tout à coup qu'après tout, il n'y a qu'une grammaire française et un dictionnaire français.

I ask the driver if he speaks French; he responds: No, I speak Cajun. And as the conversation goes on, he suddenly realizes that after all there is but one French grammar and one French dictionary.[33]

The use of *Cajun* is better documented. At the turn of the century, the term was either used as a derogative or avoided. Until the 1960s there were no newspapers, literary publications, or Acadiana businesses using it. Scholars did not use *Cajun/cadien*; their writings refer to *Acadian/Acadien, French-speaking, Louisiana French*, and *French*; when *Cajun* was used, it was printed in a different type or accompanied with explanations.[34]

The use of *Cajun* by outsiders was notably different. In 1925, a record company labeled Louisiana French folk music *Cajan* whereas local terms included *French, Acadian*, or *French Acadian*,[35] Cajun dialect and simple-mindedness were portrayed by humorists such as Walter Coquille, caricaturesque mayor of fictitious Bayou Pom Pom. Among writers, playwright Ava Jack Carver penned *The 'Cajun* in 1926—a dark affair of cousin marriage and broken hearts[36]—and a *National Geographic* contributor rubbed "elbows with the famous 'Cajuns' " during his incursion among the trappers of Terrebonne Parish:

The language of the Cajun is a French patois, but occasionally he makes forays into the English tongue, and weird and fantastic are the results. Although a vast deal of fun is had at the expense of the Cajun, chiefly on account of his linguistic lapses, Louisiana has leaned heavily upon his stalwart shoulders and he endures the hardships of the trapper's life with admirable bonhomie.[37]

Accompanied with transcriptions in vernacular Cajun English and photographs of Cajuns fishing and logging, these works contributed to build the image of the rural, illiterate Cajun living on the edge of civilization; this excerpt by Daniels helped publicize the negative connotation of *Cajun*:

Terrebonne is another land in the same state. It lies across the instep of the boot of Louisiana from Feliciana. But this parish of the Good Earth has by no means been a land of riches. Sometimes even it must seem to its Cajun fur trappers, oysters tonguers, shrimp seiners and fishermen that *le bon Dieu* had forgotten them. And devout, even superstitious as they have remained, they have in some cases of poverty had to forego [*sic*] the expensive services of priests. . . . But such Cajuns, of course, [. . .] are not typical. But they are there and they have been desperately poor. But its fish and its fur as well as its fertility made it ripe for opening before Huey ran in his roads to take Cajun votes and produce out as well as carry new wealth in.[38]

Gone are the explanations of the term and the typographical hints; symbolically, *Cajuns* are a group in their own right, disconnected from their Acadian heritage. Whereas *Acadians* are lauded and studied, *Cajuns* are derided and stereotyped. Even attempts by fair-minded scholars to "clear up a maze of misunderstandings about the Cajuns" ended up reinforcing the cliché:

The term Creole has always been synonymous with excellence. . . . And Cajun was a fighting word. Here an old Negro mammy did not say "poor white trash." She said "Cajun"—or "blue bellied Cajun." When the old Creoles wished to designate some ignoramus in their midst with whom they were exasperated, they tacked on an adjective [. . .] "*maudit* Cajin." . . . As another educator, a man from *La Côte des Acadiens*, laughingly puts it, "Me, I am a Creole; the other fellow, he is a Cajun."[39]

In her assessment of the representation of Cajuns in literature, Pecot acknowledged that some descendants of the Acadians have risen to become

some of the most distinguished citizens the state has produced. . . . But [such] personalities, although retaining some features particular to their countrymen, have, in the larger sense, succumbed to the dominating influences of American culture and have become hybrid by-products. . . . Not so the typical 'Cajun, who has been neither amalgamated nor assimilated by the Americans, but is today the same sturdy Breton peasant who fished and trapped and farmed over two hundred years ago in the environs of Nova Scotia.[40]

By the 1950s, approximately a century after its emergence in writing, the usage of *Cajun/cadien* followed a clear pattern: the English orthography was the dominating norm, it had eclipsed *Acadian*, it was used derisively or stereotypically by outsiders, and it was avoided or used carefully by insiders.

TOWARD A POSITIVE ASCRIPTION

Despite some continuity in the use of these labels, there were signs of gradual change. The English term began to be applied to groups outside Louisiana. Publications revealed the existence of *Cajan* communities in Alabama, Mississippi, and Texas; accounts focused on miscegenation and poverty:

> Cajans in the hilly areas of Washington, Mobile and Clarke Counties [Alabama] as well as adjoining parts of Mississippi . . . are a poor hill people of the wooded country who subsist by lumbering, turpentine extraction, and various odd jobs. . . . Cajans are a mixture of white, Indian and Negro types.[41]

Though the distinctiveness with Louisiana Cajuns was noted, the common French heritage and similarity of the names leave "little doubt that at least some of their ancestors included members of the original migrants from Acadia or other early French settlers."[42]

On the other hand, two derogative terms applied to Cajuns appeared presumably in the late 1940s: *coonass* and *bougalie.* Despite its rather clear denotation (a racoon's behind), the etymology of *coonass* remains a matter of debate. Some argued that the term originated from the French word *conasse*, a feminine term indicating either a prostitute or a person doing stupid things; the term would have been used by French and American soldiers to address French-speaking Louisianian soldiers who would have brought the term back home after the war. Others believed that *coonass* was derived from the name given to Andrew Jackson's Tennessee volunteers when they came to New Orleans wearing their coonskin caps. Folklorist and Cajun activist Barry Ancelet proposes that "it is not unlikely that *coonass* evolved simply as an expression of the doubly racist notions that Cajuns were even lower on the social scale than *coons* (a disparaging term for African Americans)." Recently, yet another possible origin has surfaced: the Caribbean Indian term *cunaso* applied to "someone who lives simply, off the land." Whatever the disagreement on the origin, there was consensus on several points: the term is recent, used as a derogative by non-Cajuns, and by Cajuns as "a term of endearment much in the same way that African-

Americans have used the word 'nigger' among themselves to try to disarm that hurtful word."[43]

In the 1970s, the use of the term came under scrutiny. Edwin Edwards, the self-proclaimed Cajun governor, was chastised for using the term liberally; in 1977, a Cajun employee filed suit against his employer, who had fired him because he objected to the use of the derogatory term *coonass*; the case was settled out of court in favor of the employee. In 1981, amidst extensive media coverage and prompted by Cajun activists, the Louisiana legislature condemned the use of the slur and forbid the sale of items displaying it. The endeavor was met by reactions ranging from support to derision. More than twenty years later, the controversy lingers on with the same protagonists and the same arguments. Stirred by use of the term on the airwaves or its discussion in a New Orleans *Times-Picayune* newspaper article, it prompted a participant in an ensuing Internet forum to write, "It doesn't bother me a bit. I think it all depends on HOW it's used, just like any other word. We're a little to sensitive these days and need to lighten up." Despite these developments, *coonass* remains used among Cajuns, "primarily by young working-class males of Cajun extraction who [. . .] see the term as a kind of macho assertion of their earthy, pungent masculinity."[44]

Another derogative term addressed to Cajuns was *boogerlee/bougalie* ['bugʌli]. Also spelled *boogalee* and *bougalee*, it referred to a French person of mixed black and white ancestry; "a contemptuous or taunting name for a lower-class Cajun,"[45] it was considered a synonym of *Cajun* and *coonass*. Scant data indicate a limited use, confined to the New Orleans area.

Discussion of racial purity of *coonasses, boogerlees*, and out-of-state *Cajans* represented a relative improvement of the prestige of *Cajun*: after all, descendants of the Acadian exiles in Louisiana could be called names more pejorative than *Cajuns*. In a shift similar to the turn-of-the-century split between *Acadian* and *Cajun*, *Cajun* came to embody positive qualities that other derivatives were described as lacking; in 1966, an editorialist proposed to name the fledgling football team in New Orleans the Louisiana Cajuns: "Pro gridders should have a name that denotes courage, valor, stamina, boldness and daring—in short all the virtues that are inbred in the manly Cajuns of Louisiana."[46]

Even though the NFL franchise was to become the New Orleans Saints, the endeavor symbolized a drastic evolution in the use and meaning of the word: *Cajun* no longer carried the stigma with which it had been associated. Again, writers for the popular press reflected this evolution; reporting for *National Geographic*, Keating wrote,

> The estimated quarter of a million French-speaking dwellers of the Louisiana coastal marsh do not accept strangers easily. Louisiana Frenchmen show an un-Gallic reserve, possibly because their English-speaking neighbors have often misunderstood them.

For instance, before I began my latest tour of Acadiana, I chatted with an Anglo-Saxon state official who expressed alarm at my free use of the word "Cajun."

"Don't let them hear you call them Cajuns," he said. "It's a dirty word to them."

Like most of his Anglo-Saxon neighbors, the nervous official has managed to spend his life among the French-speakers of southern Louisiana without once noticing that Cajuns is precisely what they call themselves.[47]

Positive ascription by outsiders was mirrored by an increasingly positive self-image; Table 1.3 documents the appearance of *Cajun* in the Lafayette telephone directory and its ever-increasing use by businesses in the heart of Cajun country. By the mid-1960s, the use of *Cajun* was acceptable to both insiders and outsiders.

The factors of this shift are found in Louisiana's changing social structure. The postbellum Acadian/Cajun split had left *Cajun* with a negative ascription; the rapid acculturation of Cajuns to the American way of life resulted in positive ascription and self-image. As Cajuns became more American, *Cajun* became more acceptable. The Americanization of Cajuns was itself the result of changes in American society. Of these, mechanization, industrialization, and urbanization had the strongest effect on the rural Louisiana population and especially on Cajuns. The integration of Cajuns into the larger American culture was evident in the decreasing use of the French language, the decline of agricultural occupations and the rise of industry and service jobs, the encroachment of Protestantism, and the adoption of American consumer habits from foodways to entertainment. The growing homogenization of the Louisiana cultural landscape apparently blurred the distinction between Cajuns and others. Nevertheless, the visibility of Cajuns increased dramatically; the less objective the difference, the more symbolic it became. This development was reflected in the use of *Cajun/cadien*.

First, *Cajun* and *Acadian* were once again used as synonyms. The distinction that separated *Cajuns* from *Acadians* at the beginning of the century had weakened. The reversal of ascription was extended to the etymology of the term: long characterized a "corrupted term," *Cajun/cadien* had become a "natural and legitimate linguistic derivative." A Louisiana senate resolution provided a definition of "Acadians (Cajuns)":

Louisianians originating from the province of Acadia in Canada were named and identified as Acadians and likewise as Cajuns since the word Cajun is a natural and legitimate linguistic derivative of the word Acadian in the English language.[48]

A typical example of the joint use of both terms is found at the University of Louisiana at Lafayette. Located in the heart of *Acadiana*, the "*Université des Acadiens*" has a "*Ragin' Cajun*" mascot that supports teams playing at *Cajun Field* or in the *Cajundome*.

Secondly, *Cajun* experienced a dramatic increase in usage both by insiders

Table 1.3
Listings Using Ethnic Code Words in the Lafayette Telephone Directory, 1905–2000

	1905	1906	1907	1908	1909	1912	1914	1928	1941	1944	1946	1951	1956	1961	1962	1963
Evangeline	○	1	1	1	1	○	○	3 (a)	6	8	8	11	12	18	19	18
Acadian								1	3	2	2	3	3	9	10	7
Acadia								10 (b)			1					1
Acadiana																
Cajun																
Creole										1 (c)	1					

	1964	1965	1966	1967	1968	1969	1970	1971	1972	1973	1974	1975	1976	1977	1978	1979
Evangeline	16	18	20	16	17	20	21	20	24	25	25	26	25	26	27	28
Acadian	8	10	14	16	21	23	24	28	29	36	37	39	38	42	42	46
Acadia	1	1	1	1	2	2	2	1	2	2	4	4	3	3	3	5
Acadiana	1	3	4	3	6	10	16	23	30	36	42	45	58	68	77	85
Cajun		1	2	1	3	3	2	8	13	11	10	11	8	7	12	13
Creole															1	1

	1981	1982	1983	1984	1985	1986	1987	1988	1989	1990	1991	1992	1993	1994	1995	2000
Evangeline	26	28	27	28	26	23	20	23	21	21	19	20	19	19	20	17
Acadian	52	54	60	53	54	49	48	43	54	52	55	50	54	59	48	45
Acadia	9	9	11	11	12	13	8	8	7	8	7	6	6	6	6	4
Acadiana	120	141	144	152	144	155	142	147	157	153	151	165	172	175	182	210
Cajun	24	21	34	37	41	36	32	41	46	40	41	42	46	50	50	56
Creole	4	6	5	4	3	3	3	3	3	3	6	5	5	4	4	7

Source: Adapted from Barry J. Ancelet, "From Evangeline Hot Sauce to Cajun Ice: Signs of Ethnicity in South Louisiana," paper presented at the meeting of the American Folkore Society, October 1994, New Orleans, LA.

Notes: Listings starting with the mentioned ethnic code words were counted in the commercial telephone directories covering the Lafayette area. Variations are noted in the area covered (starting in 1949, listings outside of Lafayette are omitted) and the organization of listings (businesses are listed separately starting in 1984).

○: no recorded use of any term;¦ : indicates a break in time sequence; (a): in Saint Martinville only; (b): in Rayne and Crowley only; (c): *Calais Creole Café* in Breaux Bridge and outsiders. It is a consequence of the movement of ethnic renewal that developed in the late 1970s after the creation of the Council for the Development of French in Louisiana (CODOFIL). The ensuing French Movement, as it was dubbed, is widely credited for promoting ethnic awareness among Cajuns. Beside its increased use in the Lafayette area, *Cajun* became a statewide brand name used in areas where Acadians had not settled and no Cajuns lived; a computer search of businesses in contract with the state of Louisiana yielded fifty-six hits in 1987 and seventy-five in 1994.[49] Now "hot," *Cajun* was reportedly helping sales and promotion not only in Louisiana but nationwide. Indeed, *Cajun* became associated with a great variety of products, items, and techniques; so, in French and Anglo Louisiana alike, appeared "Cajun popcorn," "Cajun Computers," "Cajun Police Supply," "Cajun Beauties," and a whole range of culinary products such as "Cajun Pizza," "Cajun Whaler," and many "Cajun" hot sauces. The popularity of Louisiana's French culture also led to a 300% increase in the use of ethnic identity markers based on *Acadia* between 1975 and 2000; the most used term is now *Acadiana*, a combination of Acadia and Louisiana, coined in 1964 and adopted as the official name of the southwest area of the state in 1971 (see Table 1.3). Alternate, stylicized spellings have also appeared: *Kajun* (in the name of several businesses in Southwestern Louisiana), *Kajon* (a convenience store in Baton Rouge with a *fleur-de-lys* in the o), *KAJUN* (a radio station in Baton Rouge whose logo was adorned by an alligator and cowboy boots), *KAJN* (a radio station in Abbeville), *KJIN* (a radio station in Houma), and even *KJN* seen on personalized license plates in Acadiana.

THE MOVE TOWARD SELF-DEFINITION

In parallel, the French term also experienced changes in context, form, and frequency of use. In 1978, a debate within the Louisiana French community centered on the spelling of *Cajun/cadien/cadjin*. The English spelling was normalized, but the French spelling was not. Cajuns writing in French and/or English had no clear guidelines to follow; some used the abbreviated term, whereas others declared *Nous Sommes Acadiens/We Are Acadians* because, as Arceneaux wrote, "It is therefore proper to insist on the word Acadian in its ancestral accuracy as opposed to the meaningless unorthographic corruption Cajun which obscures the literary association and historical significance of the name."[50]

Prompted by necessity, the editors of the newsletter published by CODOFIL asked their readers to choose between "Cajun or Cadjin" to designate Louisiana Cajuns. A handful of responses proposed *Cadjin, Cajun, 'cadien, Cadien, Cajin, Acadien*, and *coonass.* A repeated attempt in 1980 yielded some forty comments but also failed to gather a consensus. Commented a disappointed editor, le mot "Acadien" vient largement en tête, avec 13 supporters. Cajun vient en deuxième place, mais loin derrière: sept votes. Ensuite viennent Cadien et Cajin avec cinq voix chacun; Français-Acadien, Acadien-Louisianais, Acadien-Franco-Américain et Franco-Américain-Acadien, 1 chacun.

De plus, deux petits comiques, ou deux inconscients, ont suggéré "coonass," bien que cette possibilité n'était pas prévue.

the word "Acadien" is clearly ahead with 13 supporters. Cajun places a distant second with seven votes. Then come Cadien and Cajin with five votes each; Français-Acadien, Acadien-Louisianais, Acadien-Franco-Américain et Franco-Américain-Acadien, one each.

In addition, two comics or two ignorants suggested "coonass" which was not even offered as a choice.[51]

A decade elapsed before another attempt at formalization. The effort developed in a different context. The publication of texts in Cajun French and debates on the type of French to teach had occupied cultural activists for the better part of the decade; there was a greater awareness of the difficulties in defining and writing the various brands of Louisiana French. The popularity of *Cajun* and the persisting demand for a French name contributed to create a sense of urgency. "If we do not choose a 'standard' name, somebody else is going to do it for us," wrote one Cajun activist.[52] Normalization was due. Ultimately, a group of Louisiana writers gathered under the auspices of CODOFIL and organized a committee to standardize written Louisiana French.

The first order of business was the coining of a French name. The exclusion of *Cajun* was unanimous because it reflected the English pronunciation. Two positions emerged. One favored *cadjin* because it was unique to Louisiana, adequately noted the pronunciation, especially the [dj], and gave the morphologically correct feminine *cadjine*; the other opted for *cadien* because it clearly established Acadian ancestry, had been used to designate Acadian settlements outside ancestral Acadie, and accounted for the difference between oral and written communication.

Of course, the debate involved issues larger than the correct spelling of a word, no matter how symbolic, or the novel interpretation of old definitions. The issue was of boundary maintenance or, perhaps more accurately, boundary construction. Some called for a French Louisiana reaction to cultural imperialism. Guidry, for example, urged CODOFIL to put an end to the linguistic exploitation of "Cadiens" and promote the traditional orthography " 'Cadien' to name us." Ancelet concurred: "It's a colonialist crime to impose on us a spelling which reflects pronunciation . . . If we begin to change the orthography to reflect all the different accents in Louisiana, we risk alienating the French spoken in Louisiana, driving it back further into its corner. We have . . . to establish a means of communication between us and the rest of the French-speaking world."[53] On the other side, Marcantel argued for *cadjin* because its unique spelling objectified the ethnic diversity of Cajuns and de-emphasized the Acadian connection; *cadjin* is not a synonym of *acadien* because:

Pour être cadjin, on n'est pas obligé de faire des recherches généalogiques. . . . Si on accepte volontier (et je pense que c'est généralement admis) que la musique cadjine et la cuisine cadjine résultent d'un mélange d'influences espagnoles, africaines, américaines, acadiennes, françaises, allemandes, etc. pourquoi est-il difficile à admettre que le peuple cadjin est un mélange de ces mêmes cultures?

To be Cajun, one does not need to trace its genealogy . . . If it is agreed (as I think it widely is) that Cajun music and Cajun cuisine are the result of Spanish, African, American, Acadian, French, German and other influences, why is it so hard to admit that the Cajun people is a combination of these same cultures?

In the end, the committee recommended the spelling *cadien* and recognized the variant *cadjin*, in line with the guidelines adopted for the writing of Louisiana French. Recent observations suggest that *cadien* may emerge as the leading spelling among French-speaking and French-writing Cajuns; it is used by organizations (Renaissance Cadienne, Action Cadienne, Association des Etudiants Cadiens), Louisiana authors, and French-language publications.[54]

These developments are clearly linked to the recent evolution of Cajun ethnicity. Once a marker used by outsiders to delineate a social difference and exclude a group, the label is now controlled by Cajuns to denote a cultural difference from the inside. This control was achieved mostly by manipulations of symbols, including a group name, but also by the adoption of a flag in 1969 and a name for the geographical area. First, the context of reference in which Cajunness is defined has been changed; it is not limited any longer to the American society and culture. The inadequacy of an official frame of reference, defined by outsiders, is expressed in this excerpt of a play performed by the Théâtre 'Cadien. A census worker visits a Cajun family:

"Elle a dit: 'Est-ce que vous êtes Américain?' 'Ben non,' j'y ai dit. 'Les Amaricains, ça reste au Nord des Avoyelles, pis dans les aut' états, pas par icitte.' 'Est-ce que vous êtes noir?' J'ai dit, 'Non.' 'Chinois' 'Non.' 'Mexicain?' 'Non.' 'Puerto Ricain?' 'Non.' 'Amérindien?' 'Non.' J'ai dit, 'Non, j'ai jamais attendu parler de cette qualité de monde-là.' 'Bien,' a dit, 'c'est la finde la liste. Alors vous n'êtes pas une minorité reconnue!' J'ai dit, 'Madame, ti veut dire que tous les Cadjins se ressemblont?' A dit, 'Non, je veux dire que vous n'êtes pas une minorité. Que diable êtes-vous alors? J'ai dit, 'Madame, à Bayou St-Pierre, tout le monde est Cadjin, Acadien.' A dit, 'Non, pas possible. Ce n'est pas sur la liste. Le gouvernement fédéral à Washington n'a jamais entendu parler de vous.'

"Pensez-donc. On est icitte en Louisiane depuis au-dessus de deux siècles et y'z'ont jamais attendu parler de nous-aut'. Le gouvernement envouaye le C.I.A. tout partout dans le monde pour sa'oir quoi-ce qui se passe, mais y z'ont jamais fouillé à Bayou St-Pierre pour nous découvert.

"A dit, 'Est-ce que vous parlez une langue étrangàre?' J'ai dit, 'Ouais, l'amaricain.' 'Est-ce que vous êtes en Amérique depuis longtemps?' 'Ouais, on est en Louisiane depuis au-dessus de deux siéc', mais on est en Amarique depuis plus de 370 ans. On était en Amarique avant les Amaricains." (. . .) 'Alors,' a dit, 'il n'y a plus de question. Je sais maintenant exactement ce que vous êtes. Vous êtes des sauvages!' J'ai dit, 'Ouais, madame, asteur je connais exactement ça que t'es toi itou. T'es eine couillonne!'

"She said: Are you American? 'Well no,' I said. 'The Americans live north of Avoyelles, and in the other states, but not around here.' 'Are you Black?' I said, 'No.' 'Chinese?' 'No.' 'Mexican?' 'No.' 'Puerto Rican?' No.' 'Amerindian?' 'No.' I said 'No, I never heard of this kind of people.' 'Well,' she said, 'that's the end of the list. Then you are not an official minority!' I said, 'Miss, do you mean to say that all Cajuns look alike?' She said, 'No, I just mean that you are not a minority. What the hell are you?' I said, 'Madam, in Bayou Saint Pierre, everybody is Cajun, Acadian.' She said, 'No, that's not possible. This is not on the list. The federal government in Washington D.C. has never heard about you.'

Think about it. We have been here in Louisiana for over two centuries and they never heard about us. The government sends the CIA all over the world to find out what's going on, but they never looked in Bayou Saint Pierre to find us.

She said, 'Do you speak a foreign language?' I said, 'Yeah, American.' 'How long have you been in America?' 'Well, we've been in Louisiana for over two centuries but we've been in America for over 370 years. We were in America before the Americans' (. . .) 'Then,' she said, 'no more doubt. I know who exactly what you are. You are Savages!' I said, 'Yeah, madam, now I know exactly what you are. You're a jerk!'"[55]

The favored French label is now *la francophonie*, the French-speaking world. The rejection of *Cajun* and the adoption of a French term is necessary not only for French Louisiana but the positioning of Cajuns within the French-speaking world. Just as the emergence of *Cajun* symbolized the advent of an American ethnic group, the emergence of *cadien* symbolizes the inclusion of Cajuns in the *francophonie*. From this perspective, after more than two centuries in Louisiana, the descendants of the Acadian exiles are no longer *français, acadiens*, or *créoles* and even less *Cajuns*: they are *cadiens*. As Daigle put it,

the words Cajun and Acadian do not have the same meaning. The word Cajun applies only to those whose Acadian ancestors came to Louisiana after the eviction of 1755, whereas the broader term Acadian applies to all the descendants of the original Acadians, regardless of where they now live. Thus, all Cajuns are Acadians but not all Acadians are Cajuns.[56]

The distinction is not only symbolic, but is found in social practice. The debate on the type of French to teach in Louisiana classrooms highlighted the difference between standard French and French-based languages found in the state. The criticism by Cajun activists of the academic French bend of the initial CODOFIL endeavors focused on the specificity and variety of Cajun culture. From this emerging Louisiana francophone perspective, *Cadien* now labels a discrete group.

In addition, the control now asserted by Cajuns over their self-conception is marked by inclusiveness. Linguists have already pointed to a linguistic "continuum" and interrelations between French, Cajun, Creole, and English, a unique characteristic.[57] The acceptance and integration of the numerous cultural influences that shaped today's Cajunness is articulated in this definition of Cajuns by Reed, author of the first book published in Cajun French:

Alors pour moi, un vrai Cajun est une personne qui reste dans le sud-ouest de la Louisiane ou Est-Texas, et qui a demeuré avec les Français, les Allemands, les Anglais, les Espagnols, les Italiens, les Indiens et les Noirs; et depuis 1804, avec les Américains; mais qui a gardé la langue française-acadienne, qui a préservé la culture acadienne pour 200 ans et qui a toujours été fier de son héritage. (. . .) S'il a accepté la langue française, l'a apprise, l'aime, et la parle le mieux qu'il peut, ça, c'est un vrai Cajun! S'il a accepté la culture, les traditions, et la musique des Cajuns, il est un Cajun; et s'il garde son héritage acadien malgré tout les grands changements depuis le "grand dérangement" des Acadiens en 1755, il est un Cajun. Il est peut-être un pauvre ou un riche, un catholique ou un Baptiste, bien informé dans l'éducation ou pas du tout; mais s'il parle cajun, aime la musique cajune, garde les vieilles manières de vivre, lui aussi devrait être qualifié comme un Cajun. Finalement, un Cajun est un Cajun, qu'il demeure dans le sud-ouest de la Louisiane ou Los Angeles, Houston ou les pays étrangers. Ça c'est ça le Cajun qui croit qu'il est un Cajun."

Then for me, a real Cajun is a person who lives in southwestern Louisiana or East Texas, and who has lived with the French, Germans, English, Spanish, Italians, Indians and Blacks; and since 1804, with the Americans; but who has kept the French-Acadian language, who has preserved Acadian culture for 200 years and who has always been proud of its heritage. [. . .] If he has accepted the French language, learned it, loves it and speaks to the best of his ability, he is a real Cajun; and if he has kept his Acadian heritage despite all the changes since the "great displacement" of Acadians in 1755, he is a Cajun. He may be poor or rich, Catholic or Baptist, educated or not; but if he speaks Cajun, loves Cajun music, kept the old ways, then he should be called a Cajun. In the end, a Cajun is a Cajun, whether he lives in Southwestern Louisiana, Los Angeles, Houston or abroad. A Cajun is one if he believes he is a Cajun.[58]

This statement embodies in its form the inclusiveness of its content; it displays the use of the English noun (*Cajun*) in a French text with the morphological adjustments of capitalization (*cajun* as adjective and *Cajun* as noun) and gender (the feminine *cajune*) as well as the various synonyms (*acadien, française-acadienne*).

Positive, defined from within and inclusive, Cajun ethnicity remains challenged whether in French, as exemplified by the *cadien/cadjin* debate, or in English, from the inside and the outside, or rather from the various perspectives Cajun ethnicity may be viewed.

Cajun had been problematic when used as a derogatory term to characterize the lowest class of the illiterate, poor, and altogether non-Americanized descendants of Acadian exiles. By the 1980s, the term was destigmatized, positively charged, and used liberally by Cajuns and non-Cajuns alike. Interestingly, it remains problematic. Regardless of its connotation, the term still symbolizes differences. As the all-encompassing symbol of Cajunness, *Cajun/cadien* became a contested battleground

The commercial exploitation of *Cajun* did not sit well with cultural activists who objected to the construction of a stereotype and complained of being "Cajuned-out." Renowned Cajun musician Dewey Balfa commented, "Cajun is being so commercialized. Not just Cajun music. Cajun everything. Someday it's going to be too much"; the same view "once prompted musician instrument maker and local sage Marc Savoy to answer a reporter's question, 'Are you sorry the Cajuns have been discovered?' with 'I'm sorrier the Cajuns have discovered themselves.' "[59]

The "Cajunization of Louisiana" also prompted outsiders to react. Louisiana merchants worried. A state marketing official commented, "Our problem is that Cajun is very, very popular right now. . . . What we're trying to solve is the fake Cajun problem." Reports of "Cajun" products marketed by companies in Illinois, New Jersey, and Tennessee prompted Louisiana officials and food producers to action. The legislature authorized the adoption of a logo for Louisiana products, and the commissioner of agriculture threatened to sue producers of "out-of-state, bad-tasting, red-pepper-hot, copy-cat Cajun food."[60] The logo currently in use reads "Product of Louisiana Certified *Cajun*."

In New Orleans, the liberal use of the *Cajun* label was also contested because of its inadequacy. As the economic benefits of Cajunization could be seen and taunted throughout the French Quarter, a columnist wrote,

> What those visitors probably don't know is that New Orleans isn't a Cajun town, and never was. Creole, yes; Cajun, no. But the city, curiously, has become the center of the Cajun revival [initiated by Chef] Paul Prudhomme. Prudhomme's food is not the Cajun food that settlers of yore used to eat. . . . [The French] Quarter, a place that played a role in the development of Cajun culture at two stages—the very beginning when the original Acadians arrived at the port of New Orleans; and the Prudhomme revival.[61]

In a study of the cultural diversity of French Louisiana, geographer Cecyle Trépanier proposed that the designation of twenty-two parishes in the southwest region as Acadiana, and the adoption of the Louisiana Acadian flag "made awkward the place of Italian, Spanish, Scots-Irish 'Cajuns' by referring to an old Acadian identity, and definitely prevented blacks and Indians of French culture from being Cajuns."[62]

Indeed, black legislators responded vigorously when a Cajun legislator attempted to include "French Acadians" among officially recognized minorities. Such a distinction would have extended to Cajuns the benefits of set-aside programs and other economic advantages provided to minorities. Black legislators labeled the bill "facetious" and "ludicrous"; it was widely described as an attempt to water down affirmative action and was ultimately vetoed by the governor.[63]

African American activists have been waging a campaign to protest the inclusion of Louisiana Blacks under the label *Cajun*. One of the founders of the UnCajun Committee protested the naming of the University of Louisiana at Lafayette athletic teams as Ragin' Cajuns: "Southwest Louisiana is pluralistic in every sense of the word with Acadians, Afrikans (30%), French, Germans, Puerto Ricans, Spanish, etc. who together made and make the area what it is. How dare the Cajuns co-opt, usurp and suck all of the honey!"

The issue generated a debate on campus. One participant noted that "Cajun" and "nigger" were both racial slurs in the past and that the "cleaning up" of Cajun could not totally erase the connotation. Other participants remarked, "If this university became home of the Ragin' Niggers, how many white students would attend this university? How many of you would go and cheer the Ragin' Niggers? This is not a mascot issue . . . This is not anti-Cajun. This is un-Cajun. It simply means that we are not Cajun."

The issue flared up again in 1997 at the occasion of the planned appearance of Nation of Islam leader Louis Farrakhan at the . . . Cajundome. The discussion took an economic turn with complaints that African American and Creole tax dollars were being used to promote a white culture.[64] The name issue is symbolic of a wider movement that contributed both to reassert the racial difference between Whites and Blacks and reinforce the French-based identity of Louisiana's black French-speakers. The 1980s saw the development of actions by Creoles to assert both their race and culture: an association, C.R.E.O.L.E. Inc. was formed in 1987 to promote Louisiana Creole culture through student exchanges, cultural activities such as zydeco dances, and discussions of *créolité*; magazines have been published (*Creole Magazine* in 1990, *Creole Experience* in 1995); and zydeco, the accordion-based folk music of Creoles, has gained significant popularity with festivals, radio programs, and Grammys awarded to Creole musicians.

Because outsiders had used it in a derogatory sense, Cajuns had long contested the use of *Cajun/cadien*. The situation is now reversed: confronted with the liberal use of the term, outsiders tend to reject its use. The cultural content of Cajunness has also changed considerably in the past hundred years. Still, there are historically consistent cultural markers of difference: race, Acadian origin, French language, religion, the maintenance of particular folkways, and a Cajun ethos stereotyped by the much-used formula *Laissez les bons temps rouler* (Let the good times roll).

ETHNIC LABELS, ETHNIC IDENTITIES, AND SOCIAL CHANGE

The definition of Cajun ethnicity has been ongoing since the arrival of Acadian exiles in Louisiana. It has taken place amidst the economic, social, and cultural changes that have happened since the eighteenth century. The names used to designate the descendants of Acadian exiles have accompanied this evolution. In this sense, the evolution of *Cajun/cadien* symbolizes the ongoing process of the definition of Cajun ethnicity.

The analysis of the written occurrences of *Cajun/cadien* shows that the term originated in early Acadian speech and that it was codified and popularized in English in the 1880s. The negative connotation emerged from the Louisiana Acadian community when it split between an Acadian upper class and a Cajun lower class. The negative ascription of *Cajun* then spread in English through mostly English-language media. With the integration of Cajuns into American culture, the term "Cajun" took on a positive connotation in the 1960s. The subsequent French renaissance movement resulted in an increased and sometimes contested use of *Cajun* and the codifying of *cadien* by Cajun activists.

The manipulation of these symbols of Cajun ethnicity has been framed by the interaction of outsiders and insiders. The assignment of a name, the ascription of qualities, and the rejection of a name are indicators of the boundaries between the Acadians and the groups with whom they came in contact. These boundaries shift with historical context, social change, and perspective. The analysis of the use of *Cajun/cadien* shows how Cajun ethnicity has been less a matter of cultural content than a dialectical process. Cajuns have been defined by what they were not rather than by what they were.

Cultural traits are used to construct, not describe, the "otherness" of ethnicity. In the past this process of constructing Cajun ethnicity was mostly controlled by outsiders, from Longfellow's *Evangeline* to portrayals by novelists and journalists. Recently, insiders have been increasingly involved. In the following chapters of this volume, we will attempt to describe the social, economic, and historical forces that have shaped and reshaped Cajun identity. The agricultural society in which Cajuns came to be defined has, we will demonstrate, largely disappeared. However, the label continues to be used, by both insiders and outsiders. Our aim, in the following pages, is to describe how the changing society of Louisiana has both maintained and transformed the meanings of the term "Cajun."

NOTES

1. Steven DelSesto & Jon Gibson (eds.), *The Culture of Acadiana: Tradition and Change in South Louisiana* (Lafayette: University of Southwestern Louisiana, 1975).

2. For various definitions of Cajuns see Dorice Tentchoff, "Cajun French and French Creole: Their Speakers and the Questions of Identities" in Steven DelSesto & Jon Gibson (eds.), *The Culture of Acadiana: Tradition and Change in South Louisiana* (Lafayette: University of Southwestern Louisiana, 1975); Larbi Oukada, "The Territory and Population of French-speaking Louisiana," *Revue de Louisiane/ Louisiana Review* 7(1) (1978):5–34; James Dormon, *The People called Cajuns: An Introduction to an Ethnohistory* (Lafayette: Center for Louisiana Studies, 1983); Charles R. Brassieur, "The Modern Atchafalaya Culture: Results of the Ethnographic Survey" in Jon L Gibson (ed.), *Archeology and Ethnology on the Edges of the Atchafalaya Basin, South Central Louisiana*, (Lafayette, LA: Center for Archeological Studies, 1982), 153–242; Lawrence Estaville, "Mapping the Cajuns," *Southern Studies* 25(2) (1986):163–171; Robert Gramling, Craig Forsyth & Linda Mooney, "The Protestant Ethic and the Spirit of Cajunism," *Journal of Ethnic Studies* 15 (1986): 33–46; Cécyle Trépanier, "The Cajunization of French Louisiana: Forging a Regional Identity," *Geographical Journal* 157(2) (1991):161–171.

3. Written occurrences of *Cajun/cadien* and other words are noted with italics; oral realizations of [kedzʌn] and other words are noted in phonetics; general references to the Cajuns or Acadians are in basic typeface.

4. Historical Records Survey, *The Favrot Papers 1695–1769* (New Orleans: Louisiana State Museum, 1940); Historical Records Survey, *The Favrot Papers 1769–1781 Volume 2* (New Orleans: Tulane University of Louisiana, 1941); Gabriel Debien, "The Acadians in Santo Domingo: 1764–1789" in Glen Conrad (ed.), *The Cajuns: Essays on Their History and Culture*, (Lafayette: Center for Louisiana Studies, 1978), 21–96; Carl Brasseaux, Emilio Fabrian Garcia & Jacqueline Voorhies (eds.), *Quest for the Promised Land* (Lafayette: Center for Louisiana Studies, 1989).

5. William Read, *Louisiana French* (Baton Rouge: Louisiana State University Press, 1931); Florence Roos Brink, "Literary Travellers in Louisiana Between 1803 and 1860," *Louisiana Historical Quarterly* 31(2) (1948):1–32; Timothy Reilly, "Early Acadiana Through Anglo-American Eyes," *Attakapas Gazette* 12(1) (1977): 3–20, 12(3) (1977):159–177, 12(4) (1977):185–94, 13(2) (1978):53–71; Carl Brasseaux & Glenn Conrad, *A Selected Bibliography of Scholarly Literature on Colonial Louisiana and New France* (Lafayette: Center for Louisiana Studies, 1982).

6. References are listed in chronological order as they appear in Table 1.1. Page numbers are omitted when mentions are repeated. Bona Arsenault, *Histoire et généalogie des Acadiens* (Québec: Le Conseil de la Vie française en Amérique, 1965), 266–267; Historical Records Survey, *The Favrot Papers 1695–1769*, 76–77, 88; Archivo General de Indias, Papeles procedentes de Cuba, legajo 188C, folios 62–63 (Seville); Chevalier Jean de Champigny, *La Louisiane ensanglantée* (Londres: Fleury Mesplet, 1773), 27; Jean Bernard Bossu, *Nouveaux Voyages dans l'Amérique Septentrionale* (Amsterdam: Changuion, 1777); Historical Records Survey, *The Favrot Papers 1769–1781 Volume II*, 60; Guillaume T.F. Raynal, *Histoire Philosophique et Politique des Etablissements et du Commerce des Européens dans les deux Indes* (Ge-

nève, 1780), 115; Baudry des Lauzières, *Voyage à la Louisiane et sur le continent de l'Amérique septentrionale fait dans les années 1794 à 1798* (Paris, 1802); Pierre-Louis Berquin Duvallon, *Vue de la colonie du Mississipi, ou des provinces de Louisiane et de Floride occidentale, en l'année 1802* (Paris: Imprimerie Expéditive, 1803); François Marie Perrin du Lac, *Voyage dans les 2 Louisianes* (Paris, 1805), 377; C.C. Robin, *Voyage dans l'intérieur de la Louisiane, de la Floride occidentale et dans les îles de la Martinique et de Saint Domingue* (Paris: F. Buisson, 1807); François René, vicomte de Chateaubriand, *Voyage en Amérique, en Italie, au Mont Blanc* in *Oeuvres Complètes de Chateaubriand* ([1827] Paris: Garnier, 1929–1938); Victor Tixier, *Voyage aux Prairies Osages Louisiane et Missouri 1839–1840* (Clermont-Ferrand, 1866), 28; Alexandre Barde, *Histoire des Comités de vigilance aux Attakapas* (Saint Jean Baptiste, LA: Imprimerie du Meschacébé et de l'Avant-Coureur, 1861); Désirée Martin, *Les veillées d'une soeur ou le destin d'un brin de mousse* (La Nouvelle-Orléans: Imprimerie Cosmopolite, 1877), 11–13; Sidonie de la Houssaye, *Pouponne et Balthazar* (1888; reprint, Lafayette: Center for Louisiana Studies, 1983), 2, 34; Paul Marc Sauvalle, *Louisiane-Mexique-Canada: Aventures Cosmopolites* (Montréal, 1891); Alcée Fortier, *Louisiana Studies; Literature, Customs and Dialects; History and Education* (New Orleans: F.F. Hansell and Bro., 1894), 190–196; Jay K. Ditchy (ed.), *Les Acadiens louisianais et leur parler* (Paris: Librairie E. Droz, 1932); Felix Voorhies, *Acadian reminiscences, with the true story of Evangeline* (Opelousas, LA: Jacobs News Depot, 1907).

7. Newton D. Mereness (ed.), *Travels in the American Colonies* (New York: Macmillan, 1916), 482; Philip Pittman, *The Present State of the European Settlements on the Mississippi* (1770 reprint, Gainesville: University of Florida Press, 1973), 24; Thomas Hutchins, *An Historical Narrative and Topographical Description of Louisiana and West Florida* (Philadelphia: for the Author and Robert Aitken, 1784), 41, 47; James Pitot, *Observations on the Colony of Louisiana, from 1796 to 1802* (1802; reprint, Baton Rouge: Louisiana State University Press, 1979); Major Amos Stoddard, *Sketches, Historical and Descriptive, of Louisiana* (Philadelphia, published by Matthew Carey, A. Small printer, 1812), 177–185, 319–330; Zadok Cramer, *The Navigator* (1814; reprint, (Pittsburgh, PA: Cramer, Spear and Eichbaum, 1966), 329; William Darby, *A Geographical Description of the State of Louisiana* (Philadelphia: John Melish, 1816), 146, 190; Timothy Flint, *Recollections of the Last Ten Years* (Boston: Cummings, Hilliard and Company, 1826), 329–338; *Journal of the Rev. Timothy Flint from the Red River to the Ouachitta, or Washita, in Louisiana in 1835* (Alexandria, LA, 1835), 15; S.S. Prentiss, *Memoir of S.S. Prentiss*, edited by his Brother (New York: Charles Scribner, 1855), 95–97; James B. McMillan, "Lexical Evidence from Charles Sealsfield," *American Speech* 18 (1943), 119; Henry W. Longfellow, *Evangeline, a Tale of Acadie* (London: Routledge and Co., 1847); Charles Lyell, *A Second Visit to the United States of North America*, vol. 2 (London: J. Murray, 1849), 93–94; Frederick L. Olmsted, *A Journey in the Seaboard Slave States* (New York: Dix & Edwards, 1856), 332, 342; Walter Prichard (ed.), "A Tourist Description of Louisiana in 1860," *Louisiana Historical Quarterly* 21(4) (1938):1–107; A.R. Waud, "Acadians in Louisiana," *Harper's Weekly*, October 20 (1866), 670, reprinted in Timothy Reilly, "Early Acadiana Through Anglo-American Eyes (Part 2)," Attakapas Gazette 1977 vol. 12(3), 160–161; J.O. Noyes, "Cotton Planting at Port Hudson," *Putnam's Magazine* 2(7) (1868):46–57, Samuel Lockett, *Louisiana As It Is*, ed. Lauren C. Post (1873; reprint, Baton Rouge: Louisiana State University Press, 1969);

Albert Rhodes, "The Louisiana Creoles," *Galaxy* 16 (1873):252–260, Edwin De Leon, "The Bayou Teche," *Eclectic Magazine* 84 (1875):353–362; Edward King, *The Southern States of North America: A Record of Journeys* (London: Blackie & Son, 1875), 85; Charles Nordhoff, *The Cotton States in the Spring and Summer of 1875* (1876; reprint, New York: Burt Franklin, 1965), 73; R.L. Daniels, "The Acadians of Louisiana," *Scribner's Monthly* 19 (1879–1880):383–392; J.F.F Finerty, "Far South," *Chicago Times*, November 1880 (on file with author; courtesy of Shane Bernard); W.H. Sparks, *The Memories of Fifty Years*, 4th ed. (Philadelphia: E. Claxton & Company, 1882), 372–389; George W. Cable, *The Creoles of Louisiana* (New York: Charles Scribner's Sons, 1886), 3, 318; George W. Cable, *Bonaventure a prose pastoral of Acadian Louisiana* ((1888; reprint, New York: Charles Scribner's Sons, 1901), 74, 260–261; Rebecca H. Davis, "Here and There in the South V: In Attakapas," *Harper's New Monthly Magazine*, (1887):913–925, T.W. Poole, *Some Late Words about Louisiana* (New Orleans: E. Marchand, 1889), 26; William Henry Perrin (ed.), *Southwest Louisiana: Biographical and Historical* (New Orleans: Gulf Publishing Company, 1891; Baton Rouge, LA: Claitor's Publishing Division, (1971), 103–104; Julian Ralph, "Along the Bayou Teche," *Harper's New Monthly Magazine* 87 (1893):870–884; Kate Chopin, *The Complete Works*, ed. Per Seyersted (1894; reprint, Baton Rouge Louisiana State University Press, 1969), 294, 320–321.

8. Michael Moerman, "Ethnic Identification in a Complex Civilization: Who Are the Lue?" *American Anthropologist* 67(5–1) (1965):1215–1230; Joshua Fishman, "Am and Goy as Designations for Ethnicity in Selected Books of the Old Testament" in Joshua Fishman et al., (eds.), *The Rise and Fall of Ethnic Revival: Perspectives on Language and Ethnicity*, (Berlin: Mouton, 1985), 15–38 Thomas H. Eriksen, *Ethnicity and Nationalism* (London: Pluto Press, 1993), 88–91. In fact, Pierre Bourdieu in *Ce que parler veut dire. L'économie des échanges linguistiques* (Paris: Fayard, 1982), 135–137 argues that labels and criteria are at the core of the struggle to define ethnic categories and impose a worldview.

9. James Hintze & Larbi Oukada, "The Lexical Item *Creole* in Louisiana," *Journal of the Linguistic Association of the Southwest* 2 (1977):143–161; Virginia Dominguez, *White by Definition: Social Classification in Creole Louisiana* (New Brunswick, NJ: Rutgers University Press, 1986); James Dormon, "Louisiana 'Creoles of Color': Ethnicity, Marginality, and Identity," *Social Science Quarterly* 73 (1992): 615–626; Gwendolyn Midlo Hall, *Africans in Colonial Louisiana: The Development of Afro-Creole Culture in Louisiana in the Eighteenth Century* (Baton Rouge: Louisiana State University Press, 1992), 157–159; Joseph Tregle, "Creoles and Americans" in Arnold Hirsch & Joseph Logsdon (eds.), *Creole New Orleans: Race and Americanization*, (Baton Rouge: Louisiana State University Press, 1992), 131–185.

10. Edward Laroque Tinker, *Les écrits de langue française en Louisiane au XIXème siècle* (Paris: Honoré Champion, 1932), *Bibliography of French Newspapers and Periodicals in Louisiana* (Worcester, MA, 1933); David Barry, "A French Literary Renaissance in Louisiana: Cultural Reflections," *Journal of Popular Culture* 23 (1989):47–63; and Becky Brown, "The Social Consequences of Writing Louisiana French," *Language in Society* 22 (1993):67–101.

11. Dudley Leblanc, *The True Story of the Acadians* (Lafayette, LA, 1932); Antoine Bernard, *Le Drame Acadien* (Montréal: Les Clercs de Saint Viateur, 1936); Alfred Martineau, "Les survivances françaises en Louisiane," *Revue d'histoire des col-*

onies françaises, 2ème trimestre (1937):113–124; and Bona Arsenault, *Histoire et généalogie des Acadiens.*

12. Arsenault, *Histoire et généalogie des Acadiens*, 266–267.

13. Bernard, *Le Drame Acadien*; Pascal Poirier *Glossaire acadien* (Moncton: Université St Joseph, 1953), 18; and Geneviève Massignon, *Les parlers français d'Acadie: Enquêtes linguistiques*, 2 vols. (Paris: C. Klincksieck, 1962).

14. *Cayens* has been used by Emile Lauvrière, "Pélerinage acadien et canadien en Louisiane," *France-Amérique*, Août-Septembre (1931) and *Histoire de la Louisiane Française* (Paris: G-P Maisonneuve, 1940), and Poirier, *Glossaire acadien; cajin* was used by Lauren C. Post, "Acadian Animal Caste in Southwest Louisiana: Some Sociological Observations," *Rural Sociology* 5(2) (1940):183–191; *Cadgiens* by Poirier, *Glossaire acadien; Cajen* by Richard Guidry, "Un Cajen en Guadeloupe," *Acadiana Profile* 3(1) (1971):4; *Cadjun* by Jeanne Castille, *Moi, Jeanne Castille de Louisiane* (Paris: Lunot-Ascot Editeurs, 1983); *Cadjein* by Ain Cadjein mailed anonymously in 1987; *Cadjien* appears on a sign at the Prairie Acadian Cultural Center, Eunice, LA.

15. Noyes, "Cotton Planting at Port Hudson," 54; Rhodes, "The Louisiana Creoles," 253; Nordhoff, *The Cotton States in the Spring and Summer of 1875*, 73.

16. *Cajan* by Davis, "Here and There in the South V: In Attakapas," 918, and Perrin, *Southwest Louisiana: Biographical and Historical*, 104; *'Cadian* by Chopin, *The Complete Works*, 320; *Cajian* in a 1906 court transcript in William A. Craigie & James R. Hulbert (eds.), *A Dictionary of American English*, vol 1 (Chicago, 1938), 384; and *Cajin* in Thad St. Martin, "Cajuns," *Yale Review* 26 (1937):859–862, 859.

17. R.L. Daniels, "The Acadians of Louisiana," 383; Ralph, "Along the Bayou Teche," 874; De la Houssaye, *Pouponne et Balthazar*, 2, 34.

18. Noyes, "Cotton Planting at Port Hudson," 54. Quotation marks were used by Nordhoff, *The Cotton States in the Spring and Summer of 1875*, 73; Davis, "Here and There in the South V: In Attakapas," 918, and Perrin, *Southwest Louisiana: Biographical and Historical*, 103. Jay K. Ditchy (ed.), *Les Acadiens louisianais et leur parler*, 65.

19. Pierre Gérin & Pierre M. Gérin, *Marichette: Lettres Acadiennes 1895–1898* (Sherbrooke, Québec: Editions Naaman, 1982).

20. Jean Bernard Bossu, *Nouveaux voyages aux Indes occidentales* (1763; reprint, Paris, 1980), and *Nouveaux Voyages dans l'Amérique Septentrionale;* Baudry des Lauzières, *Voyage à la Louisiane et sur le continent de l'Amérique septentrionale fait dans les années 1794 à 1798*; Chateaubriand, *Voyage en Amérique, en Italie, au Mont Blanc* in *Oeuvres Complète*; Paul Marc Sauvalle, *Louisiane-Mexique-Canada: Aventures Cosmopolites.*

21. Major Amos Stoddard, *Sketches, Historical and Descriptive, of Louisiana*, 319–330.

22. H.M. Brackenridge, *Views of Louisiana* (Pittsburgh, PA, 1814), Cathcart in Walter Prichard, Fred Kniffen & Clair Brown (eds.), "Southern Louisiana and Southern Alabama in 1819: Journal of James Leander Cathcart," *Louisiana Historical Quarterly* 28(3) (1945):735–921, and John Dennett, *The South As It Is 1865–1866*, ed. Henry M. Christian (1866; reprint, London, 1965) do not mention the Acadians. Timothy Flint, *Recollections of the Last Ten Years*, and *Journal of the Rev. Timothy*

Flint from the Red River to the Ouachitta, or Washita, in Louisiana in 1835; S.S. Prentiss, *Memoir of S.S. Prentiss.*

23. See note 9 and Ingrid Neumann, *Le Créole de Breaux Bridge, Louisiane: étude morphosyntaxique, textes, vocabulaire* (Hamburg: H. Buske, 1985).

24. Frederick L. Olmsted, *A Journey in the Seaboard Slave States*, 342.

25. George W. Cable, *The Creoles of Louisiana* and *Bonaventure.*

26. Perrin, *Southwest Louisiana: Biographical and Historical*, 103–104.

27. Ralph, "Along the Bayou Teche," 883.

28. Ditchy, *Les Acadiens louisianais et leur parler*, 65.

29. Dormon, *The people called Cajuns: An Introduction to an Ethnohistory*, 43.

30. Carl Brasseaux, *Acadian to Cajun: Transformation of a people 1803–1877* (Jackson: University Press of Mississippi, 1992), 87–88.

31. Davis, "Here and There in the South V: In Attakapas," 917–918.

32. Cable, *Bonaventure*, 74 and 260; Chopin, *The Complete Works*, 319–324.

33. Adolphe Robert, *Mémorial* (Manchester, NH: L'Association Canado-Américaine, 1940), 383. For other uses see Lauvrière, "Pélerinage acadien et canadien en Louisiane"; Simone Delery & Gladys Renshaw, *France d'Amérique* (Chicago: D.C. Heath and Company, 1932); Gabriel-Louis Jaray, "Le destin français en Louisiane," *France-Amérique*, Août (1937):153–158; Edouard Fabre-Surveyer, *Une journée française à Lafayette et autres récits de voyage* (Montréal, 1938).

34. See Leblanc, *The True Story of the Acadians*; H.W. Gilmore, "Social Isolation of the French-Speaking People of Rural Louisiana," *Social Forces* 12 (1933):78–84; T. Lynn Smith, "An Analysis of Rural Social Organization in Louisiana," *Journal of Farm Economics* 16(4) (1934):680–688; Vernon Parenton, "Notes on the Social Organization of a French Village in South Louisiana," *Social Forces* 17 (1938):73–82; T. Lynn Smith & Vernon Parenton, "Acculturation among the Louisiana French," *American Journal of Sociology* 44 (1938):355–364; Joel Fletcher, *The Acadians in Louisiana Today* (Lafayette: Southwestern Louisiana Institute, 1948); Harnett Kane, *The Bayous of Louisiana* (New York: Hampton Publishing, 1943).

35. See Catherine Brookshire Blanchet, Louisiana French Folk Songs Among Children in Vermilion Parish, 1942–54 (master's thesis, University of Southwestern Louisiana, 1970); Ann Savoy, *Cajun Music: A Reflection of a People*, vol. 1 (Eunice, LA: Blue Heron Press, 1984).

36. Marguerite Pecot, "The 'Cajun" (master's thesis, Louisiana State University, 1932); Howard Jacobs, "Cajun Laugh-in" in *Acadiana Profile* 3(2) (1971).

37. Ralph Graves, "Louisiana, Land of Perpetual Romance," *National Geographic* 57(4) (1930):393–482.

38. Jonathan Daniels, *A Southerner Discovers the South* (New York: MacMillan, 1938), 227.

39. St. Martin, "Cajuns," 859–861.

40. Pecot, "The 'Cajun", iii–iv.

41. William H. Gilbert, "Memorandum concerning the characteristics of the larger mixed-blood racial islands of the Eastern United States," *Social Forces* 24(4) (1946): 439–440.

42. David C. Roller & Robert W. Twyman, *The Encyclopedia of Southern History* (Baton Rouge: Louisiana State University Press, 1979), 170.

43. State of Louisiana, *Official Journal of the Proceedings of the Senate of the State of Louisiana*, vol. 4 (Baton Rouge: State of Louisiana, 1981), 3243; "Edwards under

Fire for 'Coonass' Jibe" (*New Orleans States-Item*, October 24, 1972); Ron Thidodeaux, " 'Coonass' Carries Baggage Some Prefer to Forget" (*New Orleans Times-Picayune*, July 17, 2001); Barry J. Ancelet, "On Coonass" with author (manuscript on file, 1996a); Barry J. Ancelet, *"Rapin' Cajun: What's in a Name"* (manuscript on file 1996b).

44. James Domengeaux, "Native-Born Acadians and the Equality Ideal," *Louisiana Law Review* 46 (1986):1151–1195; Revon Reed, *Lâche pas la patate: Portrait des Acadiens de la Louisiane* (Montréal: Editions Parti pris, 1976); " 'Coon Ass' Bill Passes: Haik Says It's Stupid" (*New Iberia Daily Iberian*, July 12, 1981); "I've been called a Coonass just because I'm from Louisiana" (comment on www.nola.com/forums/cajun, July 19, 2001); James Dormon, "Louisiana's Cajuns: A Case Study in Ethnic Group Revitalization," *Social Science Quarterly* 65 (1984):1043–1057.

45. Frederic G. Cassidy, *Dictionary of American Regional English* (Cambridge, MA, and London: Belknap Press of Harvard University Press, 1985), 334; see also "New Orleans Know-It-All" (*New Orleans Gambit*, November 22, 1988).

46. Editorial, *Lafayette, Sunday Advertiser*, December 4, 1966.

47. Bern Keating, "Cajunland: Louisiana French-speaking Coast," *National Geographic* 129(3) (1966):352–391.

48. State of Louisiana, *Official Journal of the Proceedings of the Senate of the State of Louisiana*, 3243.

49. On the nationwide popularity of Cajun products, see Chapter 7.

50. George Arceneaux, *Youth in Acadie: Reflections on Acadian Life and Culture in Southwest Louisiana* (Baton Rouge, LA: Claitor's Publishing Division, 1974), 5; Myron Tassin, *Nous Sommes Acadiens/We Are Acadians* (Gretna, LA: Pelican Publishing, 1976).

51. *Louisiane* 41 (1980), *Louisiane Française* 11, 12, 13, 14, 15, 16 (1978).

52. *La Gazette de Louisiane* 1(6) (1991).

53. Quoted in (1) *La Gazette de Louisiane* 1(8) 1991, 6; (2) Becky Brown, "The Social Consequences of Writing Louisiana French," *Language in Society* 22 (1993): 67–101. Material in this section comes from correspondence (on file) in 1991 with Barry Ancelet, Richard Guidry, and David Marcantel; Barry Ancelet, "A Perspective on Teaching the 'Problem Language' in Louisiana," *French Review* 61(3) (1988): 345–356; and *La Gazette de Louisiane* 1(6) 1991, 1(7) 1991, 4(1) 1993.

54. Interestingly, an anonymous writer using the name Ain Cadjein stayed out of the debate despite its interest and work in transcribing Louisiana French. Between 1975 and 1988, he mailed to local radio stations handwritten then typed Cajun French translations of classical literary works. Using a quasi-phonetic system and shunning conventional "Parisian" orthography as much as possible, he used *Cajun* when writing in English and *Cadjein* (feminine *cadjéne*) when using French.

55. Marc Untel de Gravelles, "Mille Misères—Laissant le bon temps rouler en Louisiane," *Projet Louisiane* monograph no. 5 (Québec: Université Laval, 1979).

56. Jules Daigle, (Quebec: Université Lavel, *A Dictionary of the Cajun Language* (Ann Harbor, MI: Edwards Brothers, 1984), ix.

57. Neumann, *Le Créole de Breaux Bridge, Louisiane: étude morphosyntaxique, textes, vocabulaire*, 79.

58. Reed, *Lâche pas la patate: Portrait des Acadiens de la Louisiane*, 21.

59. Kenneth Ford, "Cajuned-out," *Acadiana Profile* 11(5):16 (1984); Elizabeth Mullener, "A Cajun Journey" (*New Orleans, Times Picayune*, August 14–18, 1988);

Trent Angers, *The Truth About the Cajuns* (Lafayette, LA: Acadian House Publishing, 1990); Barry J. Ancelet, "From Evangeline Hot Sauce to Cajun Ice: Signs of Ethnicity in South Louisiana" (paper presented at the meeting of the American Folklore Society, New Orleans, LA, October 1994, 5.

60. See state of Louisiana, *Official Journal of the Proceedings of the Senate of the State of Louisiana*, 1981), and "Louisiana Battling Counterfeit Cajun" (*New York Times*, March 18, 1989); "Imitation Cajun" (*Lafayette, Times of Acadiana*, March 22, 1989).

61. "Quarter Cajun" (*New Orleans Gambit*, April 5–11, 1986).

62. Trépanier, "The Cajunization of French Louisiana: Forging a Regional Identity," 161; see also Eric Waddell, "French Louisiana: An Outpost of *L'Amérique française*, or Another Country and Another Culture?" *Projet Louisiane*, monograph no. 4 Montréal: McGill University, (1979).

63. Jacques Henry, "Un statut pour les Cajuns," (New York: *France Amérique*, 23–29 juin and 30 juin–6 juillet 1988).

64. J.J. Harmon, "What Is Authentic Cajun?" (*Lafayette Times of Acadiana*, April 12, 1989), and "What's in It for Us?" (*Lafayette Times of Acadiana*, August 13, 1993). "Free Speech Alley Reflects Racial Frustration" (*Lafayette Vermilion* 88(29), October 23, 1992). Also, Ancelet, *On Coonass*, proposed that "there may be some reverse racism involved in this protest [since] the word Cajun has in fact long been considered an ethnic slur by some members of the African-American community"; on this, also see St. Martin, "Cajuns"; Ruth Foote, "Farrakhan Plan Stirs Label Debate" (Baton Rouge, *Morning Advocate*, July 24, 1997).

CHAPTER 2

The Portrayal of Cajuns: Stereotype and Self-image

As we pointed out in the introduction, contemporary scholars tend to view ethnic identity as a multifaceted concept, with cultural, structural, symbolic, and psychological dimensions. Along these lines, one sociologist defines ethnicity as "the result of a dialectical process involving internal and external opinions and processes as well as the individual's self-identification and outsiders' ethnic designations."[1] In the preceding chapter on the coining and evolution of the Cajun label, we documented how such a process can take place.

In this chapter we look further into the construction of Cajunness and examine the portrayals and images of those who receive or take the "Cajun" label. Relying on an ethnohistorical approach similar to the one we used to chart the history of the ethnic label, we examine the emergence and evolution of the content and structure of the representations of Acadians/Cajuns. We propose that the Cajun stereotype was originally constructed by outsiders via multidimensional accounts dominated by social categories such as occupation, mundane activities, historical origin, language, and socioeconomic status. The overall image of the Cajun was composed through the emphasis placed on a handful of striking features. The accentuation of a particular trait owed more to the ascription of difference and the construction of group boundaries than to factual reporting. Content analysis of accounts found mostly in popular media shows that the portrayal of this group has remained rather stable over two centuries, subtly shifting from a depiction of Acadians as poor and happy Catholic farmers to one of Cajuns as adept agriculturalists of Acadian heritage living in relative simplicity enlivened by festive occasions.

However, the relative stability in the portrayal of Cajuns is misleading. The social situation of Cajuns has undergone profound changes. But their image has not changed accordingly, a point that requires some explanation. In addition, the characteristics associated with Acadians/Cajuns have shifted from being negatively judged to being positively appraised. The picture remained the same, but its evaluation was reversed. Finally, as those who consider themselves Cajuns began to publish accounts of themselves, they took up and reworked the stereotypes that originated with outsiders. The stereotypical image formed by others became the basis for Cajuns' self-identification. We propose that this development highlights the often neglected and complex role that outsiders' definitions play in ethnic identification.

THE LIMITED VIEWS OF OTHERS

The involvement of outsiders in the formation of group identity has been addressed from various perspectives. One approach has involved research on stereotypes, the simplistic descriptions applied to every person in some category such as race, nationality, sex, or age. Research on stereotyping has generally concentrated on individual psychological processes or on descriptions of stereotypical representations. These kinds of studies usually fail to address the issue of the provenance of the "images in our head," as Walter Lippman called them. They also leave largely unexplained the social mechanisms that operate in the social construction of stereotypical categories. Even a recent attempt at "rehabilitating" a social science approach to stereotypes from a noted anthropologist focused more on individual strategies of rational choice than on uncovering the structural patterns fostering stereotyping.[2] Research on the construction of group identity (ethnic, national, or class) has also examined the involvement of others in the process of image formation. For instance, Edward Said has proposed a groundbreaking analysis of how Western thinkers have constructed a view of the Orient. Consistent with the postmodern reassessment of theoretical assumptions and methods held dear by social scientists, Michel Touillot has examined the objectification of non-Western cultures as the Other.[3] Still, from our perspective, this branch of research is more concerned with the construction of the "we" identity than with that of "them" and does not fully assess the role of outgroups in ethnic self-identification. Noting that "externally-located processes of social categorization are enormously influential in the production and reproduction of social identities," Jenkins offers a rare glimpse at several possible scenarios for the internalization by ethnics of an external image (acceptance, imposition, denial) but does not address the issue of its formation and transmission. An analysis similar to our research, but dealing with religious texts only, documents how the people of color in Mexico have reinterpreted Mormon racist doctrine as "a fountain of [coping] imagery . . . in self-affirming manner."[4]

Research on Louisiana's ethnic groups has started to move in a similar direction. Scholarship on Creolism has established that the changing and layered meaning of "Creole" can be best explained both by historical situation and social structure rather than by the content of a Creole culture.[5] Thus, depending on the situation in which the term is used as well as on the time and place of reference, Creoles may be construed as white, black, or both, urban upper class or rural poor, proficient bilingual speakers or users of a stigmatized dialect. The case of Cajuns is different. As we argued earlier, studies of this group have, for the most part, been produced by a handful of Louisiana scholars from a descriptive and humanistic perspective. Therefore, there have been few challenges to the monolithic view of Cajuns as white, rural Southwestern Louisianians. Furthermore, the historical portrayal of Cajuns has been solidly pejorative. In his study of the image of Louisiana in nineteenth-century America, Dennis notes that Acadians were briefly mentioned by observers "who did usually found little positive to say." Ancelet remarks that twentieth-century Cajuns in films have been "consistently described as drinking, dancing, and brawling gamblers."[6] Finally, there are only limited and conflicting findings to support the claim that the ethnic renaissance movement put an end to decades of stigmatized Cajun identity. Although some propose that speakers of Cajun French and Cajun-accented English tend to be awarded less prestige than standard English speakers, others suggest that a new positive attitude toward Cajun French has been emerging in Louisiana.[7]

The evidence clearly shows that until recently Cajuns were consistently described as "others" by outsiders. Little is known of Acadians' ethnic awareness before the movement out of Canada. Historians report a strong sense of independence and the emergence of a mentality distinct from that of the home country and of Quebec. However, internal rivalries as well as commercial and political opportunism suggest that the Acadian community was not totally homogeneous or dogmatic in its solidarity. Their Canadian origin, the dire circumstances of their settlement, and their early status as destitute refugees also set the Acadians apart from other white groups in Louisiana. French and Spanish colonial administrators, Creole landowners, and French immigrants all had different origins, inhabited different geographical areas, and generally held higher socioeconomic positions than the Acadians. These groups, as well as the English-speaking population, viewed the Acadian, and later Cajun, community as distinct and of little worth. There is some evidence suggesting that the early Louisiana Acadians maintained close and peaceful relations with their nonwhite neighbors, especially with the Native Americans, with whom they intermarried and traded goods, skills, and languages. However, the fear of *sauvages*, slave ownership by

Acadian planters, and, later in the nineteenth century, overt racism suggest a solid racial identity.

Unfortunately there is scant firsthand evidence on the constitution and evolution of a Cajun self-concept until the present. Obviously, the unavailability of insiders' account until recently does not mean that Acadians and Cajuns were lacking self-image or group consciousness. Historians have documented—on the basis of archival data collected in part by colonial administrators, census takers, and religious authorities—how Acadians were deft negotiators when dealing with French and Spanish rulers, free-spirited objectors to ecclesiastical power, driven by economic self-interest when adopting slavery, eschewing commitment during the Civil War, and banding together in vigilante posses to protect their property in the Reconstruction aftermath. Their reluctance in embracing American education at the turn of the century and their negotiated adaptation to social change that promoted a selective integration into the mainstream (the language goes, religion and kinship ties stay) further demonstrate a collective will and ability to persist as a distinct group.

FROM STEREOTYPE TO SELF-IMAGE: OUR DATA

Our greatest challenge in looking at the historical emergence of the Cajun stereotype was deciding what kinds of materials to consider. Our investigation of the word "Cajun," in the previous chapter, could legitimately be limited to written sources. But it was difficult to duplicate this approach in our efforts to look at the subjective meanings behind the word. Stereotypes and self-images are created and disseminated by various written, visual, and audiovisual means. In addition to traditional media such as print material and movies, radio and television programs, advertising, the entertainment industry and Web sites are all relevant contemporary means of communication. We attempted to gather a balanced, coherent, and meaningful sample, although not necessarily one that was statistically representative. Overall we sought to capture the perception that the general public may have gathered from the depictions of Cajuns available at the time. Accordingly, we decided to retain accounts disseminated and available to the public at large, excluding for instance scientific depictions of Cajuns, because their diffusion is limited compared with popular accounts, their appearance is recent, and their objective is more analytical than descriptive. When dealing with a 250-plus-year period, management of time is essential. Accounts of Acadians/Cajuns are scarce throughout the eighteenth, nineteenth, and early twentieth centuries, but there is an innumerable multitude of them since the 1970s. Consequently, all accounts of the early periods known and available to us were included,[8] whereas we made a selection of late-twentieth-century accounts.[9] We then organized the sample by time periods. As suggested by several authors,[10] three periods meaningful to the Acadian presence in Louisiana can be constructed on the basis of the historical development of Cajun ethnicity: one from the arrival of exiles to the emergence of Cajuns as a discrete group (1756 to the 1860s), one of negative ascription of Cajun ethnicity (1860s to 1960s), and one of ethnic resurgence (from the late 1960s on). We gathered 31 accounts in the first period, 50 in the second, and 75 in the third to reflect the explosion in the interest for Cajuns and the increased involvement of insiders in portraying their own group. In addition comparable sources were retained to establish some historical continuity and coherence. For instance, all treatments of Cajuns by *National Geographic* are included, providing a time sequence from 1930 to 1990 as well as a modern continuation of feature articles published in nineteenth-century magazines such as *Harper's Monthly*. We also included recent articles written for travelers to duplicate the perspective of explorers and early documenters of American diversity.

In all, our data consist of 156 accounts of the Acadian exiles in Louisiana and their Cajun descendants. These accounts appear in various forms of writings (123) (books, memoirs, reports, essays, pamphlets, articles in popular magazines and newspapers, contributions to encyclopedia and dictionaries); in collections of pictures (4); in motion pictures, documentaries, and television programs (22); and in electronic format (7) (Internet sites, CD ROMs). They vary from detailed treatments to brief mentions. They include careful attempts at presenting Cajuns as well as crude depictions. They originate mostly from outsiders (80% of our sample) except for the past three decades.[11] Most accounts result from direct firsthand observations of Louisiana and Cajun culture. They come from primary sources except for a handful of secondary accounts of early-twentieth-century motion pictures and 1970s–1980s television programs.[12] Articles from Louisiana newspapers are juxtaposed with those of the national press, mostly the *New York Times*, and international sources, mostly France.

We adapted the Developmental Research Sequence Method proposed by Spradley[13] for ethnographic data to the analysis of archival data. First the characteristics used by writers, photographers, painters, and directors to describe or qualify Acadians-Cajuns were recorded. Only explicit references were included even when text or illustration would implicitly convey additional information; for example, if no mention of French language use was made, none were noted even if the writer labeled the population as "the French." All features were noted whether they represented a factual description of behavior ("the cabdriver spoke French") or an overarching opinion on an assumed attitude ("a Cajun likes to dance"), whether they could be attributed to the observer or the observed, whether they referred to the present or the past. We opted for such inclusiveness because the emphasis was on identifying criteria of definition (in this case, the activity), not on describing the Cajun experience. Identical traits were recorded only once per account; for instance, repeated mentions of poverty in a single account yielded one notation. Similarly long and detailed treatments of the exile, celebration of Mardi Gras, or ethnic pride yielded one mention, as did repetitive shots of watery surroundings in movies. To compensate for the disproportionate size of books compared with short definitions or news articles, we selected passages or chapters where the general Cajun phenomenon was presented or discussed. The codification of traits in movies and documentaries represented a challenge, given the combination of multiple images, sounds, and elicited feelings; we recorded only the traits objectively shown and associated with Cajuns such as Cajun music played on the soundtrack, comments about Cajuns, or comments made by characters clearly defined as Cajuns. Overall, 2,540 features were recorded.

The characteristics were then grouped in analytic cultural domains defined by Spradley[14] as categories of meaning constructed by the investigator on the basis of a semantic relationship. Overall, references yielded the following fifteen discrete categories: occupation, activities, family, language, interaction, economic status, education, religion, origin, environment, physical characteristics, personal traits, and attitudes toward work, change, and authority.[15]

We constructed taxonomies by distinguishing various levels in the identified cultural domains. Some domains were dichotomous, clearly divided between positive and negative attitudes, valued or undesired social status, attitudes favoring or detracting to interaction, and European and American origin. Two domains—education and occupation—revealed more levels. Education referred to illiteracy, formal instruction, and intelligence; occupations were classified according to a combination of nine occupational categories (farming; collecting, which includes fishing; herding; manufacturing; extraction; business; professions; services; and entertainment).

We begin to look at the historical construction of Cajun ethnicity by identifying accounts in which at least one reference to any cultural domain appears. Table 2.1 indicates the major categories with which the image of Acadians/Cajuns has been constructed. Since occupation is such an important cultural domain, we then tally references to occupations over the three periods, in Table 2.2. Figures in Tables 2.1 and 2.2 include accounts by both insiders and outsiders, given the small number of texts by the former and the large overlap between both. A comparison of recent accounts by both insiders and outsiders is presented in Table 2.3.[16]

THE PORTRAYAL OF ACADIANS/CAJUNS

The initial portrayal of early Acadians is organized around three major domains: occupation (in 74% of accounts), economic status (68%), and origin (52%). Count of references signals a similar emphasis on economic status (17% of references) and occupation (16%) with less frequent mentions of attitudes toward work, activities, personal traits, religion, and origin (from

8.2% to 6.4% of references). The content of each domain is clearly dominated by discrete dimensions: small farmers raising crops and animals for subsistence supplemented with hunting and fishing bounties, poverty, a French Acadian origin, competent but not overzealous workers, enjoying life, and good Christians. This yields the ideal typical portrait of Acadians as Catholic, poor, yet happy, farmers of Canadian origin as this passage by a French aristocrat suggests:

> The upper part of Pointe Coupée next to the Mississippi River is inhabited by the Acadians. . . . Born without much industry, they appear to be in the same state of mediocrity they were in when they arrived in the colony. Without ambition or desire, they live in a situation nearing poverty on their habitations where they mostly cultivate small plots of land without outside help. This class of settlers is exceedingly dirty; their houses seem better fit to lodge animals than men . . . Acadians are generally good and hospitable: they never let a stranger in without offering refreshments but one must be hungry to eat the dishes they prepare.[17]

The depiction of Cajuns in the second period is more complex and complete. This period, especially from 1880 to 1930, can be seen as the formative time of the Cajun stereotype. This concurs with historians' findings that "the nineteenth century writings of a handful of visitors were highly influential in forming the pervasive myths that linger to the present.[18]" Thirteen of fifteen categories appear in at least 40% of accounts and seven appear in more than 60% of accounts (see Table 2.1). Although language appears in most accounts with references to the limited abilities of Cajuns to speak either French or English, occupations, activities, and personal traits gather the greatest number of references. In addition to the less-emphasized low socioeconomic status, a slow propensity to change, limited education, and Acadian origin emerge as important traits. Domains gain in diversity. Added to the farming dimension, references to Cajuns as fishermen and collectors foraging for fur, moss, or lumber become dominant; professions are also increasingly noted especially after 1930, as are manufacturing (mostly basket making and textiles) and extracting activities. Mentions of balls, music, amusement, gambling, and cuisine occur throughout the writings.

During the second period Cajuns are described as swarthy, simple, and credulous,[19] "quixotic and intermittently excitable."[20] They also appear as "Utopian dreamers"[21] going through "life as a repetition of the same round of simple pleasures and easy work"[22] yet showing "general amenity and self-respect for their bearing."[23] Acadians/Cajuns also start to be characterized by their relation to ignorance; authors unanimously describe them as "ignorant," "uncultivated," "illiterate," "the least intelligent of the Creole population,"[24] or "not markedly advanced culturally or intellectually."[25] Their only redeeming trait is their "commendable zeal in availing themselves of the improved and increasing facilities for educational advantage" with the

Table 2.1
Accounts of, and References to, Cultural Domains in Cajun Identification by Period

	1766-1866				1873-1962				1966-2001				Total			
Domain	Acc	%	Ref	%	Acc.	%	Ref.	%	Acc.	%	Ref.	%	Acc.	%	Ref.	%
Occupation	23	74.2%	43	16.1%	37	74.0%	161	17.5%	62	82.7%	354	26.2%	122	78.2%	558	22.0%
Activities	12	38.7%	21	7.9%	35	70.0%	116	12.6%	64	85.3%	296	21.9%	111	71.2%	433	17.0%
Language	2	6.5%	2	0.7%	38	76.0%	55	6.0%	57	76.0%	83	6.1%	67	42.9%	117	4.6%
Family	3	9.7%	4	1.5%	28	56.0%	46	5.0%	41	54.7%	57	4.2%	72	46.2%	107	4.2%
Interaction	11	35.5%	12	4.5%	21	42.0%	45	4.9%	35	46.7%	54	4.0%	67	42.9%	111	4.4%
Religion	13	41.9%	18	6.7%	27	54.0%	36	3.9%	27	36.0%	41	3.0%	67	42.9%	95	3.7%
Attit. -Work	12	38.7%	22	8.2%	20	40.0%	35	3.8%	21	28.0%	31	2.3%	53	34.0%	88	3.5%
Attit.-Power	9	29.0%	14	5.2%	13	26.0%	19	2.2%	25	33.3%	30	2.2%	47	30.1%	63	2.5%
Attit.-Change	11	35.5%	12	4.5%	34	68.0%	64	6.9%	39	52.0%	60	4.4%	84	53.8%	136	5.4%
Personal Traits	14	45.2%	20	7.5%	31	62.0%	109	11.8%	44	58.7%	95	7.0%	89	57.1%	224	8.8%
Econ. Status	21	67.7%	46	17.2%	32	64.0%	56	6.1%	35	46.7%	43	3.2%	88	56.4%	145	5.7%
Education	9	29.0%	14	5.2%	28	56.0%	49	5.3%	24	32.0%	40	3.0%	61	39.1%	103	4.1%
Origin	16	51.6%	17	6.4%	34	68.0%	44	4.8%	52	69.3%	64	4.7%	102	65.4%	125	4.9%
Environment	9	29.0%	12	4.5%	28	56.0%	49	5.3%	53	70.7%	91	6.7%	90	57.7%	152	6.0%
Physical Traits	6	19.4%	10	3.7%	19	38.0%	37	4.0%	11	14.7%	13	1.0%	36	23.1%	60	2.4%
TOTAL	N=31		267	100.0%	N=50		921	100.0%	N=75		1352	100.0%	N=156		2540	100.0%

result of "increasing in intelligence".[26] Educational attainment is a yardstick used to measure change and integration into American society. It is also used by French-speaking authors to mark the difference between upper-class, educated Acadians and rural, uneducated Cajuns.[27] The data yield an ideal typical image of Cajuns as adept agriculturalists of Acadian ancestry, Catholic, speaking a French dialect, living in relative yet poor simplicity enlivened by festive occasions, and slowly adapting to the changing world around them.

The portrayal of modern Cajuns is dominated by references to activities, occupation, language, place in the environment, and Acadian origin. The moderate emphasis on physical traits, education, family, religion, attitudes toward work, and economic status noted in the previous period has declined. Activities and occupation appear as central categories present in more than 80% of accounts and representing half of all references. The occupational portrayal is considerably diversified (see Table 2.2): agricultural and collecting activities (28% of references consisting mostly of fishing) still constitute 40% of mentions, but references are made to a considerable array of occupations ranging from moss picker to computer operator and professional athlete. Professions (15%), services (12%) such as restaurateur, tour operator, and pilot, and entertainment (10%, mostly music related) emerge as important categories. Manufacturing and oil and gas extraction activities collect 14% of occupational references despite the industrialization of the area and its reportedly strong effect on Cajun culture.

Many authors[28] note the evolution from marginal rural settlers to well-integrated, productive members of a modern society. They document the disappearance or transformation of traditional occupations—"Trapper, Builder and Collector: T. Paul Robin, Last Real Cajun," writes one[29]—and emphasize the growth of nontraditional occupations:

> And lots of Cajuns are doctors, lawyers, architects, accountants, even college professors. You'll find Cajuns selling shoes at Sears, running gasoline stations, driving taxis, flying airplanes, working at chemical plants, operating computers, stringing telephone lines, raising crops and cattle, delivering the mail and running restaurants . . . doing the same things people do everywhere.[30]

Cajuns' propensity for eating, dancing, drinking, playing music, and gambling is noted almost everywhere and constitutes the bulk of nonoccupational activities recorded. Activities belong to three major classes: foodways, joie de vivre (which includes dancing, playing music, gambling, and Mardi Gras), and transportation. If we are to believe the accounts examined, Acadians/Cajuns engage in few activities other than eating and celebrating Mardi Gras. Mentions of foodways and joie de vivre account for approximately 80% of reported activities. There is a remarkable continuity between early remarks that Acadians are "excessively attached to balls and parties,"[31]

Table 2.2
Distribution of Mentions of Occupations, by Category and by Period

	1766-1866		1873-1962		1966-2001	
	n	%	n	%	n	%
Farming	17	39.5%	37	23.0%	45	12.7%
Collecting	12	27.9%	46	28.6%	98	27.7%
Herding	7	16.3%	11	6.8%	16	4.5%
Extracting	0	0.0%	3	1.9%	24	6.8%
Manufacturing	2	4.7%	17	10.6%	27	7.6%
Business	3	7.0%	12	7.5%	16	4.5%
Professions	2	4.7%	34	21.1%	52	14.7%
Services	0	0.0%	1	0.6%	42	11.9%
Entertainment	0	0.0%	0	0.0%	34	9.6%
Total	43	100.0%	161	100.0%	354	100.0%

nineteenth-century notes that they "indulged the Carnival to its wildest extent,"[32] and recent headlines claiming that "in Southwest Louisiana, entire towns party from dawn to the wee hours in a last ecstatic hurrah before Lent."[33] Games and gambling are also frequently mentioned, whether they involve horses, cockfights, or cards.[34] Another class of activities deals with transportation and mentions of Cajuns riding buggies, paddling pirogues,[35] driving on levees, boating across the Atchafalaya Basin, and occasionally flying on airplanes. Emphasis on this dimension likely owes more to traveling outsiders keen to the particulars of their journey than to a great propensity of Cajuns for moving about.

Two changes are noticeable in modern accounts. Acadians were long described as sober,[36] enjoying an occasional drink[37] but mostly fond of coffee.[38] In the past three decades, the emphasis has shifted for both by insiders and outsiders to the supposed ability of Cajuns to ingurgitate large amounts of beer and spirits.[39] During the first two periods, Cajun culinary fare was rarely discussed and then described as only adequate.[40] The image of the Cajun as a "connoisseur of good food"[41] emerged in the post–World War II era, and Cajun foodways later joined the ranks of culinary excellence. In fact, the ability to prepare and consume seafood, sweet potatoes, sausage, and gumbo has been elevated to a defining trait of Cajun identity by insiders and outsiders alike, especially in documentaries and motion pictures.

Linguistic abilities are almost invariably mentioned (in 76% of accounts) as peculiar in English and disappearing in French. Finally, references to Acadian origin, environmental fitness, and likable personal traits round up a portrayal of contemporary Cajuns as residents of Southwest Louisiana of Acadian descent, busy at many occupations and proudly celebrating a threatened heritage and simple rural way of life.

PERMANENCE OF THE IMAGE

The key historical dimensions in the representation of Acadians/Cajuns over the period are occupation, activities, personal traits, relation to the environment, and origin. Inclusion of the dominant trait of each domain yields an image of Cajuns as jolly, poor, and potentially French-speaking agriculturalists and foragers of Acadian ancestry, somehow better adapted to their natural environment than to the fast-changing society around them. The portrayal is historically consistent but it is not immobile. As seen above, the emphasis placed on different dimensions varies: language was a minor category before 1873, and references to physical traits are rare in modern accounts, but physical characteristics were quite frequently mentioned in the nineteenth century. Most noticeable is the emergence of Cajuns as violent brutes in television and movie portrayals since the 1970s whereas written portrayals tend to be increasingly sympathetic. Finally, Cajuns are increasingly defined normatively, that is, according to what they do or rather what they are expected to do, whether it is holding a job, speaking a particular language or enjoying some form of leisure.[42] References to occupation, activities, language, and interaction, an approximate measure of behavior, increased from 29% of all traits in the first period to 41% in the second period and 58% lately.

Despite changes in emphasis over time, we propose that the remarkable feature of the portrayal's evolution is its stability in structure and content. All categories identified are referred to in all three periods with great consistency in their salience, whether they are central (occupation, language, origin) or marginal (physical traits, attitudes toward power). Consistency is also manifest in the recurrent references, often made in similar terms, to occupations (farming), values (love of family, Catholicism), and folkways (gregariousness, hospitality, hardworking). This permanence is a notable trait given the considerable social change that took place over 200 years. We argue that this is not because of an innate quality of either the stereotype or the related psychological process but rather to structural conditions (geographical stability, maintenance of minority status) and human agency (transmission of the original image, adoption as a basis for self-identification).

A fundamental factor is the stability of Cajuns in their geographical and social environment. Unlike most immigrant groups in American history, Acadians/Cajuns have remained on the location of their original settlements in Southwest Louisiana. Although the natural environment has been greatly affected by human population and activities, Cajuns continue to live in the area settled by the people they recognize as their ancestors. Their lifestyles, occupations, and activities have long been framed by the rural environment, whose influence remains pervasive. Agriculture, fishing, and forestry represented a third of all jobs in Louisiana until 1940 and still one out of five in 1950, meaning that many Cajun baby boomers were born in the countryside. There is ample evidence of the ongoing intergenerational transmission of various skills (agricultural and domestic, such as cooking) related to maintaining Cajuns' environmental fitness.[43] The area remains a "sportsman's paradise" (the motto of the state) where plentiful game, fowl, and fish offer valued opportunities for hunting and fishing. As in other rural areas of modern America, these activities are today conducted for recreation rather than subsistence, and constitute a male preserve. Acquisition of a gun, and inclusion in all-male fishing and hunting parties continue to be common rites of passage for Cajun boys.

The relative position of Acadians/Cajuns in their cultural and social environment has also remained largely unchanged until recently. From the settlement of Acadian refugees to the emergence of Cajuns as a group in postbellum Louisiana and until post–World War II prosperity, Cajuns fit the definition of a minority group whose access to societal resources and power was limited and whose culture was stigmatized.[44] Dominant groups have changed but the status of Cajuns has not until now. They have been a disadvantaged group and have been viewed as a group apart by Spanish and French colonial administrators, American settlers, Creole planters, Yankee carpetbaggers, and Texas oilmen on the basis of their isolation, agricultural pursuits, French language, or value system. Acadians/Cajuns have been visited and described from a distance, both physical and social. The power of *Evangeline* in shaping a mythical image of the Acadians is a case in point, given that its author never set foot in Louisiana. To this day, accounts of Cajuns by outsiders are scrutinized with delight or outrage by individuals and organizations.[45] The out-group perspective emphasizes, and in fact creates, the ethnics' difference: the climate and topography tend to fascinate Northern writers, the rurality disturbs urban dwellers, the French influence strikes Anglo-Americans, the contented self-sufficiency aggravates the capitalist entrepreneur. Recently, the ideal of a Cajun *Gemeinschaft*, (close-knit community), complete with heartfelt expressions of ethnic pride and social conservatism, has tended to appeal to writers enjoying a taste of a mythical past before they motor back to reality. Overall, the structural relationship between the image's setting, its makers, and its subjects has experienced little change over 200 years. Just as the label "Cajun" was coined and ascribed derogatively by outsiders,[46] the image of Cajuns was originally drafted by outsiders. Over time, the Cajun has been constructed as the Other and the Cajun image continues to evoke a sense of the exotic.

The existence of favorable structural conditions is a necessary but not a sufficient condition to ensure the permanence of the image. Its continued relevance results from human agency: the original portrayal has been continuously reproduced by authors, and Cajuns have adopted it as a basis for ethnic self-identification.[47] The recurrence of similar traits in the portrayals we examined is caused in part by frequent cross-references. Unabashed plagiarism is especially rampant in the early years: Hutchins in 1784 lifted complete sentences from Pittman in 1770. Dana in 1819 and Buckingham in 1842 borrowed entire paragraphs from Darby in 1816. Gallasero in 1970 generously quoted from Kane in 1943, and "Cajuns of the net" in 1998 drew heavily from Hamm in 1972. More frequently though, citations are rightfully attributed. Longfellow's *Evangeline*, a mainstay of late-nineteenth-century accounts, remains a ubiquitous reference in contemporary accounts. The silhouette of Longfellow's Acadian heroine, often with the features of actress Dolores del Rio,[48] is a common feature in pictural representations. Lately, electronic duplication of material on Web sites and CD ROMS suggest that the diffusion of words and images will only increase.

A handful of scholars, musicians, entrepreneurs, activists, and chefs appear in written and audiovisual news reports. In documentaries and photographic books, intriguing scenes of Spanish moss–draped oak trees with aquatic settings teeming with wildlife (largely stemming from Flaherty's 1948 photographic work) appear to be obligatory shots. Hollywood treatments of Cajuns never fail to include festive occasions with exotic touches of French accent or Cajun music, very much as New Orleans scenes almost always seem to take place during Mardi Gras or a jazz funeral. Nineteenth-century travelers' accounts of the Louisiana folk "were most assuredly written to sell,"[49] a factor still very much present in today's media market. The effective dissemination of standardized information by the tourism industry continues to shape outsiders' expectations. We know from experience that few visiting writers or TV producers are satisfied until provided with shots and sounds of swamps, seafood, Cajun music, and rural bonhomie, with or without the participation of a local scout or specialist for accuracy. The popular portrayal shaped by outsiders continues to feed on itself.

On the other hand, Cajuns have appropriated the already-made image as a basis for their self-identification. The ethnic revival of the 1970s gave Cajuns an intensified interest in self-portrayal. Near-universal literacy and command of media technology gave them the means. Cajuns are now able to publicize their image and do so via books, newspapers, documentaries, films, and Internet sites, another consequence of today's media market and technology. Yet our data suggest that the increasing participation of Cajuns in representing themselves has not significantly altered the content and structure of the image. The comparison of the content and structure of modern portrayals by insiders and outsiders reveals notable similarity. In terms of content, both typically include references to the past, the extent of changes brought about by modernity, and the ensuing complex and protean nature of contemporary Cajuns. There is significant structural overlap (see

Table 2.3). The insiders' portrait is dominated by the category "Origin," present in 96% of accounts with half the categories appearing in more than 60% of accounts (activities, occupation, family, personal traits, environment, language, attitude toward change). Two categories (occupations and activities) account for 42% of mentions. The recent outsider's view is dominated by these same categories, present in almost nine accounts out of ten and accounting for more than half the listed features. Other categories central to Cajuns' self image (language, environment, personal traits) also appear as major defining characteristics. Cajuns are mostly defined by what they do and where they live, both by themselves and by others.[50] The major divergence between both portrayals is found in the lesser emphasis placed by non-Cajuns on the Acadian origin, a point we will address later in the book.

Two mechanisms are at play in the integration of the stereotype in Cajuns' self-definition: outright acceptance and limited adaptation. Although the crude and derogative descriptions of the past have mostly disappeared, some Cajuns project an image clearly inspired by the traditional stereotype. The juxtaposition of these statements by an anonymous copywriter for the Microsoft corporation and a Cajun business's Web site illustrates the convergence:

> Today the Cajuns live in small, self-contained communities along the Gulf Coast. They raise cattle and cultivate various crops. . . . Home crafts are important, and the people do much of their own spinning and weaving. The Cajuns have a mixed African, European and Native American ancestry, which helps set them apart from their neighbors. French-Canadian folk customs and traditions are preserved among this group, as well as a strong regional cuisine and a distinctive musical style.[51]

> Some 900,000 Cajuns live today in South Louisiana. Known for their hospitality and taste for celebration, these descendants of the French expelled from Canadian Acadia by the British in the eighteenth century conserve an original culture based on music, danse and cuisine. . . . South Louisiana is under water. Houses are less than three feet above sea level. Cajuns regularly fish in lakes or in the Gulf of Mexico. . . . Cajuns have always peacefully cohabitated with different people, former black slaves or Indians. . . . Many of them work on the numerous oil rigs found in Cajun territory.[52]

The continued diffusion of the traditional image is also facilitated by revisionist treatments, which, to debunk stereotypical views, still include them and so publicize them.[53] In a similar vein, a local journalist repeats and therefore reinforces stereotypes while debunking them:

> Few Cajuns sell handwoven cloth or homemade baskets anymore (or know how to make them either), but lots of them are still fishermen. Some still trap, gathering more pelts in the wild than all of the rest of the United States and Canada combined. Some Cajuns are boatmen—Louisiana operates the largest fleet of working craft in

Table 2.3
Comparison of Recent Accounts by Outsiders and Insiders, 1966–2001

	Outsiders				Insiders			
Domain	Acc.	%	Ref.	%	Acc.	%	Ref.	%
Occupation	44	88.0%	219	25.4%	18	72.0%	135	27.5%
Activities	45	90.0%	223	25.9%	19	76.0%	73	14.9%
Language	41	82.0%	59	6.9%	16	64.0%	24	4.9%
Family	23	46.0%	34	3.9%	18	72.0%	23	4.7%
Interaction	22	44.0%	30	3.5%	12	48.0%	24	4.9%
Religion	17	34.0%	23	2.7%	10	40.0%	18	3.7%
Attit. -Work	11	22.0%	15	1.7%	10	40.0%	16	3.3%
Attit. -Power	15	30.0%	16	1.9%	10	40.0%	14	2.9%
Attit. -Change	23	46.0%	38	4.4%	16	64.0%	22	4.5%
Pers. Traits	28	56.0%	60	7.0%	17	68.0%	35	7.1%
Econ. Status	23	46.0%	19	2.2%	12	48.0%	24	4.9%
Education	15	30.0%	23	2.7%	9	36.0%	17	3.5%
Origin	28	56.0%	32	3.7%	24	96.0%	32	6.5%
Environment	36	72.0%	60	7.0%	17	68.0%	31	6.3%
Phys. Traits	9	18.0%	10	1.2%	2	8.0%	3	0.6%
TOTAL	N=50		861	100.0%	N=25		491	100.0%

the nation, transporting goods on the myriad of waterways of south Louisiana and in support of our oil and gas industry.[54]

The ubiquity of historical reminders helps keep central aspects of the traditional image alive. The pioneer spirit of the early Acadians, their deportation from Canada, the hardship faced in colonial Louisiana, and the stigma endured until the 1960s are claimed to exemplify the Cajuns' resilience and adaptability. Although these types of themes concentrate on the achievements of Cajuns, they also reproduce the stereotypes. For example, ink drawings by popular Cajun artist Floyd Sonnier (1982–1987) depict only rural scenes of Louisiana at the turn of the twentieth century.

Finally, the integration of the outside image into Cajuns' self-representation was fostered by a change of attitude toward Cajun ethnicity. What had long been negatively evaluated became positively viewed in the 1960s. What had been a basis for scorn or shame became a badge of honor: "I was Cajun before Cajun was hip," claimed a slogan in the 1980s. The reversal was wholly conceptual since it took place with limited adjustment of the image, but it involved a radically different evaluation by both insiders and outsiders. From the inside, Cajuns engaged in a relatively limited reconstruction of the past. The mythical part was left to Longfellow's *Evangeline* whereas historical accuracy was sought in the work of historians. The travails of Acadians and minority status became markers of recent achievements and warrants of a bright future: "Two hundred years and we've just started," claimed a mural in downtown Lafayette. Although an Acadian activist has attempted to obtain an apology from the British Crown for wrongful deportation, there has been no shunning of American cultural items or values, no embracing of alternative lifestyles or calls for autonomy. The rurality, supposed closeness to the environment, earnestness, and wariness of a fast-paced technological modernity, which had been used to ridicule Cajuns, are now widely seen as virtues.

The reevaluation also took place among outsiders. As mentioned before, most outsiders' accounts contained some positive comments about Cajuns, and as early as the 1890s some authors clearly attempted to challenge the stereotype,[55] a disposition that became full fledged in the 1960s.[56] Our data show that both insiders and outsiders' views display signs of a reevaluation of ethnic characteristics in the 1960s, although it is not possible to determine from which side the process started. It is clear, though, that as the Civil Rights Movement and later ethnic mobilization movements developed among white Americans, the recognition of racial, cultural, and gender differences by the dominant American culture increased and a sense of ethnic and racial pride emerged among American ethnic and racial groups. The transformation of the Cajun negative stereotype into a positive appraisal is another example of this evolution. The acceptance of Cajunness by outsiders appears to be forthright and devoid of events akin to symbolic, that is, disguised, racism. The state of Louisiana has been allotting resources to French educational programs and ethnic commercial endeavors since the 1970s. Only one case of ethnic discrimination has been brought before the courts in more than twenty years, suggesting that in Louisiana Cajuns are not subjected to unequal treatment.[57]

STEREOTYPING AND THE CONSTRUCTION OF ETHNICITY

In the first chapter, we saw how the label "Cajun" developed over the centuries. Here, we have tried to identify the process by which an image, a cluster of stereotypes, became attached to that label. We believe that our data has established that the image of today's Cajuns owes much to the portrayals given by outsiders over the past two-and-a-half centuries. Now that we have examined the mechanics of the process, we must consider its rationale. Why do Cajuns rely on a symbolic representation of themselves borrowed from outsiders? Is this image representative of their actual conditions? If not, what does it represent?

The role of dominant groups in the self-identification of ethnic and racial groups (in addition to its definition of the very same groups) can also be seen in other groups. We can see, for example, the acceptance by aborigines of European-coined labels (American Indian, Eskimo, Bantu, Creole), of historical and mythical origins (Africa in black American consciousness, Cargo cults in Melanesia), and of fundamental cultural and ideological systems (the worldwide presence of English, Spanish, French; the idea of democracy; monotheist religions, etc). The process by which outsiders' conceptual systems made their way into the ethnics' consciousness is often related to situations of political and economic domination (Marx's false consciousness comes to mind), colonial oppression,[58] or religious persuasion.[59] Thus, ethnicity was usually defined by contrast to dominant cultural and linguistic groups. Members of the dominant groups shaped the images of the minorities, as reflected in what might be considered the narrative hegemony of outsiders. So English-speaking Americans were not "ethnic" but Americans of other origins were. However, now not only do the subjects of ethnic descriptions have access to accounts about themselves, but they can also produce accounts. These self-descriptions cannot simply discard the received historical imagery of the outsiders, because ethnicity is constructed from relations between insiders and outsiders. As insiders begin to describe themselves, they enter into a dialogue with the portrayals of the outsiders. For example, Jawaharlal Nehru, Mohandas Gandhi, and other prominent Indians have been influenced by theosophy,[60] a European intellectual creation based on stereotypical colonialist views of India as a "spiritual" nation.[61] Similarly, *Black Elk Speaks*, the representation of a Sioux medicine man by the American poet John G. Neihardt, has become an important, although problematic, text on ethnic identity for many contemporary Native Americans.[62] The evolution of the Cajuns' portrayal suggests that a similar process can take place among minorities within the dominant racial group and in absence of outright subjugation.

Interestingly, the acceptance of the image hinged primarily on a change in the interpretation by ethnics and nonethnics of characteristics associated with the ethnic group. The image has remained stable, but it can no longer provide even an approximate depiction of the contemporary Cajun experience. For example, the image remains dominated by traditional occupations—farming, collecting, and herding represent 45% of current references to occupations—although only about 4% of Cajuns are employed in farming, fishing, and forestry, according to the 1990 census.[63] The continued insistence on rurality in words and pictures does not reflect the growing urbanization of Cajuns, more than 70% of whom live in metropolitan areas. In addition, the south Louisiana areas emphasized by writers are not the regions where most Cajuns live:[64] the current emphasis on marshes and swamps fails to convey the fact that almost all Cajuns live on dry land. Similarly, the more Cajuns are integrated into American society, the greater the emphasis is placed on ethnic activities they engage in only ceremonially, such as weekend festivals, on a language whose usage declines, or on an Acadian origin increasingly distant and difficult to establish. On the other hand, historically recent activities have been incorporated into traditional portrayals. The large-scale practice of fur trapping, for example, appeared in the 1920s, and crawfishing and the popularity of seafood-based Cajun cuisine exploded in the 1960s.

There are arguably other examples of stereotypes that have evolved in a direction divergent from changes in social reality. Hannah Arendt describes how Jewish banking had ceased to be a major force in Europe when the Nazis and other anti-Semites were describing the Jews as an insidious conspiracy controlling the world economy.[65] Some Jews had, however, been economically important at an earlier point in European history because of their international connections and because they were outsiders to the European courts. A stereotype drawn from a distorted version of the past became a symbol for the group. It might be argued that the representation of Cajuns followed a similar, if much more benign and innocuous, process. The only historical representations of Cajuns were the stereotypical images drawn by others. Their mere existence and availability made them a ready-made choice for use in self-identification. Their legitimacy is rooted in the habitus, the fact that they were transmitted, more than in their accuracy in representing a condition. There is therefore a favorable disposition for agrarian ways of life, a sense that "authentic" identities and ways of life must all be linked with agrarian settings. Thus the image stands for an idealized vision of the past. The changing of the negative connotations into positive ones and the increasing importance of historical origin in the representation of Cajuns help support such a hypothesis. Our view suggests that perceptions of ethnicity can be seen as results of two interlinked dialogues: one between the accounts of insiders and the accounts of outsiders, and the other between historical portrayals and contemporary conditions. After an extensive look at central symbols of ethnicity (the label and the image) we now turn to the objective conditions in which contemporary Cajuns live and work.

NOTES

1. Joanne Nagel "Constructing Ethnicity: Recreating Ethnic Identity and Culture," *Social Problems* 41(1) (1994):152–176.

2. See James L. Hilton & William von Hippel, "Stereotypes," *Annual Review of Psychology* 47 (1996):237–272 for a review of research on stereotypes; also see Pierre van den Berghe, "Rehabilitating Stereotypes," *Ethnic and Racial Studies* 20 (1997):1–16.

3. Edward Said, *Orientalism* (New York: Random House, 1979); Michel-Ropl Trouillot, "Anthropology and the Savage Slot: The Poetics and Politics of Otherness" in Richard Fox (ed.), *Recapturing Anthropology: Working in the Present.* (Santa Fe, NM: School of American Research Press, 1991), 17–44.

4. Richard Jenkins, "Rethinking Ethnicity: Identity, Categorization and Power," *Racial and Ethnic Studies* 17(2) (1994):197–223; T.W. Murphy "From Racist Stereotype to Ethnic Identity: Instrumental Uses of Mormon Racial Doctrine,"*Ethnohistory* 46(3) (1999):451–480.

5. Virginia Dominguez, *White by Definition: Social Classification in Creole Louisiana* (New Brunswick, NJ: Rutgers University Press, 1986); Arnold Hirsch & Joseph Logdson, *Creole New Orleans: Race and Americanization* (Baton Rouge: Louisiana State University Press, 1992); Jacques Henry & Carl L. Bankston III, "Propositions for a Structuralist Analysis of Creolism," *Current Anthropology* 39(4) (1998):558–566.

6. David C. Dennis, *The Image of Louisiana in America 1800 to 1890* (master's thesis, University of Southwestern Louisiana, 1995), 52; Barry J. Ancelet, "Cajuns in Film," (paper presented at the meeting of the American Association of Teachers of French, New Orleans, LA, July 990), 1.

7. Sherri Condon & Pamela Pittman, "Language Attitudes in Acadiana," in A. M. Scott (ed.), *Cajun Vernacular English: Informal English in French Louisiana, Louisiana English Journal* (Lafayette: University of Southwestern Louisiana, 1992), 56–72; Sylvie Dubois, W. Gautreau, H. Margot, M. Mélançon, & T. Veler, "The Quality of French Spoken in Louisiana: Linguistic Attitudes Towards the Varieties of French in Cajun Communities," *SECOL Review* 19(2) (1995):126–150.

8. Although we do not claim to have reviewed everything ever written about Acadians/Cajuns in French and English, all eighteenth-, nineteenth-, and early-twentieth-century texts about Louisiana referred to in the literature and bibliographical essays, such as William Read, *Louisiana French* (Baton Rouge, Louisiana State University Press, 1931); Florence Roos Brink, "Literary Travellers in Louisiana Between 1803 and 1860," *Louisiana Historical Quarterly* 31(2) (1948): 1–32; and Timothy Reilly, "Early Acadiana Through Anglo-American Eyes," *Attakapas Gazette* 12(1):3–20, 12(3):159–177, 12(4):185–194, 13(1):53–71 (1977–1978) were examined. They were included if they contained unambiguous references to Acadians/Cajuns and at least one descriptive item. For example, mere mentions of Cajuns with no descriptive characteristic were not included.

9. To gather accounts from the 1970s on to the present, we made extensive use of the collection of press clippings maintained by the Council for the Development of French in Louisiana and by the Center for Louisiana Studies at the University of Louisiana at Lafayette. We selected accounts that provided detailed presentations of Cajun ethnicity. In addition to have already been singled out, these accounts have been frequently referred to by insiders in print and even in court. Consequently, articles solely dedicated to Cajun cuisine, Cajun music, French education programs, or individuals' portrait were not included since they did not give a general account of Cajun identity. It is obvious that local radio and television news reports and programs contributed to form and broadcast images of modern Cajuns. However, old programs are largely unavailable and the constitution of a meaningful sample of contemporary programs is quite problematic given the sheer volume of production and the immediacy of the medium. Thus none were included. We realize that selecting

seventy-five accounts from the thousands printed, broadcast, or filmed is inherently a risky proposition. However, our knowledge of a large part of the rejected accounts and extensive familiarity with Southwestern Louisiana and the development of Cajun ethnicity since the 1980s support our contention that our sample provides an accurate representation of the view of Cajuns at the end of the twentieth century.

10. James Dormon, *The People Called Cajuns: An Introduction to an Ethnohistory* (Lafayette: Center for Louisiana Studies, 1983); Carl Brasseaux, *Acadian to Cajun: Transformation of a People 1803–1877* (Jackson: University Press of Mississippi, 1992); Jacques Henry, "Un statut pour les Cajuns," New York: *France Amérique*, 23–29 juin & 30 juin–6 juillet (1988).

11. The distinction between outsiders and insiders is inherently challenging. We categorized accounts mostly on the basis of unambiguous signs (author's name, biographical information) of Cajun ethnicity or outsider status and occasionally by interpreting indications of a "we" or "they" perspective.

12. Modern versions of original material in the form of reprints and edited collections were occasionally used, such as Herbert Eugene Bolton, *Anastase de Mézières and the Louisiana-Texas Frontier 1768–1780*, 3 vols. (Cleveland, OH: Arthur Clark Company, 1914); Carl Brasseaux, Emilio Fabrian Garcia & Jacqueline Voorhies, *Quest for the Promised Land* (Lafayette: Center for Louisiana Studies, 1989); Walter Prichard, "A Tourist Description of Louisiana in 1860," *Louisiana Historical Quarterly* 21(4) (1938); and Reilly, "Early Acadiana."

13. James Spradley, *Participant Observation* (Fort Worth, TX: Harcourt, Brace, Jovanovich, 1980).

14. Ibid.

15. Terms related to religion, environment, origin, physical traits, education, and language were mostly self-evident and easily grouped. Occasionally categories did not always clearly emerge from folk categories, i.e., designed by the writers or their subjects. In cases of ambiguity, the dominant dimension was retained; for example, statements on interracial relations were included in "interaction" when referring to casual contact and to "physical characteristics" when explaining physical appearance; similarly, terms were included in the domain "personal traits" on the basis of the assumed extent of interaction necessary for them to be revealed; for example, "proud" and "unworthy"—inherent personality traits independent of actual interaction—were coded as a personal quality whereas "communicative" and "suspicious of strangers" were coded as interaction since they mostly refer to situations of contact with other people. Statements about acts of a nonoccupational nature such as riding horses, playing music, paddling in pirogues, drinking, cooking, and eating food were classified as activities (what people do), except when clearly referring to a jockey, a professional musician or chef, listed as occupations. An effort was made to adhere to the emic meaning of references to classify them. For example, nineteenth-century writers used "simple" in a largely derogative sense of being uncivilized, whereas contemporary writers tend to use it with an appreciative, humanistic outlook; similarly, references to maintenance of the ancestral heritage were largely negative in the nineteenth century and have been rather lauded recently.

16. The presentation of statistics is meant to be informative since the data does not yield itself to advanced statistical analysis given its qualitative nature and our coding procedure; for instance, occupation and personal traits are categories inherently allowing for more references in the form of lists than physical characteristics

and religion often simply appearing as "white" and "Catholics." The presentation of both variables aims at addressing the imbalance.

17. François Marie Perrin du Lac, *Voyage dans les 2 Louisianes* (Paris: Capelle et Renaud, 1805).

18. Reilly "Early Acadiana," 3; also Carl Brasseaux, "Acadian Education: From Cultural Isolation to Mainstream America" in Glen Conrad (ed.), *The Cajuns: Essays on their History and Culture* (Lafayette: Center for Louisiana Studies, 1978), 212–224.

19. Julian Ralph, "Along the Bayou Teche," *Harper's New Monthly Magazine* 87 (1893):870–884.

20. Harnett Kane, *The Bayous of Louisiana* (New York: Hampton Publishing, 1943), 9.

21. Albert Rhodes, "The Louisiana Creoles," *Galaxy* 16 (1873):252–260, in Reilly, "Early Acadiana," 65.

22. R.L. Daniels, "The Acadians of Louisiana," *Scribner's Monthly* 14 (1879):383–392, 106.

23. Margaret Avery Johnston, *The Acadians in Story and Song* (New Orleans: F.F. Hansell and Bro. Publishers, 1893).

24. Rhodes, "Louisiana Creoles," 254.

25. Marguerite Pecot, "The 'Cajun" (Unpublished master's thesis: Louisiana State University, 1924), iii.

26. William Henry Perrin, *Southwest Louisiana: Biographical and Historical.* (New Orleans: Gulf Publishing Company, 1891. Reprint 1971, Baton Rouge, LA: Claitor's Publishing Division), 104; see also Joel Fletcher, *The Acadians in Louisiana Today* (Lafayette: Southwestern Louisiana Institute, 1947); Martha Wilson, "Cajun Country: Their Unchanged Eden. After Nearly 200 Years It's Beginning to Change," *Shreveport Times*, July 15, 1954; Lauren C. Post, *Cajun Sketches* (Baton Rouge: Louisiana State University Press, 1962).

27. Marguerite Roman, "Les Acadiens au XXème siècle," *Comptes Rendus de l'Athénée Louisianais*, Mai (1924) 12–23; Jay K. Ditchy, *Les Acadiens louisianais et leur parler* (Paris: Librairie E. Droz, 1932); Gabriel-Louis Jaray, "Le destin français en Louisiane," *France-Amérique*, Août (1957):153–158; Adolphe Robert, *Mémorial.* L'Association Canado-Américaine (1940).

28. As noted by Revon Reed, *Lâche pas la patate: Portrait des Acadiens de la Louisiane* (Montréal: Editions Parti pris, 1976); Ryan Bernard, "The Cajuns," *Houston City Magazine*, October 1980: 41–43, 109–113; Trent Angers, *The Truth About the Cajuns* (Lafayette, LA: Acadian House Publishing, 1990); Griffin Smith, Jr., "Cajun Still Loving Life," *National Geographic* 178 (October 1990):41–65.

29. Gretchen Dewailly, "T. Paul Robin—Last Real Cajun," *Lafayette Sunday Advertiser*, June 28, 1981.

30. Jim Bradshaw, "Culture, not blood, defines today's cajuns," *Lafayette Sunday Advertiser*, January 13, 1991.

31. Timothy Flint, *Recollections of the Last Ten Years* (Boston: Cummings, Hilliard and Company 1826), 336.

32. W.H. Sparks, *The Memories of Fifty Years*, 4th ed. (Philadelphia: E. Claxton & Company, 1882), 377.

33. Shermakaye Bass, "Cutting Loose in Cajun Country," *New York Times*, January 4, 1998.

34. Flint, *Recollections*; Frederick L. Olmsted, *A Journey in the Seaboard Slave States*, 2 vols, (New York, 1857); R.L. Daniels, "The Acadians of Louisiana," *Scribner's Monthly* 19 (1879):383–392; Rebecca H. Davis, "Here and There in the South V: In Attakapas," *Harper's New Monthly Magazine* 74 (1887):913–925; Arden Spell, *Life in Louisiana Cajun Country* (Asheville, NC, 1956); Roy Reed, "Cajuns Resist the Melting Pot," *New York Times Magazine*, February 29, 1976; Martin Ritt (director), *Casey's Shadow* (film, 1978); Elizabeth Mullener, "A Cajun Journey," *New Orleans Times Picayune*, August 14–18, 1988; Rick Bragg, "In Louisiana, Card Games Reveal the Cajun Spirit," *New York Times*, February 18, 1996.

35. Ralph, "Along the Bayou Teche"; Alcée Fortier, *Louisiana Studies; Literature, Customs and Dialects; History and Education* (New Orleans: F.F. Hansell and Bro., 1894); Ralph Graves, "Louisiana, Land of Perpetual Romance," *National Geographic* 57(4) (1930):393–482; Frederick Simpich, "Louisiana Trades with the World," *National Geographic* 92(6) (1947):705–738; Hilda Gallasero, "Are you a Cajun?" *Acadiana Profile* 9(2) (1981):2; Dewailly, "T. Paul Robin."

36. Thomas Hutchins, *An Historical Narrative and Topographical Description of Louisiana and West Florida*. (Philadelphia: Printed for the Author and Robert Aitken, 1784); Davis, "Here and There in the South."

37. Daniels, "The Acadians of Louisiana"; Davis, "Here and There in the South."

38. Samuel Lockett, *Second Annual Report of the Topographical Survey of Louisiana: Report of Superintendent for 1870* (Baton Rouge: Louisiana State University, 1873); Charles Warner, "The Acadian Land," *Harper's New Monthly Magazine* 74 (1887):334–354; Spell, *Life in Louisiana Cajun Country.*

39. Les Blank (director), *Spend It All* (film, 1971); Reed, "Cajuns Resist the Melting Pot"; Ancelet, "Cajuns in Film"; Bass, "Cutting Loose in Cajun Country"; Jennifer Moses, "Bayou Country," *New York Times Magazine*, March 1, 1998, 53–64.

40. Perrin du Lac, *Voyage dans les 2 Louisianes*; Edmund Dana, *Geographical Sketches of the Western Country* (Cincinnati: Locker, Reynolds & Co. Printers, 1819); Warner, "The Acadian Land."

41. Fletcher, *The Acadians in Louisiana Today.*

42. Robert Gramling, Craig Forsyth & Linda Mooney. "The Protestant Ethic and the Spirit of Cajunism," *Journal of Ethnic Studies* 15 (1986):33–46.

43. Kane, *The Bayous of Louisiana*; Fletcher, *The Acadians in Louisiana Today*; Barry J. Ancelet, Jay Edwards, & Glen Pitre, eds.: *Cajun Country* (Jackson: University Press of Mississippi, 1991); Page Gutierrez, *Cajun Foodways* (Jackson: University Press of Mississippi, 1992).

44. Brasseaux, *Acadian to Cajun*; Jacques Henry & Carl L. Bankston III, "Propositions for a Structuralist Analysis."

45. Reilly, "Early Acadiana," 3; Conrad, *The Cajuns*; Angers, *The Truth About the Cajuns.*

46. Dormon, *The People Called Cajuns*; Henry, "Un statut pour les Cajuns."

47. Benedict Anderson, in *Imagined Communities: Reflections on the Origin and Spread of Nationalism*, (London: Verso, 1983) suggests that the emergence of modern media more than facilitated the production and reproduction of texts and images fostering a national identity in nineteenth-century Europe. He argues that it in fact created the basis for "imagining" communities and identities with no empirical reality within individuals' grasp.

48. Edward Carewe (director), *Evangeline* (film, 1929).

49. Reilly, "Early Acadiana," 3.

50. Our analysis is in line with most scholarly assessments of Cajun identity (Gramling, Forsyth & Mooney, "The Protestant Ethic") and with analyses of contemporary Cajuns' self-definition shown to be centered around origin and language. See, for example, Cécyle Trépanier, "La Louisiane française au seuil du XXème siècle: La commercialisation de la culture," in Gérard Bouchard & Serge Courville (eds.), *La construction d'une culture, le Québec et l'Amérique française*, (Sainte Foy: Presses de l'Université Laval, 1993), 361–394; Dubois et al., "The Quality of French."

51. "Cajun." *Microsoft Encarta Encyclopedia* (New York: Funk & Wagnall Corporation, 1996).

52. Cajun.net. "La région Cajun," www2.cajun.net (1998).

53. Beryl Stiles, *A Cajun's Persuasion: A Decade of Newspaper Columns in St Mary* (Detroit: Harlo, 1977); Bernard, "The Cajuns"; Karen Snyder (director), *Cajun Crossroads* (documentary, 1987); Angers, *The Truth About the Cajuns*; Smith, "Cajuns Still Loving Life."

54. Bradshaw, "Culture, Not Blood."

55. See, for example Davis, "Here and There in the South"; Ralph, "Along the Bayou Teche."

56. See Editorial, *Lafayette Sunday Advertiser*, December 4, 1966; Bern Keating, "Cajunland: Louisiana French-speaking Coast," *National Geographic* 129(3) (1966): 352–391.

57. Henry, "Un statut pour les Cajuns."

58. Frantz Fanon, *Les damnés de la terre* (Paris: Maspéro, 1968); Scott B. Vickers, *Native American Identities: From Stereotype to Archetype in Art and Literature* (Albuquerque: University of New Mexico Press, 1998).

59. Murphy, "From Racist Stereotype to Ethnic Identity."

60. Jeffery Paine, *Father India: How Encounters with an Ancient Culture Transformed the Modern West* (New York: Harper Collins, 1998).

61. Said, *Orientalism.*

62. Michael F. Steltenkamp, *Black Elk: Holy Man of the Oglala* (Norman: University of Oklahoma Press, 1993).

63. Henry & Bankston, "Propositions for a Structuralist Analysis."

64. Michael Forêt, "A Cookbook View of Cajun Culture," *Journal of Popular Culture* 23(1) (1989): 23–36.

65. Hannah Arendt, *The Origins of Totalitarianism* (New York: Harcourt, 1951).

CHAPTER 3

The Changing Economic Context of Louisiana

To this point, our investigation has concentrated on the development of the word "Cajun" and on the traits that came to be associated with this word. Now, we turn from the name and the image to the living circumstances of the people. Both ethnic or racial groups and social classes are shaped by the economic structures of societies and by the positions of individuals in those structures. This means that we must now focus our attention on the social and economic setting of Cajuns in the past and today. In this chapter, we describe how the socioeconomic context of Louisiana changed drastically over the course of the twentieth century and analyze the consequences of change for Cajun identity. The agricultural economy that gave rise to Cajun ethnicity largely disappeared after the middle of the twentieth century, and the children and grandchildren of the old rural poor became a regional working class.

There is a tendency to pass on class positions over the course of generations. In an agricultural economy, the children of poor farmers tend to become poor farmers themselves. In an industrial economy, despite increased opportunities for mobility, the children of working-class parents tend to become members of the working class. What happens, though, when the economic structure changes? We argue that when an agricultural economy becomes an industrial economy, this does not mean that the past is simply erased and that all individuals in a new generation simply start out afresh with completely equal opportunities for upward mobility. Instead, the children of small farmers tend to become members of a working class. Lacking resources for education or family traditions of education, the offspring of the rural poor are less likely than the children of well-to-do farmers or children of the old middle classes to acquire professional skills. Class position in an older socioeconomic context affects class position in a newer socioeconomic context.

THE MODERNIZATION OF LOUISIANA

If the establishment of the plantation system in the early 1800s and the aftermath of the Reconstruction era were major economic events of the nineteenth century, industrialization and then the emergence of a service economy have been the dominant trends in the economy of twentieth-century Louisiana. By most accounts, the modernization of Louisiana's economy began in earnest in the 1930s following a number of earlier developments. The discovery of oil in 1901 in the eastern part of the state, the diffusion of compulsory primary education, the construction of roads and bridges by the administration of Governor Huey Long, and the electrification of rural areas all helped set the stage for the state's economic transition.

The transformation of Louisiana's economy can be seen in figures on the distribution of jobs by sectors of activity (see Table 3.1). From data collected during the decennial censuses of population from 1930 to 1990, we have constructed eight categories of activities: agriculture, forestry and fishing; mining, which consists mainly of jobs in the oil and gas extraction business; manufacturing; construction; transportation and communication; wholesale and retail trade; service and administrative occupations; and finance and real estate. These numbers provide indications of drastic changes over the course of a single lifetime, shown graphically in Figure 3.1. Perhaps one of the most startling changes lies in the status of agriculture, forestry, and fishing as sources of employment for Louisianians. In 1930, this was the predominant area of economic activity, occupying well over one-third (38%) of workers aged 10 and over. In each decade from 1930 to 1970, though, workers moved out of these types of jobs by the tens of thousands. The change was especially notable during the 1950s, when the number of farmers, foresters, and fishermen was cut in half. The decrease continued through 1990, so that workers involved in agricultural production or collection represent only 2.5% of the workforce, a figure consistent with that of the U.S. economy and other industrialized nations.

The transformation of Louisiana's economy appears even more clearly when we look at occupations, rather than at industries. Machine operators, for example, who work in the agricultural industry would not properly be considered farmers. To offer a sharper picture of the state's economic transformation, Figure 3.2 uses samples from historical census data (the Public Use Micro-data Samples, or PUMS) to show percentages of Louisianians in

Table 3.1
Distribution of Jobs among Selected Industries in Louisiana, 1930–1990

	1930	1940	1950	1960	1970	1980	1990
Agriculture, forestry, fishing	310,189	256,128	160,595	78,810	47,999	42,417	41,805
(% of all jobs)	*38.0%*	*33.2%*	*18.3%*	*7.8%*	*3.1%*	*2.6%*	*2.5%*
Mining	7,135	14,869	24,201	36,335	46,584	81,327	52,329
(% of all jobs)	*0.9%*	*1.9%*	*2.8%*	*3.6%*	*3.0%*	*5.0%*	*3.2%*
Manufacturing	100,627	99,120	132,476	157,261	184,024	236,064	205,420
(% of all jobs)	*12.3%*	*12.9%*	*15.1%*	*15.6%*	*11.8%*	*14.4%*	*12.5%*
Construction	33,438	34,936	64,939	81,033	96,609	153,122	111,181
(% of all jobs)	*4.1%*	*4.5%*	*7.4%*	*8.0%*	*6.2%*	*9.3%*	*6.8%*
Transportation, communication	68,061	50,523	75,780	87,599	95,757	142,611	128,017
(% of all jobs)	*8.3%*	*6.6%*	*8.7%*	*8.7%*	*6.1%*	*8.7%*	*7.8%*
Wholesale, retail trade	79,686	112,620	169,845	200,579	245,661	346,736	361,064
(% of all jobs)	*9.8%*	*14.6%*	*19.4%*	*19.9%*	*15.8%*	*21.2%*	*22.0%*
Service	183,990	187,912	225,956	330,064	390,361	553,445	647,365
(% of all jobs)	*22.6%*	*24.4%*	*25.8%*	*32.8%*	*25.1%*	*33.8%*	*39.4%*
Finance, real estate	15,079	15,034	21,816	36,131	51,250	83,662	94,423
(% of all jobs)	*1.8%*	*1.9%*	*2.5%*	*3.6%*	*3.3%*	*5.1%*	*5.8%*
Total employment	815,725	771,142	875,608	1,007,812	1,558,245	1,639,394	1,641,414

Sources: U.S. Bureau of the Census. *Fifteenth Census of the United States—1930—Population. Vol. III. Reports by States Alabama-Missouri* (Washington, DC: Bureau of the Census, 1932) Table 20; *Fifteenth Census of the United States—1930—Population. Vol. IV. Occupations by State* (Washington, DC: Bureau of the Census, 1932) Tables 3, 4; *Sixteenth Census of the United States—1940. Characteristics of the Population, Vol. 2 Part 3. Louisiana-Michigan* (Washington, DC: Bureau of the Census, 1943) Table 18; *Census of Population—1950. Vol 2. Characteristics of the Population, Part 18—Louisiana* (Washington, DC: Bureau of the Census, 1952) Table 30; *Census of Population—1960. Vol 1. Characteristics of the Population, Part 20—Louisiana* (Washington, DC: Bureau of the Census, 1963) Tables 61, 62; *Census of Population—1970. Vol. 1. Characteristics of the Population, Part 20—Louisiana* (Washington, DC: Bureau of the Census, 1973) Tables 55, 186; *Census of Population—1980. Vol 1. Characteristics of the Population, Part 20—Louisiana* (Washington, DC: Bureau of the Census, 1981) Table 69; *Census of Population—1990. Social and Economic Characteristics, Louisiana* (Washington, DC: Bureau of the Census, 1993) Table 26.

different occupations. Because PUMS data for 1930 is not available, we begin this figure in 1920.

In 1920, a clear majority of Louisianians were classified as farmers or fishers. In the years after World War II, well within the memory of middle-aged to elderly people, this changed very rapidly. By the end of the century, only a tiny fraction of the state's population was employed in farming and fishing. The proportion of unskilled workers declined. The number of skilled

Figure 3.1
Distribution of Jobs among Selected Industries in Louisiana, 1930–1990

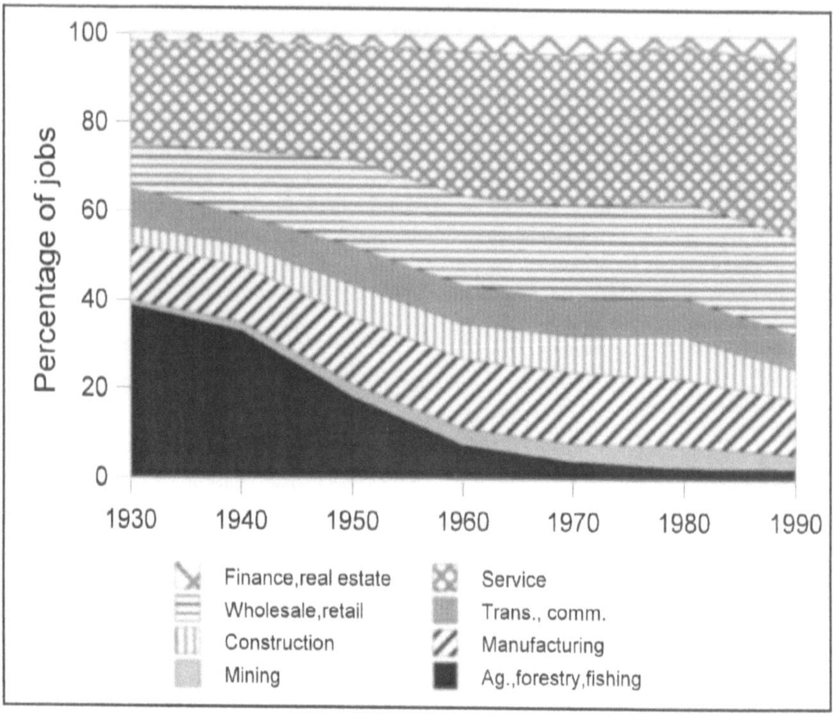

Source: Steven Ruggles, Matthew Sobek et al., *Integrated Public Use Microdata Series: Version 2.0* (Minneapolis, MN: Historical Census Projects, University of Minnesota, 1997).

craftspeople increased until about 1970 and then shrank slightly as a percentage of all workers. Although the number of professionals, managers, and technicians expanded, the most marked growth occurred in the area of sales, clerical work, and service work. Louisianians, formerly fishers and farmers, had become service and office workers.

Both fishing and agriculture, moreover, had become highly industrialized activities by the late twentieth century. Fishing and shrimping boats had become small floating factories, hauling in vast quantities of seafood. In 1997, Louisiana landed 96.2 million tons of shrimp, more than any other state in the Gulf Coast region and 35% of all the shrimp landed in the entire United States. In total commercial fisheries landings in the nation, Louisiana was second only to Alaska.[1] A relatively small number of workers, in other words, were producing seafood for a national market. As a shrimp-boat owner, a self-described Cajun, explained to us, "Shrimping today is a business and it's real competitive. If you don't approach it like a business, you won't be around very long."

Figure 3.2
Occupations in Louisiana, 1920–1990

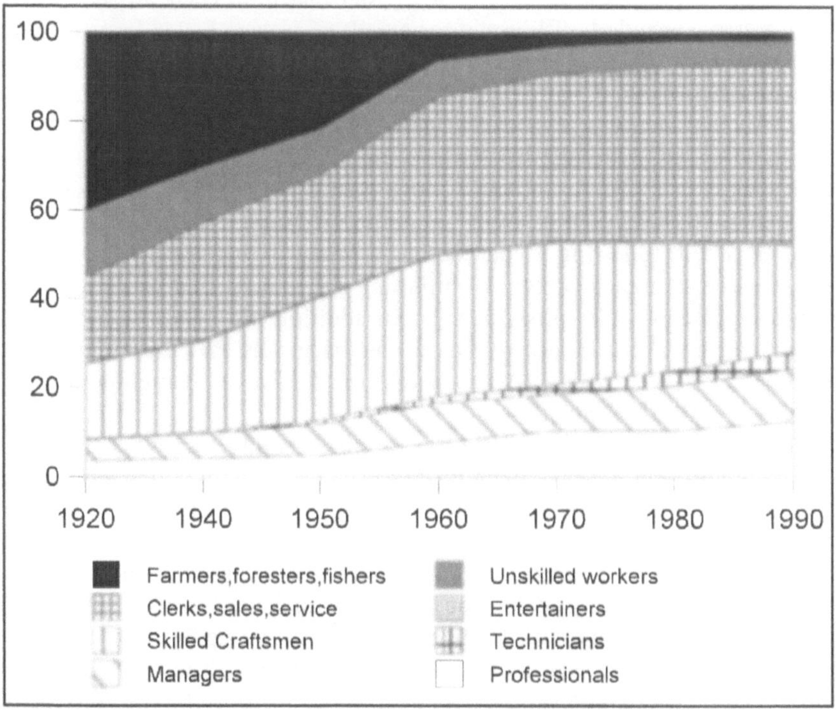

Source: Ruggles, Sobek et al., *Integrated Public Use Microdata Series.*

Farms had also become big business by the twentieth century's end. In 1930, there were 161,445 farms in Louisiana with an average size of 58 acres. In 1992, the average size had grown to 306 acres, but the number of farms had dwindled to 25,652. Agricultural jobs had declined in the state for the same reason they had declined elsewhere in the United States: farming had become a large, efficient, capital-intensive, highly mechanized business enterprise. We spoke with a Louisiana truck driver who owned and worked a small farm: "Back when my granddaddy was farming, the small farmer could make a living. It wasn't a good living, but it was a living. These days, nobody can make a living farming unless they're real big. I don't wonder there're so few small farmers left."

What replaced the jobs lost in agriculture? Although mining offered only a minority of jobs in Louisiana as a whole throughout the 1930–1990 period, its increasing economic and symbolic importance for the state cannot be underestimated. Robert Gramling, author of the most authoritative work on the offshore oil industry in the Gulf of Mexico, has pointed out that oil production in Louisiana began to expand rapidly following the 1930s with the development of the submersible drilling barge.[2] It first allowed for research and exploitation of oil in the coastal marshes. Then, in the 1950s, the industry expanded offshore into the Gulf of Mexico fueled by a constant stream of technological innovations, the settlement of the controversy on mineral rights to the Continental Shelf between the federal government and oil-producing states, and favorable geopolitical developments, especially in the Middle East. Although mining provided 7,000 jobs (less than 1% of the state's jobs) in 1930, it employed more than 36,000 people by 1960, and more than 80,000 in 1980, 5% of Louisiana's workers. This decreased somewhat by 1990, following a collapse in oil prices during the 1980s, but oil and gas continue to be centrally important for reasons that go beyond the number of people it employs directly. In addition, the regional concentration of oil mining in Southwestern Louisiana means that the industry has an especially large effect on Acadiana and on the lives of contemporary Cajuns, as we will see below.

Today, at the beginning of the twenty-first century, the oil and gas industry literally fuels Louisiana's economy. The growth or fall of mining activities has a ripple effect through all domains of the economy and society. The health of the oil business is accompanied by unmistakable signs in Southwest Louisiana: When it is good, highways are busy, urban main arteries are clogged, the price of houses to rent or buy shoots up, shops and restaurants are bustling, and Help Needed signs pop up. The oil boom of the 1960s and 1970s was accompanied by a net growth in the number of jobs in all industrial and service occupations. Unfortunately, the collapse of the oil market in the late 1980s contributed largely to a net loss of the same jobs. The fluctuations of the oil and gas industry explain in part the expansion and contraction of some entire sectors. Construction, transportation, and communication jobs have remained relatively constant as a proportion of all jobs in the state, employing an average of 16% of the workforce since 1950. But the percentage of jobs dropped from 1980 to 1990, because so much industrial and residential construction was related to oil activities by this time and the demand for transportation of goods and people dipped. State and local governments are also affected by oil. Budget officials in the 1980s estimated that a $1 variation in the price of crude oil resulted in a $1 million variation in state revenues. Louisiana state employees and citizens depending on state services have grown keenly aware of the direct consequences of the vagaries of the oil industry on their employment, wages, and even public assistance funds.

Impact studies have shown that the development of extraction activities in the Gulf Coast has had wide-ranging social consequences, both adverse and positive.[3] The prolonged absence of men from households led to the reorganization of relations in oil-workers' families and became a major source of family stress.[4] The good-paying jobs in oil heightened economic disparities between those who benefitted from the oil boom and those who did not, so that prosperity actually resulted in new pockets of poverty.[5] Although benefits in education measured by higher rates of graduation have been noted in periods of increasing extractive activities,[6] they came at a higher price and with increased strain on families and school districts.[7]

One of the most marked changes that we see in Figures 3.1 and 3.2 is the growth of the trade and service sectors. In 1930, less than 10% of all jobs in Louisiana were in wholesale and retail trade. By 1990, more than one out of every four employed persons worked in sales. Again, the decade of the 1960s appears to be the pivotal one, with trade occupations expanding from 17% to 26% of the total in this single ten-year period. By 1990 they represented a third of the workforce, and they continued to increase throughout the 1990s (see Table 3.2). If jobs in finance and insurance are added, we find that by the end of the century, more than two positions out of three were involved in the production of neither agricultural or industrial products but rather in the delivery of goods, services, information, or professional expertise.

The expansion of service occupations is the hallmark of a post-industrial economy. What happened to industrial jobs? Census figures show that although manufacturing has supplied one out of five to one out of ten jobs in the state in recent decades, Louisiana has never had the factory-based economy of the old American Northeast. At its peak in 1970, manufacturing never represented more than 17% of jobs. It grew slightly from 1930 to 1970 and then contracted. These trends reflect the state's slow development of an industrial economy to 1970, and the movement toward a service-oriented economy in the late twentieth century. This overview suggests that Louisiana's economy has experienced a drastic shift from an agricultural structure to a post-industrial design in a relatively short period, mostly between 1930 and 1970. Unlike other post-industrial economies of other regions, though, an industrial-type extractive activity (oil mining) is central to the state's livelihood. Louisiana, accordingly, has proportionately more positions for blue-collar workers than other parts of modern America do, and these positions are most heavily concentrated in Acadiana.

If we look more closely at the economy of Acadiana, we see that the modern mining industry, not hunting and trapping and fishing, now distinguishes Cajun country from the rest of the state. The Center for Economic Research of the University of Louisiana at Monroe tracks the distribution of jobs throughout the state. We consider the period from 1970 to 1995 because profound changes in the economy and the perception of ethnicity took place jointly during these years (see Table 3.2). The data show that mining is about three times more important in Acadiana that in the whole state. At the beginning of our period, 13% of all Acadiana jobs were in mining, compared with 5% of all jobs in Louisiana. Throughout the 1980s, 16% of the region's jobs were in mining, and even after the downturn, 9%

Table 3.2
Percent of Jobs in Selected Industrial Categories in Louisiana and in Acadiana, 1970–1995

	La. jobs in Acadiana	Mining		Manufacture		Construction		Agriculture, fishing		Transport		Finance		Wholesale, retail		Service	
Year		**La.**	**Acad**	**La.**	**Acad.**	**La.**	**Acad.**	**La.**	**Acad.**	**La.**	**Acad.**	**La.**	**Acad.**	**La.**	**Acad.**	**La.**	**Acad.**
1970	15.2	5.2	13.1	16.5	10.3	8.3	7.4	0.9	1.8	9.4	9.3	6.5	4.5	26.3	27.2	27.0	26.2
1975	16.3	5.1	13.7	14.9	11.3	9.1	7.6	0.8	1.7	8.4	8.6	8.5	6.0	26.4	26.4	26.7	24.4
1980	18.6	6.5	16.6	13.9	10.3	10.4	8.7	0.9	1.5	8.6	9.8	8.0	5.5	26.1	25.4	26.0	22.2
1985	18.2	6.5	15.5	12.9	8.3	9.5	7.8	1.0	1.4	8.6	10.1	8.1	6.2	26.2	25.6	27.5	25.2
1990	17.2	4.3	11.1	11.9	11.3	7.6	5.9	1.3	2.3	7.7	9.0	7.5	5.6	26.3	25.4	33.5	29.3
1995	17.3	3.2	8.7	11.1	11.7	8.1	6.9	1.9	2.1	6.9	8.2	6.4	4.8	26.9	26.7	36.2	30.8

Source: Steven Ruggles, Matthew Sobek, et al., *Integrated Public Use Microdata Series: Version 2.0* (Minneapolis, MN: Historical Census Projects, University of Minnesota, 1997).

of the Acadiana workforce were still involved in oil and gas compared with 3% for the whole state. Our calculations from samples of the census data show that if one looks only at male workers, since men tend to predominate in the oil industry, about 15% of employed men in Acadiana worked directly in petroleum mining or petroleum refining.

Figure 3.3 provides a comparison of the jobs in Acadiana and in Louisiana in 1995. The two pies look very similar. Sales and service jobs predominated in the state as a whole and in the Acadian region. Very few people worked in agriculture and fishing. The major difference is that mining was much more important for the region than it was for the state. Indeed, we will argue that its role in the regional economy extended far beyond providing jobs for about one out of every ten people (and jobs for about one out of every six to seven men).

Our statistics offer an abstract view of the socioeconomic change. Two activities, agriculture and the oil and gas industry, are the strongest sources of symbols and powerful bases of reference. As we saw in Chapter 2, farming, trapping, and fishing have become part of the stereotype and self-image of Cajuns, although most Cajuns today are not farmers or trappers or fishers. Still, preferences in locations of residence and choices of leisure activities and vehicles are often influenced by the memory of rural life. Many young couples opt to live in the "country" even if much of the "country" is fairly urbanized and no longer cultivated. A drive along the back roads of contemporary Southwestern Louisiana offers more views of residential lots than views of farmhouses. A drive through urban areas, by contrast, takes one past driveways with gleaming pickup trucks and flatboats on trailers. Agricultural activities may have been transformed into leisurely pursuits of fishing, hunting, and landscaping, but they keep area residents' lifestyles rooted in a version of rurality.

Oil mining employs many more people than agriculture, and oil provides income for many more than its employees. Although more people work in sales and service jobs, it should be remembered that the sales and service categories cover a wide variety of activities. Mining jobs in Louisiana all revolve around a single activity, the extraction of oil. It is impressive that even during a time of relative decline, this single activity employed one out of every ten workers in the Cajun region and one out of every six to seven of the region's working men. Moreover, as a profitable business, with fairly high-paid workers, it creates multiplier jobs in other sectors. Much of the construction and transportation in the Acadian region is associated with the oil business. Almost all of our interviewees referred to some economic connection to oil. But the oil industry has also acquired a symbolic importance for Cajuns. For many Cajuns, the arrival of oil rigs and crews on their lands and in their towns marked the irruption of modernity and rapid change into their lives. Various accounts by Cajuns mirror the combination of awe and expectation romantically captured by Robert Flaherty's semifictional Cajun

Figure 3.3
Distributions of Jobs in Industries in All of Louisiana and in Acadiana, 1995

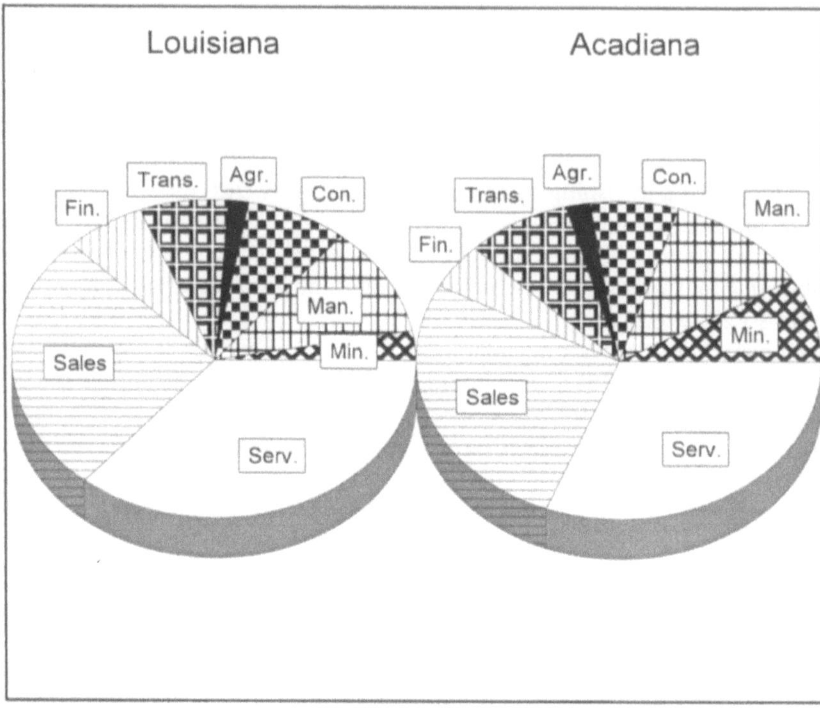

Source: Ruggles, Sobek et al.; *Integrated Public Use Microdata Series.*

family witnessing the arrival of a drilling barge in its pristine environment.[8] Witnesses have been ambivalent toward this center of the new Acadian economy. Revon Reed lists "*le pétrole*" first in its survey of the Cajuns' occupations and credits it with "saving the lives of thousands who would have starved to death."[9] But, in a series of moving monologues, Richard Guidry deplores the demands that shift work (fourteen days on and fourteen days off) places on a Cajun family. His not-so-fictional mechanic has a steady and well-paying job, but he was away when each of his three children were born, and he will miss the graduation of his son, the first in the family to attend college. He is glad, though, that his children and grandchildren will never know the hardship of the sharecropper's existence that marked his childhood.[10] Memories, images, and feelings elicited by the past coalesce to make sense of the present and build hopes for the future.

This process is expressed in real life by our interviewees. Louis Trahan, a self-described Cajun in his late 50s, contrasted his work in the oil fields with that of his parents on the small fields of their family farm: "Working on the rigs is hard work. I do it and my son does it, but I don't think I want my grandchildren to do it. I'd rather have them do something easier. But it sure is better than trying to scratch a living out of the ground the way my mama and daddy had to." Sue Arceneaux, a 90-year-old Cajun woman in Breaux Bridge, remembers her farm origins with the same ambivalence:

Là où j'ai été élevée au ras de Ossun. C'est là où mommy and daddy restaient. J'ai été baptisée au Carencro. I'm 90 years old. That was a long time ago. I was born in 1911.
[On faisait] la récolte, du maïs, du coton, des papates, des Irish potatoe. Mon papa montait des puits d'eau. Des fois il partait à trois heures du matin. Il partait en wagon et deux chevaux et là il allait fouiller l'puits. Des fois ça prenait toute la journée, ça revenait dans la nuit, ça faisait noir. Il avait ça pour lui-même. . . . C'était la propriété a Mama. Quand y en a des frères à Mama ou be des soeurs qui voulaient vendre leur property, mon père leur rachetait. Ca fait ça lui donnait plus grand. Là ça élevait tous leurs bêtes, leurs cochons, tout leurs volailles. On a fait un tas des boucheries, un tas des boudin, des gratons.
Le maïs, y'avait pas des tracteurs comme asteur c'était tout avec des ch'vaux et des charrues. . . . Là ça, quand ça levait moyèr, fallait prendre des pioches et pi piocher. . . . Marcher toujours. Là quand ça arrivait assez grand, là y avait du maïs tendre; ça aurait été cherché l'maïs tendre. On aurait tout nettoyé ça, on aurait mis ça dedans des jarres. Le lendemain ils étaient proche tout aigri parce que y avait pas des freezer comme asteur. All that work . . . Le maï quand il était sec, fallait aller l'ramasser à pied toujours. Quand fallait casser l'maï, là ça mettait les ch'vaux et l'wagon au milieu. Y'avait deux qui s'mettaient sur les côtés, ça cassait l'maï, ça l'tirait dans l'wagon. Et là quand ça c'était fini, fallair aller au magasin et rober ce maï et pi la mettre les dernières graines noires, et pis tourner et le donner à les poules, à les cochons, à les bêtes, à les ch'vaux, n'importe quoi.[11]

I was born near Ossun. That's where my mommy and daddy lived. I was baptized in Carencro. I'm 90 years old. That was a long time ago. I was born in 1911.
[We grew] corn, cotton, potatoes, Irish potatoes. My dad dug water wells. Sometimes he left at three in the morning. He left with a wagon and two horses and he went to dig wells. Sometimes, it would take all day. He'd come back at night when it was dark. He did this on his own. . . . The property was mama's. When her brothers or sisters wanted to sell their property, my dad would buy it. Like this he had more. There they raised all their animals, pigs, poultry. We did many boucheries, *a lot of* boudin, gratons.
The corn, there was no tractor like today. It was done with horses and plows. . . . There was no riding. Now when it got hard, we had to take shovels. . . . Always walking. Now when the corn got ripe, we'd get it, and clean it and put it in jars. The following day, it was almost sour because there was no freezer like today. All that work. . . . When the corn was dry, we had to go and pick it, on foot like always. When we had to break the corn, we'd put the horses and wagon in the middle, two on each side breaking the corn and then we'd pull the wagon. When this was over, we had to go to the store and "rober" the corn, pick the black kernels and give them to the chicken, the pig, the horses, anything.

Her 47-year-old son-in-law, Robert Prejean, reminisced about a life that began under similar circumstances, but changed with the economic context of Southwestern Louisiana:

My grandfather was a sharecropper and they lived about five miles just out of Church Point. He was a hard worker and coming back from the school my chore was to feed the animals, the hogs, get the corn ready for the mules when they came back from the field. I did also work in the field on weekends, during the holidays. I did break corn with my hands like my mother-in-law did. I didn't do much hoeing but I did cotton picking. It's odd because I am only 47; very few of my classmates back then lived the life that I did because my grandparents were poor. . . . I didn't know about running water in the house until I was about twelve, thirteen years old. We had an outhouse . . . and we had a hand pump. We had to go outside, get our water and bring it in the house. When I was growing up we didn't have gas in the house. It was an interesting life.

The Cajuns have always worked hard. . . . you know their fathers, their grandfathers, if they were farmers they would pretty much follow in their path but until things got real modernized where you had the tractors, where little farmers couldn't make it on twenty acres of land. When my grandfather was sharecropping, they had but twenty-two acres and you had to raise a family on that and to give some to the man who owned the property. Today they have to have probably in the neighborhood of twenty-five-hundred acres for one family to be able to live off of because of the cost of living. . . . That's why a lot of people have gotten away from farming because there's just not enough land and the cost of farming.

[My parents] had a little store. They had a blacksmith shop joined to the store. It was kind of a general store. They had a little bit of material, threads, things for the farmers, hoes, pretty much what they needed out there. Back then they didn't buy much, things they couldn't grow on the farm. . . . We didn't have much property there. I think my father had inherited the store from my grandfather which had it about four years prior to my father took it over. We had about three acres in the back. My grandfather had cattle. I always had a big interest in cattle. I would go by these dairy farms and buy calfs. I would buy them for five dollars to eight dollars. I had as many as twelve at a time and I would feed them and nurse them from a little calf that was three or four days old until they got big enough to sell. That would give me my spending money. I pretty much started to take care of myself. I had some support from them but I would never care to ask for some money. At about the age of twelve, I was making enough money to where I could buy things I wanted. I ended up graduating from high school.

My last two years, I'd go to school a half a day and the other half of the day they had this on-the-job training. I was working with a bricklayer that lived by the house. . . . I could put in a pretty good day's work. I'd make a living, I was in the eleventh grade. Then I continued bricklaying until two years after I graduated and I went into the oilfield. . . . We had the Bosco oil field that was just down from the house. We always had an interest in the oil field. I just felt it was something I wanted to try. It really didn't matter what I did. When I was laying bricks, I was pretty good at it. We could have made a pretty decent living with it but my back started to give me a little trouble. I started I was fourteen years old, doing hard labor. I started as a mechanic, in seventy-five.

I have been in the oil field ever since. I worked for two large companies, Advanced Oil and Mobil Oil, for about thirteen years between both of them. I decided to start my own business one day and I started Technical Gauging. I worked very hard at it, seven days a week for about three years, I guess, before I had my first day off. It was a bad time, in the early eighties. I was real rough getting started. It took about five, six years before I was really able to get on my feet. I finally made it through those times and things got better 'til the business got pretty successful. Today the stress that goes with owning your own business—it's unbelievable but it's very rewarding. . . . You hook up a well from scratch, you've got something you've done, you've actually created. It's rewarding.

My brother, he's in sales. He's good at it because he is a people's person. I can get in a corner and I'm fine. He's gonna be right in the middle of the crowd. I'm shy and he's not. He's working for Local Drugs. They just made him a manager for all this area pretty much. . . . It's because of his background. The Cajuns have a way. If they're in sales, they have a way of getting to your heart, they find whatever makes it tick, they can feel that. When you find a Cajun that's good at what he does, it's hard to find anybody else in that particular field to do better. . . . I don't know if it's because of the struggle that they had from way back, their ancestors—it just seems that they work real hard to achieve their goals.

From distinctive rural origins, over the course of the century, Louisiana's Cajuns became oil workers, founders of small businesses, and salespeople. Many middle-aged Cajuns like Robert Prejean experienced dramatic changes during their lifetime. Raised on farms with no modern amenities, they still live in a rural environment, albeit likely in a suburban subdivision and a house hooked to various electronic networks. The jobs have changed but long hours, hard work, and satisfaction from the task accomplished have not. When they reflect on their identity amid these changes, Cajuns turn to their experience. For instance, when parents consider their children, they turn to their own childhood. Thus the past, both near and distant, provides the basis to interpret the present. A father of two, Robert Prejean assesses the effect of the economic changes he lived through on his own family with moving sincerity.

It's not having a family life a lot but, like the work that I do. I've seen more of Rachelle growing up than I have Mark, really. We haven't done much. It's not that I don't want to. It seems like everything pulls you away. If you could make enough money doing one thing eight hours a day, I'd gladly do it, but you want to provide for them and give them things. It's tough, especially for young married people. . . . When I had a real job when I was working for Modern Oil, at some point I'd work eight days on and I was off six days. So I had a boat. I was always very active. If I couldn't find anybody to go with me, I'd go by myself. I like fishing and I could fish every day if I had the time. [I have not gone fishing in] about two and a half years. I have a lot of regrets and I feel bad about it because, Mark, I need to do things like that with him. He's gonna soon be of age to drive. I'd like to be able to give him some of the same things that I had. We got some property in Church Point.

I'd like to start raising cattle, make him responsible for it, get him started, something we could do together, teach him a little bit about life. He'll find out where the money comes from. . . . That's pretty much the life I had growing up. My father was always working. When he was home, he was in the store or doing mechanic work.

A REGIONAL WORKING CLASS

There is nothing surprising, of course, about the declining role of agriculture and the increasing role of industry, sales, and service in Louisiana's economy. This is a pattern seen in virtually all parts of twentieth-century America and the world's economies. However, the statistical series and personal accounts do not tell the whole story. What do the memories of Robert Prejean, Louis Duhon, and the others tell us about Cajun ethnicity? How has the transformation of Louisiana's economy affected Cajuns in particular?

American history provides a number of examples of the relationship between economic changes and ethnic affiliation. The slave economy of the pre–Civil War American South, for example, created the racial caste system in the United States. The heavy concentration of African Americans in unskilled, manual, and domestic labor throughout the first half of the twentieth century was, in part, a consequence of the caste status of their parents and grandparents. The Eastern and Southern Europeans who reached the United States in the late nineteenth and early twentieth centuries were largely from rural backgrounds. In the new country, though, they entered the lower rungs of the industrial working class. Even with the gains from social mobility, this social position was perpetuated, so that even today the remaining factory jobs of the Northeastern United States are still associated with descendants of the white ethnics.

Closer to home, we have seen how historians have suggested that the very emergence of Cajunism was caused by the stratification of Acadian society brought about by economic changes following the Civil War.[12] Some Acadians became Cajuns not because of their cultural heritage—upper-class Acadians shared in it—but because of their lower economic status. The rural, poorest, least educated strata of Louisiana Acadians were labeled Cajuns. Economists have pointed out the interplay between the industrialization of Southwestern Louisiana and Cajun ethnicity in the twentieth century. In a study of Cajuns in Lafourche Parish, Alain Larouche argues that the rapid and disruptive contact with American industrialized society in the 1930s forced Cajuns to redefine their ethnic identity and modes of social organization to fit the new reality. By the 1960s, the successful economic integration of Lafourche Cajuns provided them with the necessary resources to publicly claim and retool a culture that had been closeted in the private sphere. Recently, this process has been detailed by Robert Gramling, who argues that the temporal scheduling of offshore oil work, which involves offshore stays of seven, fourteen, or twenty-one days followed by an equal amount of time off from work, has helped maintain ethnic communities in Southwestern Louisiana. Instead of moving out of the area in search of work, Louisiana Cajun males have been able to work together on rigs and then return to homes in ethnic residential concentrations.[13] We propose to probe in greater detail the consequences of economic transformation on Cajuns. We suggest that within the new economy, the children and grandchildren of hunters, trappers, fishermen, and small farmers formed a blue-collar working class.

We have so far looked at the distribution of jobs in Louisiana and in Acadiana. Both are home to Cajuns and non-Cajuns alike; in fact even in the Acadian region, people who can be defined as Cajuns are most often a numerical minority. In only three of the twenty-two parishes that make up Acadiana did the population claiming Acadian descent exceed 40% of the whole population. In the parish with the largest proportion of Cajuns, only 46% claimed this descent. The figure stands at 27% for the region and 10% for the state.

To contrast the situation of Cajuns with those of other Louisianians, we again rely on census data. We first constructed categories of non-Cajuns, Cajuns, and French-speaking Cajuns on the basis of people's claim of Acadian ancestry and use of French language. To account for age differences we also created three age groups (younger than 30, 30 to 50 years old, and older than 50). Finally, we delineated three geographical areas: one where fewer than 5% of people claimed Cajun ancestry, one that we refer to as the Cajun region, where at least 5% of the population claimed Cajun ancestry, and one called the Cajun core, where at least 30% of the population claimed Cajun ancestry in the 1990 U.S. census.[14] For our look at occupational concentrations of Cajuns we computed the percentages of white Cajun and non-Cajun employed household heads over age 25 in agriculture and fishing as well as in three labor-intensive, blue-collar industries: mining, construction, and manufacturing (see Table 3.3). By looking at this specific group, we may be able to obtain a more accurate picture of what economic activities are key than we can by looking at the jobs of all employed people.

Statistically, there is a strong association between blue-collar positions and Cajun ethnicity. For example, although they were only 27% of the relevant population, Cajuns made up 39% of the white workers in mining and 42% of the white blue-collar workers in mining. Overall, with manufacturing and construction, although Cajuns made up just over a quarter of the white adult employed household heads in Southwestern Louisiana, they were about one-third of the blue-collar workers in the region. Once we look at the Cajun region where self-declared Cajuns are most heavily concentrated, we see an even closer association between Cajun ethnicity and blue-collar-type employment, particularly in the mining industry. In the Cajun core, Cajuns made up 41% of the white population of household heads and 44% of white household heads employed in mining. Further, they made up 48% of those

Table 3.3
Occupational Distribution of Cajun and Non-Cajun Household Heads in Louisiana, the Cajun Region, and the Cajun Core in the Mining, Construction, and Manufacturing Industries and in Blue-Collar Occupations, 1990

	Cajuns row pct col pct	**Non-Cajuns** row pct col pct
Percent of adult (over 25) employed Household Heads		
Louisiana	16.0 100.0	84.0 100.0
Cajun Region (Southwestern Louisiana)	26.8 90.0	73.2 47.0
Cajun Core	40.8 70.2	59.2 19.4
Percent in Mining Industry		
Louisiana	28.7 12.1	71.3 5.7
Cajun Region	38.9 12.8	61.1 7.3
Cajun Core	43.8 15.6	56.2 13.8
Percent Blue Collar Workers in Mining		
Louisiana	32.7 9.0	67.3 3.5
Cajun Region	42.0 9.6	58.0 4.8
Cajun Core		52.0 8.7
Percent in Construction Industry		
Louisiana	17.9 12.3	82.1 10.7
Cajun Region	28.9 12.4	71.1 11.2
Cajun Core	46.4 11.8	53.6 9.4

employed in blue-collar occupations in mining. In this region, in other words, members of this group are more likely than others to work at mining and they are much more likely than others to work specifically in blue-collar mining jobs. Overall, in the Cajun core, Cajuns hold 47% of all the blue-collar jobs held by white household heads. Practically, this means that one

Table 3.3 (continued)

Percent Blue Collar Workers in Construction		
Louisiana	20.7 9.7	80.0 7.4
Cajun Region	32.3 9.9	67.7 7.6
Cajun Core	52.3 10.0	47.7 6.3
Percent in Manufacturing		
Louisiana	14.7 16.6	85.3 18.4
Cajun Region	22.3 16.5	77.7 21.0
Cajun Core	33.6 16.9	66.4 19.0
Percent Blue Collar Workers in Manufacturing		
Louisiana	17.1 12.4	82.9 11.5
Cajun Region	25.9 12.7	74.1 13.2
Cajun Core	39.0 11.1	61.0 12.0
Percent Blue Collar Workers in all industries		
Louisiana	20.7 53.0	79.3 38.6
Cajun Region	32.4 54.1	67.6 41.2
Cajun Core	47.4 55.5	54.4 27.0

Source: U.S. Bureau of the Census, *Census of Population and Housing, 1990. Public Micro Use Data Samples (5%)* [Machine readable data files] (Washington, DC: Bureau of the Census 1992).

out of two white workers on oil rigs, construction sites, and factory floors in Acadiana is a Cajun. Moreover, the majority of Cajuns (56%) in this central area are blue-collar workers, compared with only 27% of non-Cajuns. What do all these numbers mean? They mean that Cajuns are vastly over-represented in oil mining, in blue-collar jobs, and in blue-collar jobs within oil mining. Although Cajuns may be a minority in their own heartland, they make up much of the region's working class and provide most of the muscle and practical know-how for the region's main working class industry.

We want to make it clear that a Cajun concentration in blue-collar jobs does not mean that all of those who consider themselves Cajuns work in these types of occupations. Emile Babin, a Cajun, president of the Chamber of Commerce of Morgan City, remarked that "Today's Cajuns do all kinds of jobs. They aren't these old country boys like a lot of people think." Indeed, there are members of this ethnic group in all walks of life, a fact that Cajuns rarely fail to mention. For example, in a book promising *The Truth About the Cajuns*, one author features "Acadians of Distinction" among which are a judge, an honor student, a college professor, the founder of a regional ambulance company, a French-language activist, a children's book author, a chef, a TV news anchor, a couple of athletes, inventors, comedians and politicians, and a Miss Louisiana.[15] In addition to this anecdotal evidence, the census statistics we analyzed show that Cajuns appear in all major occupational categories. However, they tend to be underrepresented in activities such as management and higher clerical occupations. There is a definite socioeconomic concentration for members of this group, a fact that brings them together in the same neighborhoods and that helps maintain common interests and common outlooks.

MAINTAINING SOCIAL CLASS: EDUCATION AND SOCIAL TIES

We can now turn to the question of why and how Cajun ethnicity became associated with blue-collar occupations. To some extent, Cajuns hold industrial jobs because these types of activities have become concentrated in their region along the oil-rich Gulf of Mexico. However, these jobs are also available to non-Cajuns who do not occupy them as much as Cajuns do. Among the factors that help to explain the maintenance of Cajun ethnicity as a class position, education figures prominently. First, education, like ethnicity, tends to be passed along family lines. Although educational levels in general may rise as a society industrializes, the children of those with limited formal education will tend to show lower levels of formal education than the children of those with advanced educational credentials. Since formal education is the primary avenue to white-collar professional and technical occupations, members of groups with histories of comparatively low credentialization will tend to be excluded from these types of positions. Many blue-collar job skills, on the other hand, can be learned on the job, even when those jobs actually require fairly advanced skills.

Census figures show significant differences between Cajuns and other Louisianians in education, and the statistics show that these Cajun-non-Cajun differences increase with age. Figure 3.4 shows that the youngest, as well as the oldest, Cajuns are both less likely than others to complete high school and to complete college. This comparative lack of formal education does not necessarily mean ignorance. One employer with whom we spoke

Figure 3.4
Educational Attainment of Cajuns and Non-Cajuns in Louisiana, 1990

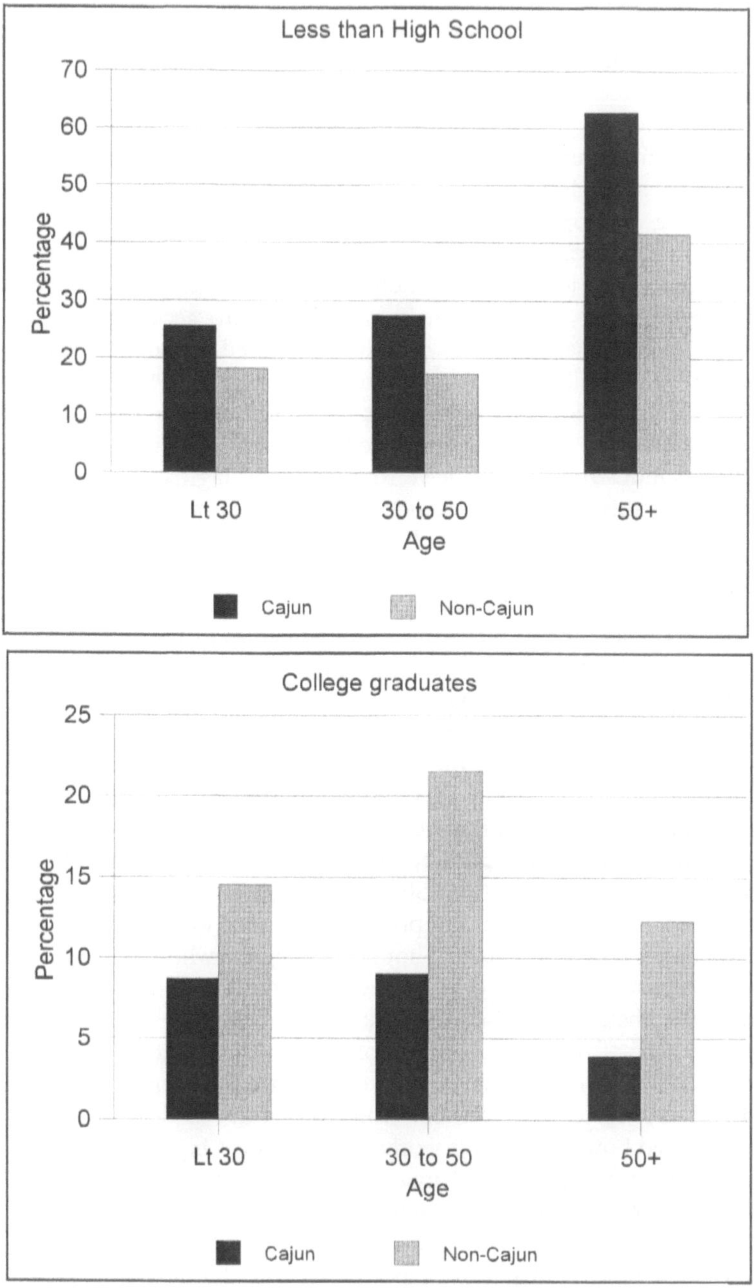

Source: U.S. Bureau of the Census, *Census of Population and Housing, 1990. Public Micro Use Data Samples (5%)* [Machine readable data files]. Washington, DC: Bureau of the Census, 1992).

in Morgan City remarked, "I'd rather hire these Cajun boys. They grow up around machines and people who work with their hands and they know how to do a lot of things that you'd have to teach the ones that have spent their lives in school." Although many of them are skillful and intelligent people, they tend to lack the credentials that would place them in white-collar jobs.

Authors have suggested two major reasons for Cajuns' relatively low educational achievement. Historian Carl Brasseaux noted a traditional resistance to formal English-language education by French-speaking Cajuns until the 1950s, a development we will analyze later. Coupled with the limited penetration of educational facilities in rural areas until World War II, this explains the lower level of education among the older age groups. Since then, however, the "Cajuns' persistent drift toward acceptance of Anglo-American educational values" may have been slowed by industrialization and particularly the availability of oil-related jobs.[16] In a 1994 report on the consequences of the boom-bust cycle characteristic of oil exploitation in Louisiana, Seydlitz and Laska suggested that well-paid employment in the oil and gas industry was conducive to completing high school but that the availability of this employment tended to detract from college attendance.

Interviews with employers and workers in Acadiana confirm that the working-class jobs that contemporary Cajuns tend to hold often make few demands of formal educational attainment. The human resources director for one of the largest oil rig fabrication companies in Iberia Parish told us that no particular level of formal education was required for employment with his organization: "As long as they can do the job," he said, "we don't care." Although he preferred to hire trained welders or pipefitters, most of them obtained their training on the job. "Let's take fitters," he explained. "Somebody who didn't know anything would start as a fitter's helper. Then they would become an apprentice. Then third class, second class, and first class." The human resources director for a large drilling company in New Iberia shared the same position. She said her company required no level of formal education, although it did prefer experienced workers. Workers without experience could be trained, though. "Someone who has no experience, we start them out as roustabouts," she explained. "Then, they become floorhands. After that, they become derrickmen. Finally, they get to be drillers. The supervisor of the rig we call a tool pusher." It would take six to eight months for a new, inexperienced worker to move from roustabout to floorhand and about five years to move from roustabout to driller.

When asked how many of his workers had finished high school, a foreman with a tugboat company in Morgan City replied, "I don't know. I don't think any of them finished high school. Including me." It is worth noting that the foreman identified himself as a Cajun. The president of an oil drilling company based in Lafayette reported that he did not know how many of his employees had completed high school or a GED, but he estimated that around half of them had, a quite accurate assessment when compared with census figures. He said some of his employees were illiterate. They had sophisticated job skills as welders or tool pushers, he said, but they had acquired these skills through experience. This accumulation of practical knowledge led Robert Prejean to start his own gauging company:

> When you know all the money you were making for everybody else and working hard at it, I just felt I could do better just by myself. You're in control. If you fail, you have nobody else to blame but yourself. I've seen it layin' bricks. You work real hard trying to make that person some money. Same thing in the oil field. One day I just said I'm using myself for someone else, let me try to do something for myself. On the gauging, it's yourself, a box of tools that you can carry is all you need for a gauger, it's experience. You have different type of gaugers, some that'll just go and read the charts and drop a gauge line in the tanks but with the background experience I have I can take a well. I don't have the knowledge to drill a well but once it's drilled I can go and complete the well, I can hook up the well and then from there we can take care of it. I have that type of knowledge.

Experience is acquired by individuals, but experiences are also passed on across generations and shared by groups of people. As the oil industry established itself in Southwestern Louisiana through the middle of the twentieth century, the industry, rather than formal education, became a major way in which the people of the Cajun region could adapt to an increasingly nonagricultural way of life. New Iberian Dwayne Meaux told us how his own family had come to specialize in oil work:

> My father was a welder in the oil field as long as I can remember. When he was really young, he quit school, my father's 75, like when he was 16, he quit school and he moved to Port Arthur. He left with some older guys because they had a shipyard in Port Arthur 'cause World War II had started going on. He went over there and learned how to weld and he was building ships. When he turned 17 he decided to join the navy. . . . I don't know if he had his mother sign a release because he was too young. But he joined the navy and he wound up going on a transport ship [in the Pacific theater]. When he got out he went back into welding and did that all his life. He never was a real high-paid guy because you're doing manual labor for an oil company or a company that's selling to an oil company. When I was a young guy, he worked for Welding Services. What they did, they took pipes—his job was to weld the end connections . . . he used what they called a submerged arc to weld. It was basically shift work. One week he'd work during the day, the next week he'd work at nights . . . making $1.59, $1.60 an hour. And finally he heard about this place called Avondale Shipyard on the other side of Morgan City. They were paying $4.50 an hour. So he took that. He went over there. But there was no Highway 90 at the time, not the four-lane highway. Every morning he'd leave at four o'clock in the morning with a bunch of guys, paid this one and he would drive his van over there. They'd all ride with him, go work there a long day and get back till it was eight o'clock at night. It wasn't a forty-five-minute ride to Morgan City back then, it was

an hour-and-a-half ride, on a two-lane road. During sugarcane season, they're hauling cane, burning cane, smoke and stuff. He did that all his life. He retired about ten years ago.[17]

With the continued availability of oil work, younger generations followed the older generations into the industry. Dwayne Meaux recounted his own experiences to us:

I work in the oil field, for Power Services, Texas Engineers. I've been working with Texas Engineers for twenty years in May and they were bought out by Power two or three years ago. We service oil-field–related tools and all and it's an up-and-down business. Right now it's very up. We're real busy, we're working a lot of hours. Last week I had eighty-one hours. You're working fifty-five hours straight when you're off call, from six to six, five days. When you're on call, you work from 6 in the morning until . . . sometimes you might go until seven or eight or whatever. You go home and they might have something come up, you might have to go back for an hour. And also the week that you're on-call you work the Saturday from seven to four minimum, maybe longer, and then on Sunday you work from seven to twelve minimum. You put in a lot of hours right now. But in the slow periods, you don't work more than forty hours. Like right now you're makin' all this overtime, after forty hours it's overtime. So you get used to spending this money, then all of a sudden they'll cut the overtime out and you have to readjust your lifestyle. That's life working in the oilfield, that's what it's like around here in South Louisiana.

I've been in the oil field basically since I got out of the air force, 1977. I went to trade school from 1976 to the middle of 1977. And after that I was working for a drilling company doing mechanical work. From there I went to Texas Engineers. I worked there about a year and a half. Then I went to work for Machinery Center, which is another oil-field–related machinery. Then that was one of the up-swings. They had 450 employees, a big company, working a minimum of 5 days a week, sometimes 6. That was the perfect job. I was working 10 hours a day, 5 days a week, sometimes on Saturday but not much, making real good money for the time. We had all these rigs to build for different oil companies. In 1982, January, you can't get enough employees. One month later, they canceled everything. Out of 450 people, they laid off 400 people. I was fortunate enough to go back to Texas Engineers. The pay was nowhere near what it was during the boom but I finally worked my way back up.

We stay at the yard. I've been trying to get in the office but they got a guy who's planted in there and I can't get him out. I'm next in line to get into the office. His advancement is up to our district manager, to move into sales or somewhere else so I can move up. It's still a lot of manual labor and with my bad back, you know [he had an operation 13 years ago].

[I chose the oil field because of] Money. In this area this is the best paying unless you have a college education. I am a high school graduate. I went to a mechanic school, but after I graduated from that I didn't want to get really into the mechanic field, as far as diesel engine mechanic or any kind of stuff like that. I had an opportunity. My first wife was pregnant at the time. I was still in trade school, just about to get out and this job came up and that was basically the beginning. I call the oil field a rut basically 'cause you get in it and it's like on an old mud road, you can't get out of the rut. You set your lifestyle according to what you make and you switch jobs, switch fields, you're starting all over again and without a college education nowadays . . . you just can't switch from one thing to the next, so that's what got me started.

Dwayne Meaux's awareness of the pivotal role of education in today's society extends beyond his own experience to that of his family:

My mother worked in a department store. I don't even remember she just staying at home. She worked all her life. . . . We had one vehicle and my dad drove that to work. She rode with some people to work. She was working with one department store, one was a clothing store, sold clothes. She worked there for dirt cheap till I was in the service. And she decided one day to go get her GED, she went get a high school education. She went to trade school. She took up accounting and worked in a bank after all those years. . . . It really surprised me. I'd go home and Mama's doing homework on the kitchen table with the adding machine and all that. She worked at the bank until she was ready to retire.

I'm trying to talk my son into sticking in school. He came to the shop the other day where I work. I said: "See what I look like right now." I was filthy, I mean you work in the oil field you get dirty big time. I said: "This is what you don't want. You better stay over there at UL. You don't want to look like this."

Still, the benefits of a college education are viewed through the lens of a working-class existence. Dwayne Meaux's son enrolled in the architecture program at the University of Louisiana in Lafayette:

He's good with his hands. . . . He draws really well. I don't know why he can't draw anything out of his head but you give him something, he'll draw it just like a picture. So when he was getting into middle school I suggested for him to take up drafting. He went through drafting all through high school. . . . So he's got a college scholarship basically. I couldn't support him to go to college. He'd have to work to go through but the state's paying for him. All we have to do is buy his books and we have to come up with $80 a semester. . . . Once he signed up for it, he comes and says "Daddy it's for five years!" So that was kind of a disappointment but he's sticking to it. I'm sure that after three or four years he'll be more or less working part time doing something like this.

As jobs in industry, sales, and services allowed generations of Cajuns to escape the hardship of sharecropping, a college degree now represents a way out of the working class. But the cost, the time it requires away from gainful activities, and the distance from practical immediate applications contribute to make a college education a difficult goal for many Cajuns to pursue. If the children and grandchildren of Dwayne Meaux and Sallie and Robert

Prejean can reasonably expect to improve on their parents' educational attainment, this remains a remote chance for some young Cajuns. Suzie Quebodeaux is a 75-year-old Cajun woman. Raised by a mother on welfare following the premature death of her father, she quit school in the eleventh grade at the age of 18 to work as a fountain clerk in a Lafayette drugstore. She places a value on education, but among her siblings and her children, high school graduation is rare and illiteracy rampant.

Central School, I went there until 1944 and I quit Lafayette High School and I had to go to work for my mommy's. She was on welfare. My daddy died young. She never worked. . . . When we got older they'd let us go at 18 years old, you see, just like my girls. They had to go to work when they were 18. They had to go work and pulled off the welfare. . . . I had to quit school in the eleventh grade. We were gonna graduate in the eleventh grade this time, *ces années là*, but I had to quit.

Mes enfants asteur, they have jobs. Becky is not well educated. I had a rough time with those girls. Amanda didn't go to school until she was 6 years old. . . . Celina start crying, she didn't want to stay in the classroom. First time, I said, "I'm gonna bring you." "Mama I don't want to go!" I said, "You're going to school young lady, I'm sorry. You have to learn!". . . . She's a good student now. [My sister] Alice brought her to technical school right here and she learned how to play with computers and stuff and she finished that, *elle a fini là*. They wanted to send her to Washington, D.C., to work in the office over there. Then she got pregnant. Then she didn't want to go. She could have gone work over there in the government's office. She was good. *Elle est bonne.* She learns fast. She finished at Acadiana and [my other sister] Mary send her right here because I could not afford for her to go finish there. Welfare, they don't give you much for school. So Mary did it for her. She learned just like that. She learned how to do everything: she knows how to work in an office, she knows about computer, she's better than I am.

The only one who graduated in my family was [my sister] Alice. Mama didn't want me to get married. . . . She didn't want my brother to get married. This boy was 11 years old. Never learned how to read and write but he went to Joe Huval and they hired him. And he drive that truck and he delivered bread. He was good. He knew how to add, how many to count, how many bread he had in his truck. Before he died, he went to school and he learned how to read and write. He was kinda old but he went to school anyway. If you have a mind you gonna learn.

Pareil comme Becky. I had a problem with her. Poor thing, they took her from Scott and they sent her over there by the underpass, which is the black one. She was crying because she didn't want to go there. They didn't have no white girls but her. She was the only one, way in the back she didn't like that. She didn't like that school over there so she quit. . . . It was just for blacks. It was for the people that are slow learners. She didn't like that. She could have finished it. She left in the twelfth grade. . . . The child don't know how to work even. *Becky a jamais travaillé, elle connait son argent.* She has a little girl that's staying with her, Vernella. She's teaching Becky how to read the big words. . . . Amanda graduated at the schoolboard. She didn't want to finish. *C'est triste.*

At the other end of the social spectrum, families of Cajun professionals also transmitted their educational status, albeit a different one. Some of the cases we encountered during our research suggest that ethnicity, place of residence, and family size had less of an influence than social class in guaranteeing access to higher education. In one case, the eleven children of a Cajun attorney all became attorneys, physicians, and other high-level professionals. In another case, the thirteen children of a Cajun entrepreneur became or married accountants, architects, and physicians. Illiteracy, very large families, and admirable educational achievements are admittedly rare situations. Still, together with the more common experiences of middle-class improvement, they help explain the role that formal education has played in the adaptation of Cajuns to their changing economic environment.

A second way in which social class is connected to ethnicity is through social ties. People associate with others who have similar incomes, backgrounds, and interests. In turn, younger people are steered into their careers by friends, neighbors, and family members. Job seekers turn to their personal connections to find work. Social ties among ethnic group members, then, are reinforced by economic specialization, and these social ties, in turn, help to maintain ethnic groups as social classes. This is especially true with a group that has a close identification with a geographic area. The president of an oil company based in Lafayette observed in an interview with us that: "people that we hire are living in the surrounding communities which are small . . . and they all know each other. They all know each other and they know where the openings are . . . probably 70 to 80% of our new hires in skilled labor is from a referral from an employee."

Contemporary Acadiana can be seen as the home of the blue-collar bayous because blue-collar types of work have become the socioeconomic center of Cajun life. Economic change in Louisiana ended the old rural way of life without erasing the memories. The children and grandchildren of farmers, hunters, and trappers moved into working-class jobs, especially in the new oil industry. A limited heritage of formal education combined with a strong stock of practical manual skills limited their entry into the upper-middle class and qualified them for necessary positions in skilled and semiskilled labor. Occupying a common socioeconomic position reinforced their sense of being in the same group, it kept them together, and it helped to perpetuate the blue-collar basis of modern Cajun ethnicity. As we will see, the new class basis also posed questions for the minority of middle-class people from Cajun backgrounds.

Social class, education, and social ties are fundamental to any group. All three of these, though, are produced by an even more basic institution, perhaps the oldest of all human social institutions. We turn, then, to another critical influence on the evolution of Cajun ethnicity: the family.

NOTES

1. Fisheries Statistics and Economics Division, National Marine Fisheries Service, *Fisheries of the United States.* (Silver Spring, MD: National Marine Fisheries Service, 1998).

2. Robert Gramling, *Oil on the Edge: Offshore Development, Conflict, Gridlock* (Albany: State University of New York Press, 1996).

3. Donald Davis & John Place, *The Oil and Gas Industry of Coastal Louisiana and Its Effect on Land Use and Socioeconomic Patterns* (Reston, VA: U.S. Department of the Interior, U.S. Geological Survey, 1983); Ruth Seydlitz & Shirley Laska, *Social and Economic Impact of Petroleum "Boom and Bust" Cycle* (New Orleans: U.S. Department of the Interior, Minerals Management Service, Gulf of Mexico OCS Region., 1994).

4. Craig Forsyth & Deann Gauthier, "Families of Offshore Workers: Adaptations to Cyclical Father Absence/Presence," *Sociological Spectrum* 11(2) (1991):177–201; Robert Gramling, "Concentrated Work Scheduling: Enabling and Constraining Effects," *Sociological Perspectives* 32:(1989) 47–64.

5. Sarah Brabant, "The Impact of a Boom-Bust Economy on Poverty" in Shirley Laska, Vern Baxter, Ruth Seidlitz, Sarah Brabant and Craig Forsyth, *Impact of Oil Exploration and Production on the Social Institutions of Coastal Louisiana* (New Orleans: U.S. Department of the Interior, Minerals Management Service, Gulf of Mexico OCS Regional Office, 1993), pp. 161–194.

6. Robert Gramling & Sarah Brabant (eds.), *The Role of the Outer Continental Shelf Oil and Gas Activities in the Growth and Modification of Louisiana's Gulf Coast* (Washington, DC: U.S. Department of Commerce, National Oceanic and Atmospheric Administration, 1984).

7. Robert Gramling & Sarah Brabant, "Boomtowns and Offshore Energy Impact Assessment," *Sociological Perspectives* 27 (1986):177–201; Robert Gramling & William Freudenburg, "A Closer Look at 'Local Control': Communities, Commodities, and the Collapse of the Coast," *Rural Sociology* 55 (1990):541–558.

8. Robert Flaherty (director), *Louisiana Story* (film, 1948)

9. Revon Reed, *Lâche pas la patate: Portrait des Acadiens de la Louisiane* (Montréal: Editions Parti pris, 1976), 49.

10. Richard Guidry, *C'est p'us pareil* (Lafayette Center for Louisiana Studies, 1982).

11. Authors' interview, February 11, 2001.

12. James Dormon, *The People Called Cajuns: An Introduction to an Ethnohistory* (Lafayette Center for Louisiana Studies, 1983); Carl Brasseaux, *Acadian to Cajun: Transformation of a People 1803–1877* (Jackson: University Press of Mississippi, 1992).

13. Alain Larouche, *Ethnicité pêche et pétrole: Les Cadjins du bayou Lafourche en Louisiane francophone.* Projet Louisiane, monographie 1(Toronto: York University, 1981); Gramling, "Concentrated Work Scheduling;" Gramling, *Oil on the Edge.*

14. The figures in Table 3.3 are based on data from PUMAs, Public Use Microdata Areas.

15. Trent Angers, *The Truth About The Cajuns* (Lafayette, LA: Acadian House Publishing, 1990).

16. Carl Brasseaux, "Acadian Education: From Cultural Isolation to Mainstream America, in Glen Conrad (ed.), *The Cajuns: Essays on their History and Culture* (Lafayette Center for Louisiana Studies, 1978), 212–224.
17. Authors' interview, February 19, 2001.

CHAPTER 4

The Cajun Family: Evolution and Endogamy

THE FAMILY AND CAJUN IDENTITY

Families are central to the life of any society. Identity and social standing are largely products of the complex set of relationships organized around birth and marriage. In most societies, the identity of an individual is primarily rooted in the father's group, the mother's group, or both, the last being the pattern of American kinship. Family is a connection to the past. Since ethnicity is based on perceived ancestral connections, family life is critical to ethnicity. Primordial views of ethnicity, in fact, conceive of the ethnic group as a form of extended family and we have seen how the social class position of parents and ancestors influences Cajuns' experience today. Everyday life in Southwestern Louisiana provides numerous illustrations of the close connection between Cajun ethnicity and family. It often starts with the name. The mention of a full name by an individual may elicit little recognition until the family connection has been established. "Who's your daddy?" is a question that Acadiana natives have to answer at some point in lieu of introduction. If that family name is known, individuals are simply referred to as "Sterling's daughter" or "Jimmie's nephew."

Genealogical inquiries are increasingly popular in Acadiana today and references to Acadian ancestors are common. Blaine Landry, 40, for example, repeated a common practice when he described his own background by explaining, "My mother was a Broussard; she got some Broussard-Préjean combination. My dad is a Landry and he comes from Landry and Hébert.

Very much rooted in Acadia."[1] For him, family also organized entertainment and residence:

On Fridays, the whole family on my dad's side would get together. It was crab boil, a huge crawfish, whatever was in season. And that was on Friday night—we just knew that we all get to get together.

The homestead, the original house that my grandparents had is now mine . . . where I live now. The seventy acres, as my dad's brothers and sisters grew up, they were each given an acre and they were allowed to build and they were given that upon their wedding. It was like a gift. They all built. They just all moved away within the last three years. The last one had sold where they were. What's interesting is they all sold but they bought property in Carencro and now they all live around each other in Carencro basically on another seventy acres. The aunt that moved out there first, her house is in the center and everybody else built around her as well as her children. They're all out there.

In fact, people's lives are almost entirely bounded by family relations. When Lafayette resident Suzie Quebodeaux, born in 1926, reminisces about her life, she offers a collection of family events:

Mama was born in Lafayette. Mama got married in Saint Genevieve Church. After that they went to Port Arthur. After that I was born. I was the first one; my brother was behind me. He was born here. We came back here then again. That's when Mary was born. And then Alice was born here in Lafayette. She never knew my daddy. She was too young. He died young . . . on Saint John Street.

Daddy moved back here when I was three or four years old. I didn't know my daddy that good. My mama never told us [what he was doing]. *Elle a jamais dit.* In Port Arthur he was working like underground. We never had any Social Security in those days. He worked but he never collected Social Security. . . .

We lived in the country when we were young, where the airport is. We stayed there, up on the hill. . . . That was like the country before they built that airport. We didn't have no screen, we didn't have nothing but one bedroom for four kids and my mama. And Aunt Leola was staying by us, on the side of us, in a *vieille vieille maison*, old house up on the hill. We had to climb some steps if we wanted to get up there. It was nice.

Aunt Leola, she's going to be ninety-two years old. Twelve kids and that was my mama's sister-in-law. My mama's brother, Adam Toce, they were four brothers. They had two or three sisters when he died. Aunt Amelia Toce Fruge stayed there. We used to go there, get some milk and stuff. She'd bring us eggs. It was like the country. That was her land. *C'était joli, on allait là.* She had twelve kids. I don't know them all; we don't even see one another anymore. Mama has one sister left; *son nom c'est Angeline Toce Calais.* She's in a nursing home not too far from my house. . . . She lived in the country. I used to go stay with her. I didn't want to stay 'cause I didn't know what the country was. I wasn't born there, I was born here! That was on the other side of Breaux Bridge. She had cows and stuff. We'd go, have picnics, pick up pecans, *et les affaires comme ça, et les vaches.* She's give us some milk. She'd make us come spend the day with her. "*Mémé faut que tu viennes coucher avec moi et ton oncle.*"

Louisianians who define themselves as Cajuns often claim that their group has a distinctive type of family, and they emphasize strong family ties that Cajuns value. They routinely stress their close kinship networks, and they say that these provide them with emotional and material assistance. For Cajun author Revon Reed, the love of family is second only to the love of land: "To understand us, you must know that the Cajun's life revolves around his personal and intimate relations with his family."[2]

There is some evidence that under exceptional circumstances, Cajun families do indeed play an essential role. Researchers who compared the aftermath of Hurricane Andrew in Florida and Louisiana in 1992 have suggested that the ability of Louisianians to help one another—and that includes kin and neighbors—probably explained the unexpectedly low need for federal emergency assistance in the region. In 1999, pan-American and even cross-Atlantic family reunions were at the heart of the worldwide meeting of Acadians held in Louisiana. Over several months, thousands of visitors were welcomed, housed, fed, and entertained on the sole basis of their Acadian names.

The uniqueness of the Cajun family under more mundane circumstances, however, is a matter of debate. Five characteristics are frequently mentioned: a large size, the existence of an extended family network, the transmission of particular folkways, domestic division of labor, and a tendency to marry within the group. An extensive review of historical and contemporary evidence suggests that Cajun families have had some distinguishing features. These features, though, have been continually changing and many of them have been magnified by both group members and outsiders. The characteristics that have traditionally been associated with Cajun families are indeed present in some fashion but they apply in part only, to some periods or segments of Cajun history and culture. For example, there is evidence that Acadian families were significantly larger than others until the very recent past.

We should also take seriously accounts of extended families and of intense kin relationships, but we should beware of making too much of these accounts. There is evidence of continued physical proximity among family members in the Cajun regions of Louisiana. Echoing remarks by Blaine Landry and Suzie Quebodeaux, students in Acadiana routinely told us that they were attending college close to home to be near their families. "I wouldn't want to be where I had to call long distance to talk to my mama," said one young man, expressing a fairly common sentiment. The residential pattern of relatives living near one another and communal activities such as *boucheries* (family-or neighborhood-based slaughtering of animals), *coups de main* (mutual assistance between relatives and neighbors), and *fais-dodo* (dances held at homes) are certainly indicative of close-knit communities, economic self-sufficiency, and high group solidarity.[3] These patterns and activities do not, however, indicate an extended family pattern. The statuses, roles, and obligations of family members in a nuclear or extended family vary significantly. When married children visit their parents, it means they do not live with them. When brothers farm adjacent strips of land, they do not work a common collective property. When relatives exchange mutual assistance, it is on the basis of reciprocity between nuclear units, not contribution to a single extended group. The evidence on hand does not fully support the existence of a different and particular family system even though it establishes intense economic and emotional relations between relatives living nearby in independent nuclear units. As for the transmission of culture and a particular division of domestic labor, referring to specific roles for Cajun women and men, caution must be exercised before accepting these traits as separating Cajuns from other Louisianians.

The sharing of a distinctive cultural heritage composed of French language, Catholicism, and distinctive folkways, particularly those related to food, music, and folk medicine, undoubtedly contributed to a sense of solidarity among early Acadians and later, Cajuns. Also, following a traditional pattern found in most cultures at some point in time, girls have tended to learn "feminine" skills, such as cooking and child care, from their mothers or other close female relatives, whereas boys have been trained to "masculine" tasks, mostly productive, by their fathers or other male relatives. These types of gender-related activities were passed on through families, and families continue to pass them on today.[4] Cajun men taught young boys about fishing, planting, hunting, trapping, woodworking, and playing music, and Cajun women passed on gardening, quilting, and cooking. A 22-year-old woman echoed the experience of many others: "My mother taught me how to make a roux from the time I was a little girl." College-age men routinely told us that they had learned to hunt and fish from their fathers, and even that these were their most common activities with their fathers, and that it excluded all women in the family. The title of a cookbook by Marcelle Bienvenu, a chef and popular food critic, sums up the assumed connection between family, culture, and Cajun ethnicity: *Who's Your Mama, Are You Catholic, Can You Make a Roux?*

The wholesale acceptance of a cultural baggage passed on through Cajun families needs to be examined more closely, however, if it is taken as the base for a claim of uniqueness. We can first notice that none of these cultural traits are individually unique to Cajun culture since there have been other types of French speakers in Louisiana (both white and black Creoles, French immigrants), other Catholics (Irish and Italian immigrants), and farmers, ranchers, and fishermen of various national origins. Still, the combination of these characteristics has distinguished Cajuns from other groups settled in Southwest Louisiana. Second, the cultural content transmitted by Cajun families is far from being uniform and uniformly passed on. The long and steady decline of agriculture and the decline of French language use attest that part of the cultural heritage failed to reach younger generations of Cajuns, especially during the first half of the twentieth century. Positive and productive traits of the cultural heritage are the ones typically emphasized, but what about the less prestigious components? Illiteracy, patriarchal domination, and racism have shaped the minds and behaviors of Acadians and Cajuns at some time and in some measure continue to do so; yet little is known about these less savory sides—by the standards of contemporary American—of Cajunism and whether they or their combination can also be claimed as unique ethnic features.

Finally, sharing a claim made by other American ethnic groups, the central role of women is often noted.[5] Beautiful maidens or dedicated mothers, Cajun mothers have been portrayed as guarantors of domestic well-being and guardians of the culture. Cajun wives have been seen as drawing non-Cajun husbands into the group. Cajun women have been described as mostly responsible for socializing their children to the sweet sound of French and the spicy taste of gumbo. Although central to the maintenance and transmission of ethnicity, this function fits the homebound role played by women in the traditional, male-dominated family typical of nineteenth-century Western societies.

The focus on mothers, more in the form of undocumented assertions than substantiated examples, has contributed to a relative ignorance of the role of fathers. Limited data suggest that Cajun fathers have played and continue to play a significant role in the passing on of their culture to their children.[6] Cajun men are cooking today and they apparently have been doing so for some time.[7] Cooking was and is still a predominantly female task. However, men's cooking is notable because it is different in nature. It usually takes place outside instead of in the kitchen, for large gatherings and ceremonial occasions instead of preparing the family's daily fare. Men cook in big quantities and they usually prepare meat or seafood, foods coming directly from the environment, not from the grocery store. In a clear indicator of cultural transmission, men learn their culinary skills from other men, reportedly on all-male hunting and fishing trips, a rite of passage for young Cajun males. Isolated in remote camps, separated from their usual food preparers, and eager to showcase their ecological fitness, men as grandfathers, fathers, uncles, or family friends engage in the demonstration, and thus the transmission, of how to catch, prepare, cook, and eat wildlife in the rough.

We are left with an apparently contradictory state of affairs. There is no doubt that the Cajun family as an institution has contributed to the transmission of Cajun culture, as all kinship and family systems do. There is also little doubt that the "cultural stuff" passed on presents a particular configuration. Still, one needs to be explicit about the period, the area, the occupation, and at least some cultural items to assess whether there has been transmission and of what through family channels. If the transmission did not take place, the question then becomes, Did the people who did not learn French, cook roux, or trap raccoons stop being Cajuns? The answers differ. Some writers claim that the Cajun family has maintained its traditional aspect, organization, or practices: "Family life has (. . .) remained largely unchanged," writes one.[8] Other researchers argue that the structural distinctiveness of the Cajun family has subsided and that its purported difference endures more in spirit than in practice. They note that the uniqueness of the Cajun family is now limited to the survival of "the Cajun spirit of pleasant merriment" or a "psychological flavor."[9] They point to increasing similarities in structure and lifestyle between the Cajun family and the standard American family: a transition from extended to a nuclear family type, increasing exogamy, urbanization, and Americanization of everyday life, and loss of French and traditional ethnic folkways.[10] After all, they argue, if relatives no longer converse in French during *veillées* on the *galerie* after a communal meal of corn bread and pork fricassée, but enjoy a TV dinner interrupted by long-distance calls from fathers on an offshore platform and children in out-of state colleges, can claims of ethnic particularism be sustained?

We address this issue by looking beyond culture. To what extent does this kind of family-bounded life characterize the modern Cajun experience? What part does family play today in shaping Cajun ethnicity and why does it play this part? To answer these questions, in this chapter we subject contemporary Cajun family life to a detailed sociological examination to determine the role of family life in contemporary Cajun ethnicity. We look at two major topics. First, we provide a structural description of the modern Cajun family to determine if and how it may differ from other types of families found in Louisiana. Next, we look in depth at marital strategies and especially at the question of endogamy, or in-group marriage, because marriage is a prime strategy to maintain social boundaries and it has been identified as a major mechanism in maintaining Cajun identity. This approach will allow us to assess whether this group really does have definable social boundaries, such as a unique form of family, and how it contributes to further its ethnic identity.

STRUCTURE OF THE CONTEMPORARY CAJUN FAMILY

To shed some light on the contemporary Cajun family, we turn to historical census data from the Public Use Microdata Samples (PUMS), which we earlier used to examine the shifting socioeconomic basis of Cajun ethnicity. Figure 4.1 examines the question of family size: have Cajun families been larger than others and do they continue to be larger? The answers are

Figure 4.1
Average Family Sizes in Acadiana and Elsewhere in Louisiana, 1920–1990

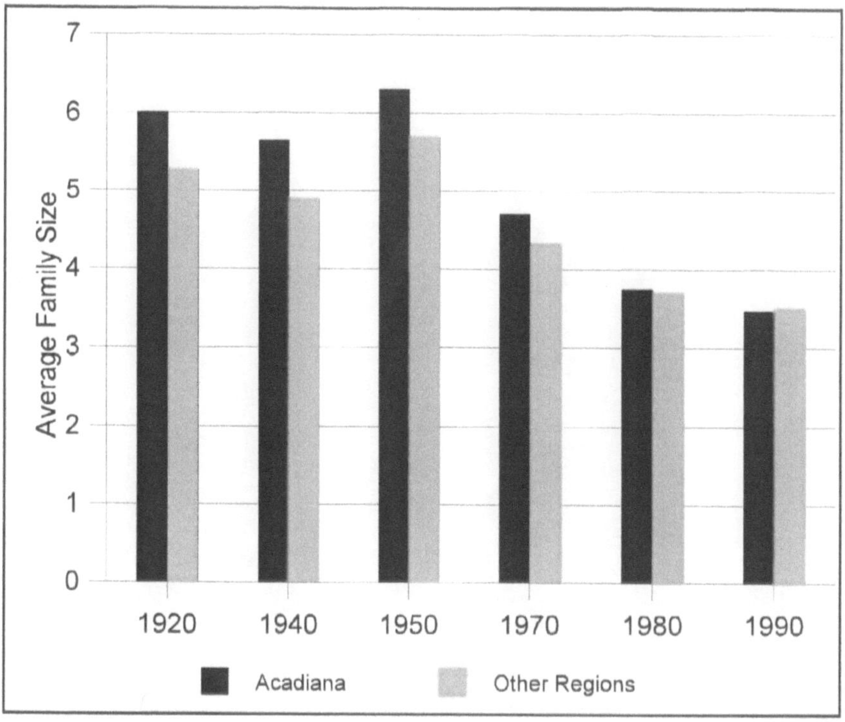

Source: Ruggles, Sobek et al., *Integrated Public Use Microdata Series.*

"yes" and "no." In this figure, we contrast the average number of people per family in Acadiana with the average family size elsewhere in Louisiana.

As is well known, families grew smaller throughout America during the twentieth century. This was connected to the shift from the rural, agricultural way of life that we discussed earlier. Louisiana shows this same general trend. In the Cajun region of the state, families have historically been larger than in other areas. In 1920, families in what is now known as Acadiana averaged about six people. In the rest of the state, they averaged about five and a quarter. The families of Acadiana did tend to be noticeably larger, then. However, the differences diminished over the course of the century, so that, by the 1990s, family sizes in Acadiana were actually slightly smaller than those in other parts of the state.

How do we know that this was a result of a shrinking of Cajun families, and not a consequence of non-Cajun families decreasing in size or people from other places moving into the Cajun region? This is a difficult question, since most demographic information comes from census sources and the

Figure 4.2
Family Sizes of Cajuns and Non-Cajuns in Acadiana, 1980 and 1990

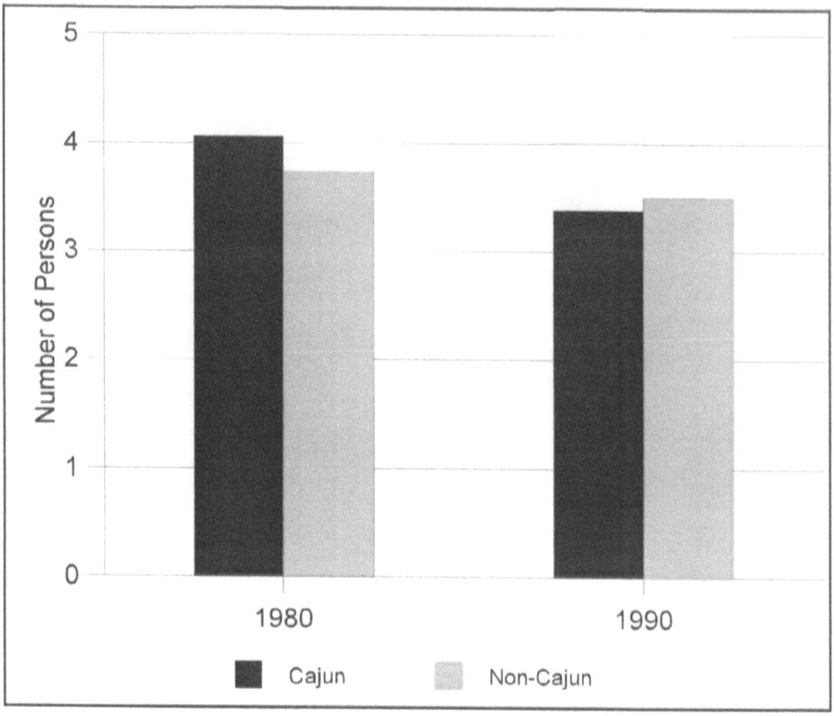

Source: Ruggles, Sobek et al., *Integrated Public Use Microdata Series.*

census began recording Cajun ancestry only in 1980. However, if we look at contrasts between Cajun and non-Cajun family sizes in 1980 and 1990, we see the same convergence. Figure 4.2 shows that in 1980, family sizes of ethnic group members and nonmembers were almost the same. By 1990, family sizes of Cajuns were slightly smaller.

Family size, of course, is closely related to fertility. People have large nuclear families because they have many children. Comparable data on fertility is available for only select years in the census samples, so Figure 4.3 shows only 1910 and 1970 through 1990. The thinnest lines show average number of children born to women 40 years of age and over, the somewhat thicker lines show children born to women aged 30 to 39, and the thickest lines show children born to women 16 to 29. We can see that in 1910, women in Acadiana did have more children than those in other parts of the state. The older the women were, the greater the difference between the Cajun region and other regions. This indicates that the difference in childbearing was not chiefly caused by early fertility, but by the fact that the

Figure 4.3
Children Born to Women in Three Age Groups in Acadiana and Elsewhere in Louisiana, 1910 and 1970–1990

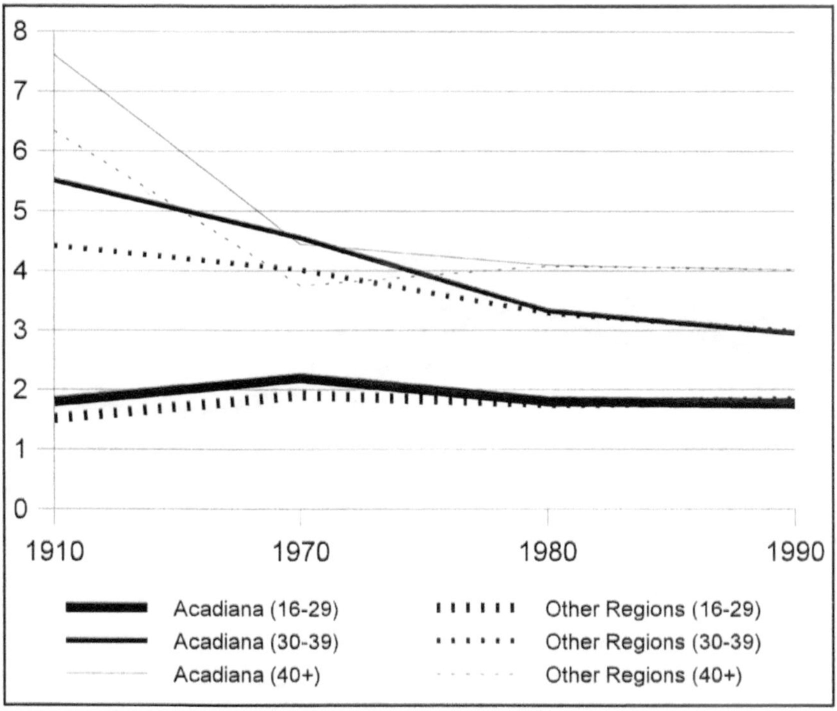

Source: Ruggles, Sobek et al., *Integrated Public Use Microdata Series.*

women of Acadiana continued to have children longer than other Louisiana women did. The difference in average, approximately one child, is statistically considerable and explains both the larger size of families and the recollections of large families by elderly Cajuns.

Sixty years later, childbearing in Cajun country had become more similar to childbearing in the rest of the state, but the women of Acadiana still had more children. Twenty years later, though, the fertility figures had converged. Childbearing in the Acadian homeland was no different from childbearing in other places. Further, if we compare Cajuns to Non-Cajuns (rather than using a regional comparison) for 1980 and 1990, the fertility figures look almost identical to those shown in this chart.

Extended or semi-extended families, as well as fertility, can affect family size. Big families may include grandparents or uncles and aunts. As readers will have noted, our interviews are filled with reminiscences of living with or around kin. Figure 4.4 shows percentages of households in Acadiana and

Figure 4.4
Percentages of Households Containing Grandchildren, Grandparents, and Other Non-nuclear Family Members in Acadiana and Elsewhere in Louisiana, 1920–1990

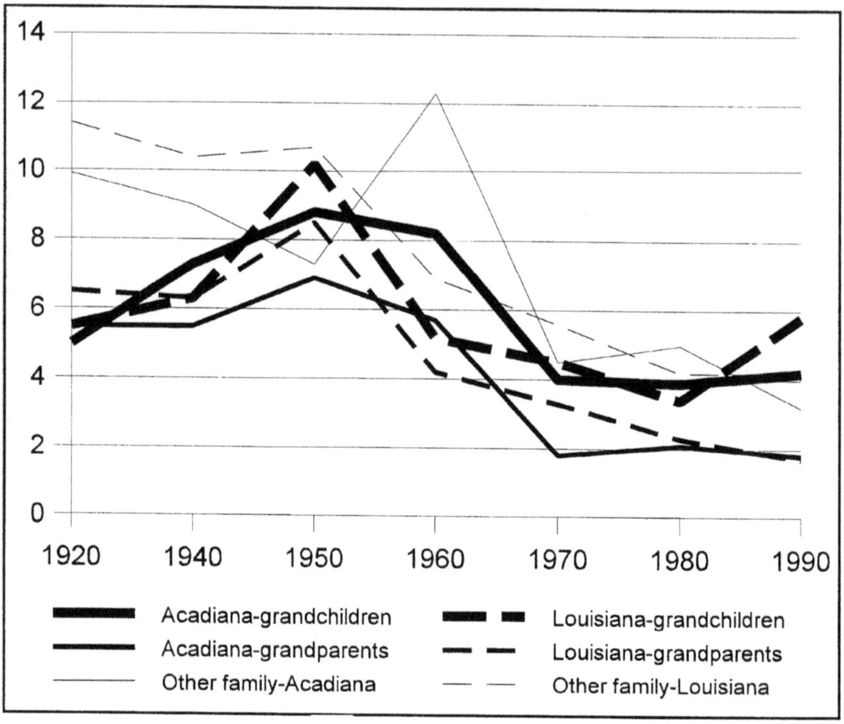

Source: Ruggles, Sobek et al., *Integrated Public Use Microdata Series.*

in other regions of Louisiana, from 1920 through 1990, that contained grandparents or great-grandparents (i.e., parents or grandparents of those listed as householders), grandchildren, and other non-nuclear family members, such as siblings, uncles, aunts, and cousins of householders. It is true that living in extended-family households was more common in the past than at the end of the twentieth century. But this was the case throughout Louisiana. It was not a distinctive characteristic of the Acadian region.

There was a general decrease, throughout the century, in the likelihood of "other family members," the uncles, aunts, and cousins, being included in households. In 1920, about one out of every ten households contained these non-nuclear family members. When our older respondents remember living around their uncles and aunts, they are not suffering from some version of false-memory syndrome. Still, these are memories that older people of every ethnic background might have. Our Cajun respondents did have more uncles and aunts than other people, until about the 1970s, but in most cases these relatives did not live with them.

The probability that households would contain grandparents or grandchildren increased somewhat in the middle of the century and then began to go down. A moment's reflection will supply a clear explanation for this pattern: life expectancies increased throughout the century and the economic position of older people improved from the 1960s onward, so that they could live on their own. The census data show that in 1920 only 2.9% of the people in Acadiana and only 3.2% of the people in the rest of the state were aged 65 or over. Proportionately, there weren't very many grandparents around to live with. By 1990, though, 11.0% of those in Acadiana and 12.0% of those in other places were seniors. Further, in 1920, about 50% of seniors in non-Acadian Louisiana and 55% of seniors in Cajun country were listed as heads of household. This remained roughly constant until about 1960, and the probability that an older person would head her or his own household increased, so that two out of three seniors in every part of the state were householders by 1990. In other words, older people were more likely to live with their children and grandchildren in earlier years, but there were fewer older people around.

Let's pause to think about what all of these numbers mean. We do not think they mean that the "Cajun family" is just an illusion or an advertising ploy invented by local chambers of commerce. They do mean that objective structural differences between Cajun families and other families have lessened steadily over the years and have now disappeared. People in the Cajun region did have larger families than those in other parts of the state. Women in Acadiana's past had longer childbearing years than women in other parts of the state. Although people in Cajun country did not live in extended family households to any unusual degree, the fairly large families and the geographic concentration of the group in the past meant numerous contacts with relatives.

To the extent that Cajuns, and observers of Cajuns, have seen large families as characteristic of the group, this has been a matter of emphasizing differences. We discussed in the earlier chapters how Cajuns were defined as a distinctive group of people in the course of Louisiana history because of their geographic and socioeconomic locations. Once people are seen as different, others tend to concentrate on the traits that distinguish them from others. Even when the traits disappear, they still exist in memory and in self-image. They play a very real part in how people think about themselves, about their relations to others, and about their relations to the past.

Many of their experiences growing up around grandparents, uncles, and aunts would have been similar to the experiences of other Louisianians (and probably other Americans). We do need to keep in mind, though, that our evidence has indicated that Cajuns occupy a definite geographic and socioeconomic location. This means a lot of contacts, including family contacts, with other members of the group. They may not have lived with their non-nuclear relatives to a greater extent than others, but they did have a lot of contact with them. Low levels of geographic and economic mobility meant dense social networks, in which family members played important parts. We turn to this matter of social networks and family contacts now, as we consider the question of marriage.

ENDOGAMY AMONG LOUISIANA CAJUNS

Endogamy, the tendency to marry inside a group, can be a central part of maintaining ethnicity. Historically, marriage has played a double role in perpetuating Cajun ethnicity. Marriage within the group enabled members to pass on cultural traits, and marriage outside the group made it possible to absorb non-Cajuns who moved into the region. Acadians traditionally married endogamously. Given the small size of early settlements and their relative isolation, this marriage pattern led to unions between relatives. There are reports of sets of siblings marrying one another and of cousin marriages. In her examination of marriages in an early Acadian settlement, Maureen Arceneaux notes that "6 of the couples were not related while 10 were," the degree of kinship of the bride and groom varying from second to fourth cousin. Anecdotal data such as clusters of family names and recent ethnographic accounts further show that marriage within kin groups has been and remains a pattern found among Cajuns. It is not rare to find two Leblancs who are not closely related married to each other or spouses sharing more or less distant cousins.[11] The marital choices of Suzie Quebodeaux's daughters are indicative of the enduring strength of the combination of ancestry, residence, and language. Benoit, Alleman, and Lavergne are common names among Cajuns, and Cecilia is a small community in Saint Martin Parish near Lafayette.

> They're all married. Celina is Thomas, it's Benoit. *Thomas vient de Cecilia.* Darren and Bryan and Jojo are from here. All five of them speak French. Darren, *le mari à Celina*, his mama's French . . . but he don't talk much French. Mona is Alleman. Paulette is Lavergne. Amanda is Alleman too. They married the brothers, Bryan and Darren. Becky is Carter.

However, as Becky's exogamous marriage suggests, endogamy has its limits. In his account of the cultural integration of Cajuns in postbellum Louisiana, Carl Brasseaux documents a "pervasive" exogamous pattern among "Acadians of all social and economic backgrounds." Brasseaux found that between 1865 and 1876, 58% of Acadian wives and 55% of Acadian husbands had married non-Acadian spouses. However, linguistic endogamy remained strong since 82% of spouses of Acadian wives and husbands were

French-speakers, either Creoles or foreign French.[12] These exogamous marriages allowed for the integration of non-Cajuns into Cajun families. It was suggested that such assimilation took place because "the Acadian and the French maidens" had their male spouses adapt to their Cajun ways.[13] Although the frequency of non-Acadian names among Cajuns certainly supports this explanation, it does not address other potential scenarios. Brasseaux's data clearly show that Acadian men were as likely to marry non-Acadian spouses as Acadian women were. The possibility that Acadian husbands would Cajunize their wives cannot be discarded and neither can the resistance of non-Acadian husbands to raising their children in a language and culture different from theirs, especially in a period when both were stigmatized. One of our interviewees illustrated the historical process of becoming Cajun through marriage: "My grandfather [*mother's father*] was a Broussard. On my daddy's side, my dad's mom was Spanish. She was Romero and Lopez. My dad was a Meaux and Derouen." Following the profound socioeconomic changes of the twentieth century and the increasing similarity between Cajun and non-Cajun families, the examination of marital strategies will allow us to gauge the depth of the transformation of Cajun ethnicity. Who do Cajuns marry and why?

The Public Use Microdata Sample provides valuable data on individuals. Based on self-reports it allows us to compare the characteristics of each person in a household. We distinguish between the statewide situation (Figure 4.5) and regional variation (Figure 4.6).[14] Figure 4.5 shows percentages of marriages in Louisiana involving either a self-described Cajun wife or Cajun husband. The other ethnic groups that we include are "French" (for those who described themselves as being of French, but not Cajun or Acadian, ancestry) and "non-Cajun." In more than 60% of these marriages, Cajuns were married to other self-described Cajuns. Only one out of five of these marriages were between Cajun men and non-Cajun women, and only about 15% were between non-Cajun men and Cajun women. This is a remarkably high rate of ingroup marriage for an American white ethnic group, higher than almost all other white ethnicity in the United States.

These percentages may be somewhat misleading, though, because Cajuns are not evenly distributed around the state, but concentrated in the southern to southwestern areas. It is possible, then, that endogamy may be a purely geographic phenomenon: Cajuns may marry co-ethnics because these are the people they find in their regions. Propinquity, the tendency to marry someone living nearby, is well documented by social science in the United States and indeed throughout the world. Long settled in Southwestern Louisiana, fairly stable, Cajuns may marry the boy or girl next door because he or she is there. For two of our informants, proximity of residence in the country or in town certainly fostered interaction. Sue Arceneaux met her future husband because

Figure 4.5
Ethnicity of Husbands and Wives in Louisiana Marriages Involving a Cajun, 1990

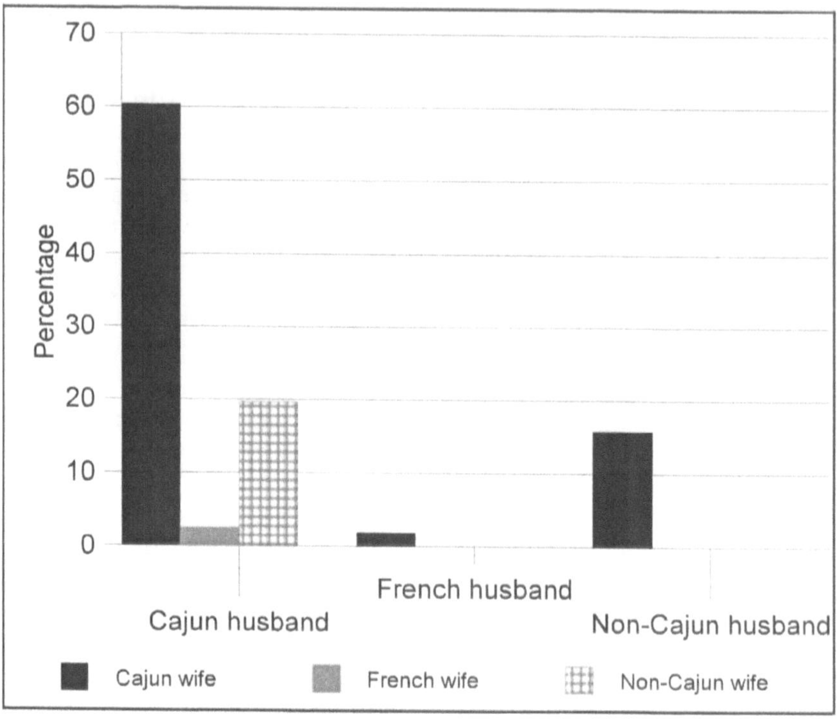

Source: U.S. Bureau of the Census, *Census of Population and Housing, 1990.*

on allait au bal à la même place, des bals de maison. Lui il avait d'la famille, moi j'avais d'la famille qu'était marrié ensemble. On s'est connu comme ça là aussi parce que on était pas trop trop loin, un bon three or four miles apart.

we were going to the same dance, house dances. He had relatives, I had relatives who were married to each other. We met like this because we were not living too far apart, about three or four miles apart.

Suzie Quebodeaux's fiancé lived with his mother one street over and would visit her on his way back home. To examine this question a little more closely, we will look now at the distribution of Cajuns around the state and at their marriage patterns in the various geographic regions of Louisiana.

The map in Figure 4.6 shows the percentage of the white population in each U.S. census Public Use Microdata Area (PUMA) that claims Cajun ancestry (in bold), the percentage of Cajun men who report being married to Cajun women (in italics), and the percentage of Cajun women who report

Figure 4.6
Percentages of Cajuns in the White Population, of Endogamously Married Cajun Men, and of Endogamously Married Cajun Women, 1990

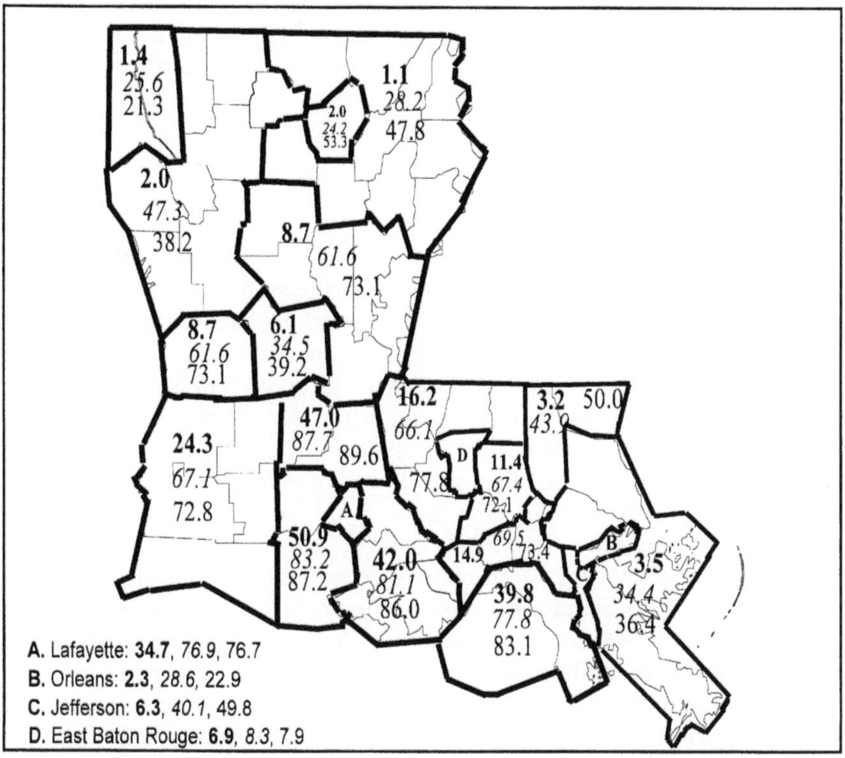

Boldface type indicates Cajuns in the White population, *italic* type indicates endogamously married Cajun men, and regular type indicates endogamously married Cajun woman.

Source: U.S. Bureau of the Census, *Census of Population and Housing, 1990.*

being married to Cajun men. For the major urban areas of Lafayette Parish, Orleans Parish, Jefferson Parish, and East Baton Rouge Parish, the percentages are reported below the figure, for reasons of space. We note that endogamy is indeed related to geographic representation: the larger the percentage of the population reporting Cajun ancestry, the greater the rates of endogamy. We also note, though, that geographic concentration cannot fully account for the tendency toward endogamy in this group. In each PUMA, rates of intermarriage are far above the percentages of Cajuns. In the north of the state, the Shreveport–Bossier City area where Cajuns represent 1.4% of the population, they have one chance out of four to be married to a co-ethnic when statistically their chances should be about one in a hundred. In the Cajun heartland, in the southern to southwestern region, Cajuns are in the minority in all but one PUMA; nevertheless, men and women in the ethnic core show rates of endogamy that are generally higher than 80%. When we consider geography, then, the high rate of intermarriage is even more impressive than when we look at it statewide. Although many of the structural characteristics of Cajun families differ little from those of other families, one structural characteristic stands out: Cajuns overwhelmingly marry other Cajuns.

WHY DO CAJUNS MARRY CAJUNS?

There has been a strong tendency toward out-marriage among most American minorities. Marriages of Jews to non-Jews, for example, have been rising sharply since the 1970s and some researchers have maintained that a majority now marry non-Jews.[15] Exogamy continues to be rare for African Americans, but this very rarity is evidence of the continuing socially constructed boundaries between black and white Americans. A high rate of endogamy among a white ethnic group such as Cajuns is a phenomenon that demands explanation. When a high rate of endogamy is found among members of a minority who bear no traits of appearance that distinguish them from the majority, the phenomenon is especially curious.

Focusing first on cultural characteristics, we can ask if Cajuns tend to marry other Cajuns because they share a language, a set of family values, or a religion. Since French is the traditional language of Cajuns, they may choose Cajun partners because they can talk to them. This may have been the case in the nineteenth century when all Acadians spoke French and most of them spoke only French, but it would not fully explain today's situation, since only a minority of Cajuns today still speak French.

Other cultural characteristics may also direct marriage choices. Expectations regarding family may promote intermarriage because individuals are likely to seek mates who share their values in matters such as family size and family roles. Even though, as we have seen, Cajun families have been structurally similar to other families, they may have distinctive ideas about family life. For instance, the cultural role of women in Cajun families as bearers and guardians of traditions may make them especially likely to marry in the group or to cause the non-Cajuns they marry to be absorbed by the group. Indeed, the slightly greater tendency of Cajun women to marry in (see Figure 4.5) offers some support for that view. Family roles and expectations, however, face the same trend toward assimilation that other cultural characteristics do. The evidence presented in the previous section and findings by other writers show that there are increasing similarities in structure and lifestyle between the Cajun family and the standard American family.[16] Whether a Cajun marries another Cajun or not, the couple is likely to establish its own residence, have between one and three children, and interact with relatives who live within a short driving distance for work-, entertainment-, or family-related purposes.

The role of religion is harder to establish clearly. Southwestern Louisiana where Cajuns reside is predominantly Catholic and Cajuns are overwhelmingly Catholic. In addition, limited but strong evidence suggests that Catholicism is still transmitted from generation to generation. Finally, contrary to nationwide trends, intermarriage appears to be rare although it is on the rise among younger generations. Although it is not possible to present up-to-date statistical evidence on religion here, since U.S. census data do not contain any information on religion, we should note problems with a purely religious explanation of endogamy. First, there are non-Cajun Catholics in Southwestern Louisiana who can provide co-religionists as marital partners. In 1980, for example, data by the Archdiocese of New Orleans showed that fully 65% of people living in the Diocese of Lafayette (an eight-parish diocese in the center of Acadiana) were Catholic. In Acadiana's second primary Catholic diocese, the Diocese of Houma-Thibodaux (Terrebonne and Lafourche parishes), 63% of the people were Catholic.[17] Since self-described Cajuns make up only a minority, about 40%, of the population in virtually all of this region, it seems evident that there are more Catholics, even white Catholics, than there are Cajuns. Second, religious endogamy does not preclude other cultural or structural factors from affecting marital strategies. For instance, there are socioeconomic correlates of religious affiliation. Jews and liberal Protestants tend to be more educated and upper-class than middle-class Catholics and moderate Protestants. Religion and class also intersect with ethnic origin, race, and residence. If a religious explanation clearly cannot be rejected in the case of Cajuns, it also cannot be viewed as sufficient to account for continued endogamy amidst a trend of cultural—if not religious—assimilation.

It is our view that, given the steadily declining cultural distinctiveness of Louisiana Cajuns, structural characteristics are likely to provide important sources of similarity among members of this group that can promote endogamy. One of these structural characteristics is the group's numerical representation in geographic areas. Another important structural characteristic, one that is often overlooked or underemphasized in studies of the maintenance of ethnicity, is the class position of Cajuns.

If an ethnic group is large enough to predominate in a geographic region, it can absorb others, literally turning outsiders into insiders. There is some historical evidence of exogamous marriages by Cajuns resulting in the integration of non-Cajuns into Cajun families. Cajuns' "capacity for absorbing the extraneous population elements" is attested to by families of German, Spanish, Irish, Scotch, and English origins speaking French despite non-Acadian last names such as Waguespack, Hernandez, O'Brien, or McGee.[18] Contemporary South-western Louisiana has become a highly diversified society. There are no distinctively Cajun towns, parishes, or neighborhoods but rather "a cultural continuum in a bicultural community."[19] There is intensive interaction across flexible ethnic lines. The combination of residential stability and a strong regional presence may result in sustained endogamy as follows: a Cajun marries a non-Cajun, socializes the newly formed family and especially the children to Cajun ways, one or more children marry a Cajun, and so on. Hard evidence to support such a scenario is lacking, but anecdotal evidence abounds.

Social class constitutes a second type of structural influence on marriage patterns. On this note, we have seen that Cajuns now constitute a blue collar segment of Southwestern Louisiana. Ethnically endogamous marriage among Cajuns, then, could also be a case of class homogamy: Cajuns tend to marry one another because people tend to marry those who are economically and socially similar to themselves. To clarify the respective roles of cultural and structural factors, and especially that of social class, we conducted a statistical analysis of the census data already presented.

We constructed a set of logistic regression equations to first identify predictors of endogamy among Cajuns and then to measure their effect in the three geographical areas we have defined (see Tables 4.1 and 4.2).[20] For readers who are not familiar with logistic regression, we provide here a nontechnical summary of our findings. We found that living in the Acadian region, occupying a low socioeconomic status, remaining in the same residence for a long time, having French spoken in the house, being female, and living in a rural area are the most important predictors of endogamy. The age of the couple, the number of children born to the family, and the educational gap between husband and wife show no association with the ethnicity of the marriage partner. The results show some support for both cultural and structural explanations of endogamy; the high ranking of the socioeconomic variable suggests that indeed socioeconomic status is negatively associated with endogamy, meaning that the higher the social class, the less likely Cajuns are to in-marry and vice versa. However, since location appears as a prime factor and Cajuns are unevenly distributed throughout the state, we wanted to ascertain that once again these statewide results were not flawed by the effect of the geographical variable, living in Acadiana. We repeated the analysis for Cajuns who live outside of Acadiana, for those who live in the Acadian fringe, and for those in the Acadian core. Outside of Acadiana, of all the variables, socioeconomic status appears to be the strongest predictor followed by remaining in a residence for a long time, and the age of couples, age and status both being associated with decreased probabilities of endogamy. The pattern in the Acadian fringe shows some differences. Residential stability and speaking French in the household are the most strongly related to endogamy; the emergence of language in this region makes sense since there are virtually no French-speakers outside of Acadiana. The negative association with socioeconomic status remains: in

Table 4.1
Logistic Regression Coefficients for Predictors of Endogamy for Louisiana Families Containing a Cajun Spouse

	Logit (WALD)	Standard Error
Acadian region	.820** (441.868)	.039
Nonmetropolitan area	.321** (16.294)	.079
Length of residence	.156** (40.816)	.024
French spoken in home	.253** (19.935)	.057
Age of couple	-.002 (.342)	.003
Number of children	.016 (.623)	.020
Cajun female	.835** (28.017)	.158
Educational gap	-.243 (.882)	.258
Socioeconomic status	-.266** (97.963)	.027
Intercept	-2.337** (135.546)	.201
N	7,440	

* $p < .05$ ** $p < .01$

the fringe, Cajuns of comparatively lower social class are more likely than others to marry in the group.

In the Acadian core, Cajuns make up a large portion of the population and it is therefore much easier to find co-ethnics as mates. In this region, socioeconomic status appears to be the variable most strongly associated with in-group marriage. Living in a nonmetropolitan area and length of residence are also related to greater probabilities of endogamy. People living in rural areas and people who show relatively little residential mobility are likely to have and marry into long-established ties within a group. Speaking French is positively related to endogamy, indicating that cultural characteristics do play some part in maintaining in-group marriage. Cajun women in the Acadian core, as in the fringe, are more likely than men to take co-ethnics as mates.

Table 4.2
Logistic Regression Coefficients for Predictors of Endogamy for Louisiana Families Containing a Cajun Spouse, by Geographic Region

	Outside Acadiana		Acadian Fringe		Acadian Core	
	Logit (WALD)	Standard Error	Logit (WALD)	Standard Error	Logit	Standard Error
Nonmetropolitan area	.040 (.024)	.256	-.097 (.233)	.200	.465** (23.834)	.095
Length of residence	.249** (8.909)	.084	.297** (32.269)	.052	.098** (11.041)	.029
French spoken in home	.288 (1.643)	.225	.585** (19.234)	.133	.200** (9.137)	.066
Age of couple	-.025* (4.089)	.012	.004 (.253)	.008	-.001 (.083)	.005
Number of children	.044 (.410)	.069	-.031 (.363)	.051	.024 (1.003)	.024
Cajun female	1.207 (3.688)	.629	.986* (5.968)	.404	.742** (16.778)	.181
Educational gap	-.916 (1.074)	.482	.398 (.682)	.451	-.551 (2.812)	.329
Socioeconomic status	-.497** (31.605)	.088	-.250** (15.984)	.063	-.240** (56.221)	.032
Intercept	-2.289** (10.446)	.708	-2.090** (21.068)	.455	-.511* (5.276)	.223
N	900		1488		5052	

* $p < .05$ **$p < .01$

We can, then, identify two structural characteristics that perpetuate endogamy in this Louisiana ethnic group. First, the concentration of Cajuns in certain areas of Louisiana does help to maintain in-group marriage. However, this is not simply a matter of women and men marrying the people who happen to live around them. Everywhere, rates of endogamy tend to be higher than one would expect, given the percentages of Cajuns in each parish. Moreover, Cajuns constitute a minority of the white population even in their core areas. This means that almost everywhere there are nongroup members theoretically available as marriage partners.

The second important structural characteristic is socioeconomic status. Consistently, the higher the socioeconomic status of individuals, the more likely they are to marry outside the group. Since Cajuns have been identified as occupying a specific socioeconomic status in Louisiana, we believe that socioeconomic homogamy may offer much of the answer to the question of Cajun endogamy.

Cajun families do still display some differences from other families. However, these differences are slight and are primarily associated with older people and with French language ability, a cultural trait that appears to be in steady decline. Despite the fact that Cajun families are becoming more like others, though, the family continues to be a means by which the ethnic identity is passed on across generations. This tends to perpetuate the sense of connection to ancestry, even as ancestral traits decline. Readers will note that we are not maintaining that Cajun ethnicity has been reduced to nothing more than social class. Instead, we are suggesting that the regional working-class position of many Cajuns plays a critical part in passing on the ethnic identity.

In Chapter 3, we suggested that the rural setting that gave rise to the Cajun identity has largely disappeared. However, we argued that Cajuns have not disappeared, nor is their ethnic identification somehow a matter of self-delusion. There are people in Southwestern Louisiana who share a self-concept as Cajun, who have social ties to one another, and who feel strong emotional attachments to a historical tradition. This continued existence as a group and not just as a memory, though, is made possible by the fact that a new setting has taken the place of the old one. Cajuns are now disproportionately the blue-collar working class of Southwestern Louisiana, with a heavy representation in the new oil industry and related activities. Although not all members of the group fit into this economic category, sharing an economic position helps maintain them as a distinctive set of people by giving them things that they have in common and by helping maintain connections among them. These connections include the most important ties of all, the ties of family life. Even though Cajun families today look similar to others in matters such as family size and composition, the Cajuns we interviewed for this book still see their families as something special, and their choices of husbands and wives still distinguish them from the general population.

Cajun family life is shaped by the group's geographic and socioeconomic position, by the fact that its center of gravity is a modern regional working class. But, as we have seen in the interviews with our respondents, Cajuns draw on images of the past to understand and interpret their present-day lives.

NOTES

1. Authors' interview, March 20, 2001.

2. Revon Reed, *Lâche pas la patate: Portrait des Acadiens de la Louisiane* (Montréal: Editions Parti pris, 1976), 28.

3. T. Lynn Smith, "An Analysis of Rural Social Organization in Louisiana," *Journal of Farm Economics* 16(4) (1934): 680–688; Charles R. Brassieur, "The Modern Atchafalaya Culture: Results of the Ethnographic Survey" in Jon L. Gibson (ed.),

Archeology and Ethnology on the Edges of the Atchafalaya Basin, South Central Louisiana, (Lafayette, LA: Center for Archeological Studies, 1982), 153–242; Mathé Allain, "Twentieth-Century Acadians" in Glen Conrad (ed.), *The Cajuns: Essays on Their History and Culture*, (Lafayette Center for Louisiana Studies, 1978, 129–141); Barry J. Ancelet, Carl Brasseaux & Jay Edwards, "Acadian Folklife" in Barry J. Ancelet, Jay Edwards & Glen Pitre (eds.), *Cejun Country* (Jackson University Press of Mississippi, 1991), 33–65.

4. On use of French see Smith, "An Analysis of Rural Social Organization"; on Catholicism see Cécyle Trépanier, *French Louisiana at the Threshold of the 21st Century*, Projet Louisiane, Monograph 2 (Quebec: Laval University, 1989); on familism see Brassieur, "The Modern Atchafalaya Culture" and Dorice Tentchoff, *Speech in a Louisiana Cajun Community* (Ph.D. dissertation, Case Western Reserve University, Cleveland, OH, 1975); on division of labor see Sarah Brabant, "The Acadian Family: Anachronism or Paradigm?" *Attakapas Gazette* 12(4): (1977) 201–208, Stella Jones, "The impact of acculturation on Cajun husband/wife role/perception and values within the family structure" (master's thesis, University of Southwestern Louisiana, 1982), and T. Lynn Smith & Vernon Parenton, "Acculturation among the Louisiana French," *American Journal of Sociology* 44: (1938) 355–364; on occupational skills see Ancelet, Brasseaux & Edwards, "Acadian Folklife" and Edward Kammer, *Four Southwestern Louisiana Parishes* (Washington, DC: Catholic University of America Press, 1941); on music see Barry J. Ancelet & Elemore Morgan, *The Makers of Cajun Music* (Austin: University of Texas Press, 1984); on folkways see Page Gutierrez, *Cajun Foodways* (Jackson: University Press of Mississippi, 1992) and Jay Edwards & Maida Bergeron, "Folk Medicine" in Ancelet, Edwards & Pitre, *Cajun Country*, 95–100.

5. David Schneider, *American Kinship: A Cultural Account* (Englewood Cliffs, NJ: Prentice-Hall, 1968).

6. Kammer, *Four Southwestern Louisiana Parishes*; Harnett Kane, *The Bayous of Louisiana* (New York: Hampton Publishing, 1943); Ancelet & Morgan, *The Makers of Cajun Music.*

7. Kane, *The Bayous of Louisiana*; Joel Fletcher, *The Acadians in Louisiana Today* (Lafayette, Southwestern Louisiana Institute, 1947); Patricia Harris, "Cuisine in Acadiana" in Steven DelSesto & Jon Gibson (ed.), *The Culture of Acadiana: Tradition and Change in South Louisiana*, (Lafayette: University of Southwestern Louisiana, 1975), 79–85.

8. Allain, "Twentieth-Century Acadians," 139; see also Trent Angers, *The Truth About the Cajuns* (Lafayette, LA: Acadian House Publishing, 1990); Lauren C. Post, *Cajun Sketches* (Baton Rouge: Louisiana State University Press, 1962); Carolyn Ramsey, *Cajuns on the Bayou* (New York: Hastings House, 1957).

9. Clyde Collard, "The Cajun Family: Adjustment to Modern Trends" in DelSesto & Gibson, *The Culture of Acadiana: Tradition and Change in South Louisiana*, 118; Jay Edwards, "Family Organization," in Ancelet, Edwards & Pitre, *Cajun Country*, p. 69.

10. Rodrigue Landry, Réal Allard & Jacques Henry. "French in South Louisiana: Towards Language Loss," *Journal of Multilingual and Multicultural Development* 17(5) (1996): 442–466; Trépanier, *French Louisiana.*

11. Maureen Arceneaux, *Acadian to Cajun: Population, Family and Wealth in Southwest Louisiana, 1765–1854* (Ph.D. dissertation, Brigham Young University,

1982), 79; Marjorie Esman, *Henderson, Louisiana: Cultural Adaptation in a Cajun Community* (New York: Holt, Rinehert and Winston, 1985).

12. Carl Brasseaux, *Acadian to Cajun: Transformation of a People 1803–1877* (Jackson: University Press of Mississippi, 1992).

13. Brasseaux, *Acadian to Cajun*, 105; T. Lynn Smith & Lauren C. Post, "The Country Butchery: A Co-operative Institution," *Rural Sociology* 2 (1937): 335–337; Smith & Parenton, "Acculturation among the Louisiana French," 364.

14. In Table 4.5 the row percentages represent the marriage partners of women and the column percentages represent the marriage partners of men. For the map (Figure 4.1) we use PUMAs rather than parishes as in the map in Chapter 3, because data on individuals in households that can be connected with data on other individuals (such as spouses) is not readily available at the parish level. Differences between figures in both maps result from aggregation and different sampling procedures and do not invalidate our findings.

15. Barry Kosmin, Sidney Goldstein, Joseph Waksberg, Nava Lerer, Ariella Keysar, and Jeffrey Scheckner, *Highlights of the CJF 1990 National Jewish Population Survey* (New York: Council of Jewish Federations, 1991); Neil C. Sandberg, *Jewish Life in Los Angeles* (Lanham, MD: University Press of America, 1974).

16. Collard, "The Cajun Family"; Edwards, "Family Organization"; Landry, Allard & Henry, "French in South Louisiana."

17. Ancelet, Edwards & Pitre, *Cajun Country*; Trépanier, *French Louisiana*; Jacques Henry, "Le Mouvement Louisianais de Renouveau Francophone: Vers Une Nouvelle Identité Cadjine?" (Ph.D dissertation, Université Paris V, René Descartes, 1982).

18. Smith & Post, "The Country Butchery," 335.

19. Larbi Oukada, "The Territory and Population of French-speaking Louisiana," *Revue de Louisiane/Louisiana Review* 7(1) (1978): 5–34; Lawrence Estaville, "Mapping the Cajuns," *Southern Studies* 25(2) (1986):163–171.

20. Table 4.2 presents results of a logistic regression analysis in which we examine predictors that may be associated with an increase or decrease in the probability that someone of Cajun ancestry will be married endogamously. Our sample here consists of all married Louisianians who claim Cajun ancestry. Logistic regression coefficients are difficult to interpret, as the logarithmic scale does not readily lend itself to comparing magnitudes of effects (Richard Alba, "Interpreting the Parameters of Log-Linear Models," *Sociological Methods and Research* 16 (1986): 45–77). Even if we were to convert the coefficients to odds ratios or percentage differences, we would still have only the odds or increase in likelihood of endogamy associated with one unit increase in the independent variable. This would still leave the puzzle of how to compare an increase in likelihood of being endogamous associated with one unit increase in socioeconomic status with, for example, the increase in likelihood associated with being male rather than female. One answer to this problem can be to compare Wald statistics, since these can be used as rough indicators of strength of association. If we examine these statistics, given in parentheses below the logit coefficients, we see that the regional variable appears to have the strongest association with endogamy. This is consistent with the evidence presented, but using a contextual variable in single-level model can result in some inflation of the value of the coefficient; it can also overlook the fact that the coefficients of other variables may vary

from one context to another (Anthony Bryk & Stephen W. Raudenbush, *Hierarchical Linear Models: Applications and Data Analysis Methods*, Newbury Park, CA: Sage Publications, 1992). Table 4.3 presents the results of logistic regression equations for the three regions.

Chapter 5

The Bases of Cajun Ethnicity

We have seen that as the socioeconomic setting of Louisiana changed over the course of the twentieth century, the economic center of gravity of the state's Cajuns shifted. They had emerged as French-speaking rural people, concentrated in a fairly isolated region. Although they largely stayed in this region, though, they became a local blue-collar group, in somewhat the same manner that other white ethnics became the blue-collar groups of America's Northeast. Many of the Cajuns' social structures and practices came to be indistinguishable from those of other Louisianians, and from those of other Americans. The relatively high fertility rate and large families of the Acadian region vanished as statistical averages. The Cajun version of French, a major cultural distinction, survived to the beginning of the twenty-first century, but it is becoming increasingly rare.

Despite these changes, though, the Cajuns themselves did not disappear as a group. Claims of Cajun ethnicity increased, and these claims were not based on sentimental illusions. Three major factors served to hold the group together through the change. First, people who had ancestral or contemporary family ties to the group did not move away. They continued to be defined by geography. Second, even though the past was indeed past, it continued to be a reality in the present. People did transmit a stock of symbols—language and self-images—that continued to influence how Southwestern Louisianians thought about themselves and about others. Third, the new economic concentration, like the geographic concentration, kept people who thought of themselves as Cajuns in contact with each other and helped to maintain common attitudes and ways of life. The fact that increasing numbers of descendants of Cajuns did not fit into the new regional working-class category meant, as we will see, that many middle-class people in the region had questions about their relations both to the past and to the present.

Before we describe, in our final chapters, some features of the new economy of ethnicity, we want to paint a comprehensive picture of Cajun ethnicity. Given the complex and evolving nature of social arrangements and the conflicting assertions of competing theories, especially in the social sciences, it should be apparent that the answer will reflect some ambivalence. The discussion should not be limited to a rigorous "either-or" proposition, but it should consider the interplay between perceptions and structural realities. Our data clearly show that there are both objective and subjective factors leading people to call themselves Cajuns and causing others to agree with them. Cajun ethnicity is both an idea in people's heads and a hard fact of socioeconomic life. In this chapter, we look at how ideas and socioeconomic life work together to create and maintain contemporary definitions of Cajun ethnicity.

A SHIFT IN THE BASIS OF CAJUN ETHNICITY

All the data we have presented in this book come from people who identified themselves as Cajuns when they filled out their census forms or when they agreed to talk with us. In doing so, they claimed a heritage. We have relied on this affirmation of ancestry to collect accounts and statistics on different aspects of their experiences but we have not yet looked at this variable in detail. Before we proceed with a recapitulation of the factors associated with Cajun ancestry, a brief assessment of the relevance and reliability of ancestry claims is in order.

Although we have no doubt that most people tell the truth on census questionnaires or in interviews, the truth about ancestry and ethnicity can be pretty slippery at times. Clearly people with no Acadian connection whatsoever in their family history are unlikely to count themselves as Cajuns. Still, the affirmation of such a heritage relies on much more than documented evidence. There is no requirement of a quota of Acadian blood, of place of birth, or of a direct and uninterrupted lineal connection to a male or female Acadian ancestor. Thus ancestry depends very much on what people believe: Is it beneficial to claim or to reject the heritage? Does it fit one's personality, lifetime goals, beliefs, upbringing? Does one simply care?

When people in Louisiana call themselves Cajun or Acadian, by any definition they choose, they are neither lying nor misrepresenting themselves. Still, they may choose different definitions at different times, and answers about ethnicity may depend on questions. For this reason, there might be some skepticism about the accuracy of census data. The way questions are phrased, the manner in which they are answered, and the coding of responses by census takers all point to a need for a critical assessment of the data. Throughout our research, we have come across examples of data sets that are incompatible, because of different questions asked on language use or inconsistent occupational categories, for instance. The placement of a question and an example in a questionnaire matters. The insertion of "Cajun" as a possible choice of ancestry in the 1990 census has probably increased the number of answers compared with previous years when it was not offered as explicitly.[1] Then there is the human factor. Researchers have suggested that white ethnics are typically vague, unsure, and manipulative of their ethnic backgrounds;[2] for instance, fathers are the most likely to fill out census questionnaires, and their response may reflect their own views of ancestry more than those of their spouse and children. These are valid objections and we have taken them into account when proposing interpretations of census data. However, they do not warrant the wholesale rejection of census information, since this does reflect the more or less official designations that people give themselves. It does mean that we need to consider this information in the light of richer, more detailed reporting from interviews.

Although data on the basis of self-identification of Cajun is limited, the various sources strongly suggest that a connection to Acadian ancestors is the most important criterion of Cajun ethnicity. According to the 1990 census, about one-quarter of Louisianians identified themselves with the Acadian ancestral category. It was mentioned by 80% of respondents to a question on the definition of a true Cajun in 1995.[3] The emphasis on the Acadian heritage remains strong despite the growing distance in time and kinship ties separating the Cajun experience from its ancestral past. As one informant put it, "Usually, a real Acadian or Cajun is somebody who has Acadian roots. To prove that you are a Cajun you have to go back to the roots, to the genealogy: Should be one who can claim some ancestry to Nova Scotia or New Brunswick; otherwise, he's not a pure, true Cajun."

In addition, Cajuns are pretty secure in their ethnic identification and do not feel hyphenated to the same extent that say Italian-Americans, Irish-Americans, or Albanian-Americans do. Fewer than 1 percent of those who selected "Cajun" as a first ancestry gave a second ancestry. The majority of those who did select a second ancestry chose "French." This contrasts with ancestry claims made by other white ethnics: approximately one-third to two-thirds of native-born whites listed multiple ancestries.

The importance of ancestry indicates that claims of contemporary ethnicity are partly based on ideas about the past. But what influences who will have these ideas about the past? We have already seen how those who claim Acadian ancestry and use of French tend to share occupational categories and marital strategies. We now want to broaden our investigation to other dimensions of social life and and identify the characteristics shared by those who label themselves Cajuns. To do so, we use logistic regression equations to examine predictors of self-identification as Cajun and predictors of being a self-identified Cajun who can speak French (Tables 5.2 and 5.3). In this way, we can look at individual relevant predictors while controlling for others. We introduced this statistical technique earlier, one that allows us to look at increases or decreases in probability of one variable associated with other variables. Does, for example, the ability to speak French make it more or less likely that individuals will claim a Cajun heritage? If we hold the ability to speak French constant, does working in the oil industry make claims of Cajun background more likely or less likely both for French-speakers and non-French-speakers? Further, how much more likely than other people are French-speakers or workers in the oil industry to claim Cajun history?[4]

We have retained nine variables providing information on individuals' date and place of birth, residence (where and how long), ability to speak French, and socioeconomic status (employment categories, income, education level). We have introduced three occupational variables to the logistic regression equation. Employment in fishing, farming, and forestry represents occupations that are traditionally and stereotypically associated with being Cajun. Employment in oil industry occupations has been brought into the equation because the oil industry is a major employer in Southwestern Louisiana and because of its complex effect on Cajun ethnicity. We have also included employment in textile mills because they have become a major source of employment for women in the region. Table 5.1 summarizes the characteristics of Louisiana Cajuns and non-Cajuns, by age groups.

The analysis shows that the predictors of a person claiming Cajun ancestry are, in order of importance, the following:

1. *Ability to speak French.* French-speakers are more likely than non-French-speakers to report this ancestry by a difference of 28%, indicating that, despite the generational decline in French-speaking ability, competence in this language remains the trait most strongly associated with Cajun ancestry. Cajuns have retained their original tongue in greater proportions than other white ethnics. For example, a third of Cajuns reported speaking French or Cajun at home. By contrast, Richard Alba reports that 74.1% of his sample of white ethnics in the Northeast had no knowledge of their mother tongue and 84.1% did not use it at all. In addition, among those who retained knowledge of the ancestral language, less than half (10.9%) reported a speaking ability and, overall, less than 5% used it in speech. An analysis of the age distribution further supports the distinctiveness of the Louisiana situation. Alba reports that among white ethnics, 18.2% of those over 60 and 4.3% of 19–33-year-olds spoke a non-English language at home. Among Franco-Americans, the rates of language retention vary between a high of 34.5% among those 81 and over with French as mother tongue to a low of 1.2% for 11–20-year-olds with English as mother tongue.[5] Respective rates for Cajuns show most of the oldest Cajuns (72%)

Table 5.1
Selected Characteristics of Non-Cajuns and Cajuns in Southwestern Louisiana, by Age Groups, 1990

	Non-Cajuns			Cajuns		
	-30	**30-50**	**50+**	**-30**	**30-50**	**50+**
Total Percent	73.9	77.1	79.4	26.1	22.9	20.6
(N)	(28,005)	(17,122)	(15,305)	(9,871)	(5,093)	(3,980)
Language						
Speak French	2.9	8.4	20.5	8.1	34.5	71.8
Fluent English	98.7	97.5	91.7	98.0	93.9	72.4
Linguistically isolated	0.5	0.8	5.1	1.0	1.8	17.6
Ancestry						
French 1st ancestry	20.4	20.1	23.3	—	—	—
French 2nd ancestry	6.3	5.2	4.4	0.0	0.0	0.0
Residence						
La. native	81.4	68.6	73.6	96.2	96.2	98.0
5 year residence in area	93.1	93.2	97.4	98.2	98.3	9.44
Live in central Cajun area	37.8	37.6	40.0	76.3	76.9	78.8
Live in non-metro. area	18.9	17.7	22.1	27.1	27.1	34.7
Marital status						
Married	19.5	79.9	67.6	21.3	80.6	68.2
Divorced	2.1	9.9	6.1	2.0	9.1	4.9
Never married	77.2	6.2	3.7	75.4	6.1	3.4
Education						
Not HS grad	18.2	17.2	41.5	25.6	27.4	62.7
HS grad only	67.3	61.3	46.2	66.4	62.8	33.4
College grad	14.5	21.5	12.3	8.0	9.7	3.9
Occupation						
Manager-professional	16.5	30.8	28.3	12.2	20.1	17.8
Technician	3.9	4.4	2.5	3.4	3.6	1.9
Sales	17.9	12.6	15.1	16.8	12.6	13.3
Admin.-clerical	20.1	16.3	15.4	18.6	16.2	12.9
Service	16.1	10.2	13.0	15.2	12.5	19.1
Farm, fish, forestry	2.9	2.3	3.8	4.3	3.1	6.8
Production, craft	13.8	15.4	15.1	16.7	20.3	18.4
Operator-laborer	8.9	8.0	6.8	12.7	11.6	9.8
Income						
Median HH income ($)	(30,000)	(36,180)	(21,714)	(26,730)	(30,263)	(15,702)

Source: U.S. Bureau of the Census, *Census of Population and Housing, 1990. Public Micro Use Data Samples (5%)* [Machine readable data files] (Washington, DC: Bureau of the Census, 1992).

Table 5.2
Predictors of Cajun Ethnicity among Whites of Southwestern Louisiana

	Logit Coefficient	Odds Ratio	Percentage Difference
Age Group	-.500**	.606	-8.4
Residence in Cajun center	1.329**	3.777	10.3
Louisiana native	1.978**	7.225	15.8
In area for five years	.380**	1.462	7.9
Ability to speak French	1.190**	3.286	27.6
Fishing, hunting, farming occupation	.067	1.070	1.3
Oil industry occupation	.166**	1.181	3.3
Textile factory occupation	.450**	1.569	9.5
Educational attainment	-.275**	.760	-4.9
Household income	-1.300**[1]	1.000	0.0[2]
Constant	-3.595**		

** p <.01
1. The decimal point should be moved six places to the left.
2. Since household income is a continuous variable, the percentage decrease in probability of being a Cajun associated with each unit increase in income is too small to compute, even though household income shows a significant negative relationship to being Cajun.

could speak French and only a small yet sizeable minority of the youngest Cajuns (8%) could.

2. *Regional identification.* Being born in Louisiana and residing in the central Cajun area for at least five years are all strongly and positively related to seeing oneself as a Cajun. This is consistent with findings by other researchers who found that residence in Southwestern Louisiana was mentioned quite consistently over the last twenty years in an average 20% of answers to "What is a Cajun?"[6] It is made very clear by Cajun people. "Cajun is when you grow up here in this area and all of your family is from around here. We are a lot closer to our families than other people. We don't leave or move away," said a 34-year-old woman in Lafayette. It echoes a comment by a 38-year-old Church Point resident: "I am born and raised here. My mom and dad and all my other family were raised here . . . and all my relatives live near us."[7]

3. *Jobs in the oil and textile industries.* Interestingly, traditional occupations such as farming and fishing are not significantly related to a Cajun self-identification. Employment in oil jobs and employment in textile jobs are significantly and positively associated with claims of Cajun background. It is interesting that those in textile jobs were more likely than those in

other jobs to call themselves Cajuns by 10%, whereas those in oil jobs were more likely than those in other jobs by only 3%. This may indicate that Cajuns are more heavily concentrated in textiles than in oil, but this speculation should be treated carefully. The oil industry is cyclical in nature and at the time of the 1990 census it had not yet recovered from the 1985–86 drop in oil prices that created a sharp downturn in employment in the region. Thus, it may be meaningful that oil jobs are sufficiently strongly related to Cajun ethnicity so that this relationship shows up even in data collected when such occupations were in serious decline.

4. *Youth.* The older people are, the less likely they are to identify themselves as being of Cajun descent. On the average, each age increase among the three age groups is associated with a decrease of 8% in the probability of a claim of Cajun identity. This is a greater age difference than observed in Table 5.1, before controlling for other relevant variables. These results provide convincing evidence that, other things being equal, younger people are significantly more likely than older people to identify themselves as Cajuns, suggesting an expanding rather than a declining ethnic identification.

5. *Comparatively low socioeconomic status as measured by income and lower levels of education.* As we have discussed extensively above, contemporary Cajuns tend to be concentrated in the working class of Southwestern Louisiana.

We have seen that the use of French language is the strongest predictor of self-identification as Cajun. However, we have also observed that many of those who consider themselves Cajuns do not speak French. Do French-speaking Cajuns differ from the others? To investigate this question, we calculated predictors of being a French-speaking Cajun (see Table 5.3). The results show two kinds of differences. French-speaking Cajuns differ from non-French-speaking Cajuns in terms of age and occupation. The association of age with being a French-speaking Cajun is the opposite of the association of age with simply being a self-identified Cajun. Each older age group is associated with a 7% increase in the probability of being a French-speaking Cajun. Also, in contrast, those who are employed in fishing, hunting, and farming occupations are significantly more likely than other Louisianians to be French-speaking Cajuns. Neither employment in the oil industry nor employment in textiles are significant predictors. In other words, the kinds of jobs that are characteristic of most people who call themselves Cajuns tend not to occupy the French-speakers.

The other distinctive characteristic found among French-speaking Cajuns is the reinforcement of traits found among ethnic Cajuns. Both residence in the center of the Cajun region and being a Louisiana native are much more strongly related to language-based Cajun ethnicity than to a simple claim of Cajun ancestry. Also, low income is more strongly related to being a French-speaking Cajun than to being a self-identified Cajun.

This has been a rather technical discussion, but it has yielded some inter-

Table 5.3
Predictors of French-Speaking Cajun Ethnicity among Whites of Southwestern Louisiana

	Logit Coefficient	Odds Ratio	Percentage Difference
Age Group	.614**	1.847	7.3
Residence in Cajun center	1.992**	7.330	35.8
Louisiana native	2.963**	19.352	58.9
In area for five years	.577**	1.781	6.8
Fishing, hunting, farming occupation	.316**	1.372	3.3
Oil industry occupation	.082	1.086	0.8
Textile factory occupation	.159	1.172	1.6
Educational attainment	-.586**	.556	-4.3
Household income	-3.200[1]		0.0[2]
Constant	-7.181		

** $p < .01$
1. The decimal point should be moved six places to the left.
2. Since household income is a continuous variable, the percentage decrease in probability of being a Cajun associated with each unit increase in income is too small to compute, even though household income shows a significant negative relationship to being Cajun.

esting findings. Louisianians may be seen as fitting into different classes of Cajun ethnicity. French-speaking Cajuns tend to reside in the core ethnic area, they continue to show a significant connection to the rural and wilderness occupations, and they tend to be older people. A general self-identification as Cajun, on the other hand, tends to be associated with youth, residence in the central ethnic area, and employment in the oil and textile industries. In sum, to use Milton Gordon's term, there are indications that Cajuns, whether they speak French or not, continue to be a structurally distinctive "ethclass," a group that combines ethnicity with class position. It appears that the ethnic group, over the course of three generations, has moved into a new socioeconomic niche. Cajuns, according to our evidence, are becoming an ethclass characterized by employment in areas such as mills and oil production, rather than by farming, fishing, and trapping in the swamps and bayous.

A SHIFT IN THE PERCEPTION OF ETHNICITY

This shift has been accompanied by a profound change in Cajuns' perception of their heritage. However, the perception of ethnicity and the socioeconomic basis of ethnicity appear to move in opposite directions. First, as Cajuns become more integrated in an industrial economy, the perception of identity is increasingly oriented toward the past, particularly the Acadian origin. Second, the French language remains a major factor in the definition of Cajun ethnicity despite its declining use. Third, the maintenance of Cajuns in a relatively disadvantaged socioeconomic position—and especially French-speaking Cajuns, the most disadvantaged group among whites—has been paralleled by a renewed sense of ethnic pride.

Although the connection between Acadian ancestors and contemporary Cajunness may now seem obvious, this was not the case in the distant and even recent past. As we saw in previous chapters, historical origin was never the predominant domain in earlier representations of Cajuns. If most Cajuns now consider ancestry to be pivotal to their identity, it was mentioned by less than a third of respondents to a study on "What is a Cajun" in 1977–78 and by half of them in 1981. However, over the last few decades, the use by businesses of ethnic identity markers based on *Acadia* has dramatically increased; the argument over the coining of a proper French-language label for Cajuns revolved around the emphasis on Acadian heritage. Furthermore, the team of researchers who conducted the latest study in 1995 also concluded that the image of the true Cajun tended to fit the personal characteristics of the respondents, that is a Cajun fluent in French viewed language as important, whereas non-French speakers emphasized nonlinguistic dimensions such as lifestyle or place of residence. Accordingly, as the number of speakers of French continues to decline, and Acadian ancestry is revalued, its centrality in the definition of Cajunness will be reinforced.[8] Indeed the data of other researchers, as well as our own, document the increased claims of Cajunness among the younger generations: 26% of all those under 30 years of age identify themselves as Cajuns compared with 21% of those 50 and over. Since fewer younger people speak French, this means that paradoxically, those who speak little or no Cajun French are more likely to claim Cajun ethnicity than those who speak it well.

The practical difficulties of tracing genealogies do not seem to hinder identification with Acadia. A manipulation of the genealogical information can help solve problems of identification. Our informants suggest two ways by which it can be accomplished: making an unsupported claim of Acadian ancestry and situating one's ancestry in the larger frame of "French" ancestry:

> It's difficult to come up with a definition of the Acadians naturally because we are all mixed up with the Anglo-Americans; but if somebody wants to research his ancestry, it's easy. He has to say that his ancestors were among the Acadians who settled here and he is an Acadian.
>
> A Louisiana Cajun though doesn't necessarily have to have ancestry in Acadia but it has become more, like, French descent.[9]

Acadia is increasingly viewed as the ancestral land, the point of origin, the source of Cajunism, whether the connections of today's Cajuns with it are real or mythical in a Weberian sense. The renewed interest in Acadian history has been more than symbolic, and it goes beyond a mere sentimental attachment to a glorified past, a typical and well-described trend among third-generation white ethnics. During the 1930s, the pilgrimages and publications of the populist Cajun politician Dudley Leblanc emphasized the Acadian heritage. Acadia was noticeably absent from the initial endeavors of the French-language movement in Louisiana, but a shift took place in the 1990s. Relations with governments and associations of the Acadian provinces were strengthened. Cultural programs began to organize the exchange of teachers and students, and Louisiana Cajuns joined an emotional worldwide gathering of Acadians in 1994. In addition, numerous Cajuns embarked on quests to search for their Acadian roots. Many have been helped by the publication of exhaustive records of Acadian migrations and assorted genealogical guides. Travel agencies and Francophone associations have also facilitated their enterprise by organizing tours of Acadia under the theme "Back to Our Roots." An Acadian Center opened its doors in downtown Saint Martinville in 1998; it houses an exhibit of the exile, a commemorative wall with the names of the deportees, and a computerized database allowing people to trace their genealogy.

In addition to Acadian ancestry, French-language use continues to be a major aspect of ethnic self-identification, despite the language's rapid decline. Qualitative analysis sheds some light on this point. In interviews, Cajuns showed a strong confidence in the resilience of French because it is part of the Acadian heritage:

> I don't think that the French language is facing much of a threat because it has survived all this time.
>
> We are not too pessimistic about our culture because I don't think a lot of the good traits of the culture are going to be forgotten; I don't think our cuisine, our music are going to be forgotten. Somebody must be seeing something good in this culture.
>
> We have a lot of young people who know how to play the guitar, the fiddle. They like Cajun music and I think the music is gonna help us keep our French language and everything else. As long as we have the music, young people will be interested in it, French will not be lost for me.

These comments express a fatalistic and holistic view of Cajun culture in which the language is but one element. Knowledge and use of French are not viewed as being isolated but rather integrated into a traditional culture. The language is not viewed in dualist terms (those who speak French are Cajuns, those who don't are not). Instead, any part of the French-language heritage can be sufficient for Cajun self-definition. Cajun ethnicity can be based on the past significance of French, the occasional use of French words or phrases, French lyrics in songs, or the existence of French-speakers in someone's family. The linguistic criterion is thus removed from its objective basis, that is whether people actually know or speak the language. This conceptualization of ethnic identity allows the language to remain at the center of Cajun self-identification despite our observations of its declining use.

Finally, the changing socioeconomic position of Cajuns affects perceptions of ethnicity. There are two separate issues, class consciousness and stigma/pride. It may be fruitful to consider ethnicity in the light of the Marxist concept of social class. Just as Marx saw class consciousness as the subjective manifestation of an objective class position, we may see ethnic consciousness as a manifestation of a socioeconomic position. Even within the ethnic group, we can see variations in ethnic self-perception depending on class. Historians have described the social stratification process that took place within nineteenth-century Acadian society. Building on this analysis, Dormon proposed "a crude taxonomy" of five groups with different senses of Cajun ethnicity: the CODOFIL elite, genteel Acadians, plain Cajuns, young activists, and the "coonass." Without clearly defining the class situation of these groups, he suggested that genteel Acadians constitute a bourgeois elite, whereas the coonass is mostly a "young working class males" phenomenon.[10] Cajun activists have in fact criticized the elitist bend of the initial endeavors of the state-sponsored French revitalization movement of the early 1970s; both the social status and cultural objectives of CODOFIL's personnel were described as being out of touch with the real, genuine Cajun grass roots.[11] This position, however, did not evolve into a class-based view of Cajun ethnicity. Dormon concluded that the various factions "share some sense of ethnic distinctiveness and identity . . . , a broadly 'Acadian' ethnic tradition."

We do not want to suggest that a rejuvenated Cajun ethnic consciousness emerged solely as the direct reflection of changes—both internal and in relation to the Louisiana economy—in Cajuns' social class position. Shared interests or disadvantages alone do not create a sense of identity. Cajuns do not define themselves as Cajuns just because they tend to share a common socioeconomic niche after having moved from traditional to industrial occupations. These comments by Cajun informants reflect the apparent weakness of class consciousness among Cajuns:

> We have the same needs all Louisianians have; we're not really struggling for rights for Acadians, so we don't rally together for any cause. . . . We are individuals and we don't need to band together to achieve anything. We have what we want as individuals in the society. There was no threat, there was no need to band together. Maybe it's to our advantage that there isn't a hard-core push, that we are more open, and not assimilated, instead of becoming a militant band-together group that's always charging for something.[12]

The evidence clearly shows that the Acadian reference provides for individual identification and group unity. How can it be then the source for both the positive subjective manifestation and a relatively disadvantaged socioeconomic situation? We propose that the answer is to be found in the manipulation of the stigma traditionally attached to the Acadian origin and reversed to become a source of pride. Social changes are often accompanied by identity crises and attempts to reconstruct value systems. In E.P. Thompson's 1963 classic description of the development of English working-class culture, for example, the crisis of rapid change stimulated working people to draw on national and religious mythology to build a collective identity. It has been argued that Laotian Buddhists in the United States have employed an idealized cultural heritage to develop a group self-image that enables them to adjust to greatly altered circumstances.[13] Similarly we suggest that the shifting structural base of longtime inhabitants of Southwestern Louisiana has stimulated new questions about group identity. Idealized histories and cultural traits enable them to transform membership in a relatively disadvantaged group into a celebration of ethnic unity.

A telling episode provides an adequate example of the process hypothesized. In 1988, a Cajun legislator introduced a bill in the Louisiana legislature that would have granted Acadians a minority status with subsequent economic advantages through set-aside programs. Said the author, "Last year we passed a law to define minorities and in this law they put Blacks, Hispanics, Indians and Eskimos. When I read this I said: 'Why not the Acadians?' "

The endeavor generated two types of reactions. First it was viewed by Cajuns as unnecessary because, as one informant put it, "Cajuns do not feel economically disadvantaged. Culturally yes but not economically." On the issue of discrimination, only one case has been brought to court by a Cajun employee in the past twenty years. The author of the bill acknowledged this fact but the rationale for his action was different; it involved reparation for past discrimination:

> I don't know that the Acadians have been discriminated against in recent years for employment. I think in the past they have. They were because of the fact that they spoke French, they were made to feel inferior because many of them were uneducated, and because they didn't have the opportunities. We were in a rural environment.

Another reaction dealt with the stigma long associated with Cajunism. The attempted ascription of a "minority" status was viewed as stigmatizing. It was raising an issue that Cajuns thought had been successfully resolved by the movement of the 1970s. "So I think I've paid my dues now that we're the in crowd I'm thoroughly enjoying it" wrote one "pure Cajun."[14]

Comments by two Cajun activists in 1988 are indicative of the evolution from ethnic shame to ethnic pride:

When I went to school in the '40s and to USL [Univeristy of Southwesten Louisiana] in the '50s, it was the first time I left home. I didn't talk to anybody. I was scared to talk to anybody for a whole week, you know. How did we feel about ourselves then? Did we really take a lot of stock in being an Acadian or a Cajun?

I think we fared very well having come to the United States. I think that we—and when I say "we" I mean all of our ancestors—we were very tough, determined survivors. But it paid off in a way and we then became Americans. We now have Acadian culture and Cajun cuisine and Cajun music, but we are Americans and we have all the privileges and nonstigma of being part of the United States instead of the little isolated pockets. We were isolated for a long time and became slowly assimilated; but I think in a way that gave us pride or security in our mind. But I am what I am—like it or not—I'm not going to apologize for it or explain it.

The positive ascription of the Acadian label gained from the ethnic revival of the 1970s has allowed it to be used as a basis for self- and group definition. Socioeconomic and cultural changes have, however, led to a transfer in the objective basis for such an identification. From the nineteenth century through the 1930s, Cajunism was based on a cultural content and a socioeconomic position. Contemporary Cajun ethnicity continues to be supported by an objective socioeconomic basis, but this basis has changed since the early twentieth century. The cultural content of Cajun ethnicity (ability to speak French, rural folkways) has decreased greatly, but it has been replaced by a subjective sense of cultural continuity, a feeling of connection to the past. The resilience of Cajun ethnicity, then, has many characteristics of symbolic ethnicity. There are, however, traits that suggest that today's Cajunism consists of more than the consumption of symbols or nostalgia for a vanishing past.

The evidence that we have presented above suggests that there is a socioeconomic base to Cajun ethnicity; it indicates that a shift occurred from traditional occupations in farming, fishing, and trapping to places such as textile mills and oil wells. However, the redefinition of Cajun ethnicity did not seem to reflect this structural evolution. On the contrary, the qualitative data could be interpreted to show that Cajun ethnicity moved closer to the Acadian past and away from an objective footing in social reality. The move is not akin to the nostalgic celebration of a lost history or the symbolic consumption of ethnic cultural goods; it can be seen as the subjective manifestation of the objective changes in social structure made possible by the transformation of a disadvantaged status to ethnic pride. This transformation is made possible by drawing on an idealized ethnic heritage to interpret a shifting socioeconomic situation. Thus, ethnic symbols provide collective self-images for those, such as the youngest Cajuns, living in changing social and economic situations that create questions about who they are. To find the answers, they reevaluate significant symbolic systems such as the French language and selectively interpret a stock of images from the past. Today's Cajuns are not the passive recipients of such a cultural capital. As we will see in the next two chapters, traditional behaviors and ideas about the past are adapted to the ways that people live in the present. This process is part of what we have termed the new economy of ethnicity marked by the differential effect on a modernizing economy on a group and the commodiication of its identity.

NOTES

1. Indeed, publication of data from the American Community Survey in 2001 emphasized the role of the "example effect" discussed by Levin & Lapham (Michael J. Levin & Susan J. Lapham, "Ancestry Reporting in the 1990 Census: Towards the 2000 Census" (paper presented at the Annual Meetings of the Population Association of America, Cincinnati, OH, April 3–5, 1993). Testing a new selective sampling method, the census Bureau reported that there were 42,000 claims of Cajun ancestry in Louisiana in 2000, roughly 10% of the total reported ten years earlier. Although the extent of Cajun ancestry may not have changed so drastically, the omission of the term "Cajun" in the question is probably a factor in the estimated decline.

2. Richard Alba, *Ethnic Identity: The Transformation of White America.* (New Haven: Yale University Press, 1990), 45; Mary Waters, *Ethnic Options: Choosing Identities in America* (Berkeley: University of California Press, 1990), 42–43.

3. Authors' interview, June 1985; Sylvie Dubois & Megan Mélançon, "Cajun Is Dead: Long Live Cajun. Shifting from a Linguistic to a Cultural Community," *Journal of Sociolinguistics* 1(1) (1996):63–93

4. To present these statistics in a manner that will be approachable to general readers, we use the measures of likelihood (the logistic regression coefficients) to calculate percentage differences and concentrate on discussing the percentage differences. This enables us to say not only whether speaking French or working in the oil industry makes it more likely that a Louisianian will claim Cajun ethnicity, but how much these characteristics increase the likelihood of making this claim.

5. Alba, *Ethnic Identity*, 11, 96–7; Calvin Veltman & Benoît Lacroix, *L'avenir du français aux Etats-Unis* (Québec: Editeur officiel du Québec, 1987), 51–53.

6. Larouche 1981; Trépanier 1991; Dubois & Melançon, "Cajun Is Dead: Long Live Cajun."

7. Interview by Melissa Hoffman, spring 1998.

8. See Alain Larouche, "Les Cadjins du Canal Yankee," in Dean Louder & Eric Waddell (eds.), *Du continent perdu à l'archipel retrouvé: le Québec et l'Amérique Française*, Québec: Les Presses de l'Université Laval, 1981), 235–258; Cécyle Trépanier, "La Louisiane française au seuil du XXème siècle: La commercialisation de la culture," in G. Bouchard (ed.) *La construction d'une culture, le Québec et l'Amérique française* (Sainte Foy: Presses de l'université Laval, 1991), 361–394; Dubois & Melançon, "Cajun Is Dead: Long Live Cajun." It should be noted that because of differences in the size of samples (120 for Larouche, 1,440 for Dubois & Melançon), composition of the samples, and interview format and categorization, the comparability of these data is limited. Their comparison is then meant to be anecdotal.

9. Authors' interviews, June 1985, June 1988.
10. James Dormon, "Louisiana's Cajuns: A Case Study in Ethnic Group Revitalization," *Social Science Quarterly* 65 (1984): 1043–1057, 1054–1055.
11. Barry J. Ancelet, "A Perspective on Teaching the 'Problem Language' in Louisiana," *French Review* 61(3) (1988): 345–356; Randall P. Whatley & Harry Jannise, *Conversational Cajun French 1* (Baton Rouge, LA: Chicot Press, 1978).
12. Authors' interview, June 1985.
13. Carl L. Bankston III, "Bayou Lotus: Theravada Buddhism in Southwestern Louisiana," *Sociological Spectrum* 17 (4) (1997): 453–472.
14. "Cajun Happy with Status," *Lafayette Daily Advertiser*, June 1, 1988.

CHAPTER 6

The Interrupted Transmission of Cajun French

The map of French-speaking Louisiana (Figure I.2) and the map showing the location of people claiming Acadian descent (Figure I.1) we presented in the introduction are very similar. They show that the regions of the state in which French is widely spoken are the regions containing large percentages of people claiming a Cajun ancestry. Using the same scale for language ability and ethnicity (less than 5%, between 5% and 30%, and more than 30%), both maps show that the limits of non-Acadian and non-French Louisiana coincide, and that the Acadian fringe and French-speaking fringe also largely overlap. Clearly, there is a strong and positive association between the percentage of individuals in each parish (county) claiming Cajun ancestry and the percentage of individuals in each parish who report speaking French. In fact we can predict with 84% accuracy the percentage of French-speakers with the percentage of Cajuns in parishes.[1]

The coincidence is not absolute. First, the size of the French-speaking core is much smaller than that of the Acadian core; it is clearly located within it but provides a vivid illustration of the imperfect fit between Cajun ethnicity and French language in the heart of Acadian country. It displays what statistics measure—that more people claim Cajun ancestry than speak French. In addition, it is clear that Cajuns are not the only Louisianians who speak French; in a few parishes (Avoyelles, Saint Martin), the reverse trend is observed: there are more French speakers than there are people of Cajun ancestry. Further, as we have documented, the social circumstances of those claiming Acadian ancestry only and those who speak French differ significantly. Clearly, then, the transmission of Acadian descent (or the belief in Acadian descent) and the passing on of French language abilities take place in different manners and at different speeds. This suggests that we should look at the question of language transmission, rather than of language use. To examine the relationship between French language transmission and Cajun ethnicity, we need to ask under what conditions French-speaking households, in the Acadian parts of the state or elsewhere, pass on their language to minor children.

THE CONTEXT OF FRENCH IN LOUISIANA

A key element of Louisiana's cultural history, the conditions of the existence and transmission of French have long been and continue to be problematic. Moreover, the native language of the Acadians and their Cajun descendants faces an uncertain future. Although it continues to be fairly widely used throughout the region, it is apparently in rapid decline. The dispassionate observer of Louisiana's history and current situation might respond to these observations by shrugging and asking, So what's new? In Louisiana history, the Cajun language has often looked like an enduring problem in search of a fleeing solution. A French aristocrat traveling in Colonial Louisiana observed that the Acadians "spoke a more or less corrupted French." From his perspective, of course, this was also true of the versions of French spoken by Creoles, Francophone German and Spanish descendants, and other settlers, not to mention peasants in the various regions of France. Midway through the nineteenth century, the historical record contains abundant references to the "mixture of French and English" spoken by the Acadians. Their "patois" or "dialect" was widely described as puzzling and barely comprehensible, a characterization that endures to this day.[2] By the beginning of the twentieth century, the French spoken by the Acadians was largely viewed by English-speakers as an unfortunate attachment to a primitive past. French-speakers in the Acadian and white Creole bourgeoisie agreed with this judgment. Unlike the English-speakers, though, the Francophone bourgeois did not blame the supposed "backwardness" of the Cajuns on the use of the French language itself. Instead, they simultaneously lamented the persistent archaisms of Cajun speech and accused the Louisiana peasants of bastardizing the noble Gallic tongue with Anglo-Saxon innovations.[3]

The status and role of French in public life was a continual point of contention from the moment Louisiana became an American state in 1814. The abrupt inclusion of the Louisiana territory in the United States immediately posed the problem of the coexistence of two languages, and of the cultures and worldviews they expressed. Predictably, the place of French in law, education, business, and politics became increasingly jeopardized. Louisiana's constitutional history provides a revealing example of official ambivalence toward French. The constitutions of 1812, 1864, 1868, 1913, and 1921 make no provisions for French and even explicitly assert the primacy of English; those of 1845, 1852, 1861, 1879, and 1898 grant French some official status along with English. This ambiguity still survived late in the twentieth century. When Louisiana legislators drafted the state's constitution in the early 1970s to replace the outdated 1921 charter, Cajun activists entertained high hopes that the final text would grant French a solid legal basis. A bilingual Cajun, the colorful Edwin Edwards, had just been elected governor, Louisiana was in the midst of an energetic French renaissance movement, and the recognition of racial and ethnic diversity was high on the national agenda. Despite numerous displays of sympathetic ethnic awareness and intense lobbying by Cajun activists, the status of French language was not upgraded or even mentioned by name; only "the right of the people to preserve, develop, and promote its historical, linguistic, and cultural origins" was guaranteed.[4]

Ambivalence has also characterized the past and present situation of Louisiana French in other official areas. Throughout the nineteenth century, laws were written primarily in English. Nevertheless, unabrogated dispositions of the Civil Code ensured that contracts written in French were legal and valid; thus deeds, commercial settlements and testaments continued to be drafted in French by French-speaking notaries. Until the 1930s, elected officials in the Acadian region drafted or upheld English-language laws, but they had to be able to converse in French to be elected or to go about their business with any efficiency.

The fate of French in education and in the press, indeed in writing, was sealed by the 1920s. French had been the language of the first school established in Louisiana, in 1723, by the Capucine monks, and for long had remained with Spanish the only language of education. In 1811, the first French language college, the *collège d'Orléans*, was founded, ironically, under the American regime. But French education never thrived despite these auspicious beginnings. Faced with limited state funding, ferocious competition from English-language educators, disinterest and then wariness from Acadian families, French barely made the curriculum as a foreign language for a few members of the elite. So when a directive from the superintendent of education in 1921 forbade the use of French on the school grounds, it clearly signaled that French was no longer acceptable in education under any guise, even if it was the native and only tongue of many Cajun students. No longer a language of teaching, French was not even tolerated in most educational settings.

Two years after the superintendent's directive, the only remaining French-language newspaper, *L'Abeille* of New Orleans, folded, marking the temporary end of French-language media. Until the 1850s, most urban areas in Southwestern Louisiana had been served by a newspaper published wholly or partially in French. Between 1820 and 1830, New Orleans counted no fewer than six bilingual dailies. Weakened by fierce competition and poor editorial quality, ignored by English-speaking businesses reluctant to advertise their wares to an increasingly insular Creole French pseudo-aristocracy, and irrevocably confronted with a shrinking readership, the French press withered and disappeared.

Once the prestigious and official language of the ruling class, French, now spoken mostly by Cajuns, had become the stigmatized idiom of the hinterland. After decades of ridicule, communication problems, and missed opportunities, Cajuns had received the message that all corners of society had been sending them: no more French. Inheriting a language deprived of constitutional protection, locked out of school grounds, no longer in print, and of limited value in the business world, Cajuns started not only to speak English but also to discard French. Anecdotal but convincing evidence shows that the process happened quite rapidly.[5] Over three generations, roughly between 1900 and 1960, a drastic linguistic shift had taken place. By the thousands, elderly Cajuns recount stories of French-speaking children attending English-language schools and learning the hard way about the pains and virtues of bilingualism. Cajuns who grew up in the second half of the century reminisce about their parents' care in limiting the use of French around the house; "my parents spoke French when they didn't want us kids to understand; so I picked it up a little but I could never speak it fluently" is a generic statement repeated like a mantra in Southwestern Louisiana. Suzie Quebodeaux, whom we quoted earlier on Cajun family life, illustrated the casual nature of French transmission in Cajun families:

> I learned it [French] by myself. Nobody taught me. I just picked it up listening to the family, grandma on my daddy side. . . . Mom speak more French than Dad. He died young, 30-something. Alice *savait pas du tout*. Eugene my brother just like that. The Toce spoke French but the Evans are English, call that Irish. . . . My girls don't speak French. My sisters don't speak French. They didn't want to learn or they didn't want to pay no attention to French. I was the oldest. . . . My mother she could speak both. I just listened and just went to my grandma. You know you love your grandmother, that's the way it goes. Mama, she did speak French but English too. She never finished school, she never went to school but she was not dumb. Nobody could fool that lady. [I spoke French] with my grandmother, my mother and my daddy and nobody else. When I worked at the drugstore, I had to go speak at the prescription room because they don't know how to speak French. I was the interpreter. They call me: "Miss Suzie, come see, I don't understand!"[6]

As the passively bilingual generation of the midcentury gave birth to another, increasingly limited French abilities and reliance on English sealed the process. A linguistic divide had split Cajuns families, often leaving monolingual grandparents and grandchildren barely able to communicate with one another. Even among members of the older generation, language abilities and language use frequently complicated relations. Breaux Bridge resident

Sallie Prejean observed of her father's language use: "*On croyait pas que Pa parlait en anglais du tout parce que quand on allait fallait nous aut' parle avec lui en français chaque fois.*" (We didn't think Dad could speak English because when we'd visit we had to speak English with him.) Hearing this, her mother interjected, "*J'connais il y a des fois où j'l'ai entendu parlé en anglais. Toi, il savait que tu pouvais parler en français. Peut être il craignait que Robert aurait pas compris.*" (I know sometimes I heard him speak English. He knew you could speak French. Maybe he was afraid that Robert would not understand.)[7]

Spoken by the majority of Louisianians until the 1850s, the use of Louisiana French declined steadily over the course of the twentieth century. The concentration of speakers among rural Cajuns, the inferior status of French relative to English, and the lack of French education all contributed to this decrease and lessened the passing of the language from generation to generation. It is, however, remarkable that faced with such adverse conditions in homes and schools for decades French still did not disappear. Weakened and marginalized, French survived among the Cajuns. Census figures accurately document both the decline and resilience. In 1940, 298,420 whites or 19.7% of the white population claimed French as their mother tongue; in 1970, 487,626, or 19.1% of the same population laid claim to French. Population growth and different statistical methods explain the increase in number and stability in ratio. In the later census, people were asked what language was spoken in their parents' homes when they were young, not what language they spoke themselves. People who answered "French" in 1970 were much less likely to be fluent French-speakers than their parents, who had been recorded as native speakers of French thirty years earlier. We have seen that figures from 1980 and 1990, after the wording of the census changed to reflect actual language use, documented a steep decline to a level of about 260,000 French-speakers or 6.7% of the population.[8]

Interestingly, this downward trend continued despite a large-scale effort to revitalize Louisiana French in the 1970s. Launched by a coalition of individuals concerned about the possible extinction of French in the state, the enterprise centered around the teaching of French as a foreign language in elementary schools statewide. Well aware of the problems of language transmission through families, the movement's leaders opted to save French through the schools. Formal education became the focal point for hopes of reviving and retaining Louisiana French. We will present later in this chapter the circumstances and issues that surrounded this ambitious endeavor, but its outcome after thirty years is unambiguous: the French education program has, apparently, been a pedagogical failure.[9] No assessments of linguistic abilities or language acquisition by students were ever systematically conducted on a large scale, so hard evidence does not exist. However, the limited but consistent evidence that we have does not present an optimistic picture of school-taught French. Pedagogical assessments by outside specialists, French teachers, and off-the-cuff remarks by the movement's leaders largely concur. By all accounts, of the tens of thousands of students who have been exposed to French classes over the past thirty years, very few have achieved fluency or even developed interest in the language.

Data gathered by CODOFIL in 1988 on enrollment in French classes between 1968 and 1987 in eleven Louisiana colleges show ambiguous results. Although some universities reported large increases, others reported large declines or little change. Complete figures for all eleven institutions show an increase from 6,617 undergraduates in 1983 to 7,330 in 1987, an 11% increase. However, growing student enrollments, year-to-year variations, and changes in college policy such as adding or dropping foreign language requirements render any interpretation rather risky. Ultimately, no increase in the number of young French-speakers has been noted, and overall the number of French speakers continues to decline. Notwithstanding the derived benefits of French educational programs, they do not appear to have succeeded in creating a new generation of French-speakers, as the French revival movement had hoped. Schools have not taken up the role of families in language transmission.

ETHNICITY AND LANGUAGE TRANSMISSION

The failure of schools to spread French in Louisiana highlights the continued importance of family in language transmission. We turn now to a closer examination of the role of relatives in this endeavor. In our discussion, we try to avoid moralizing and emotional involvements with questions of language. Whether a Cajun should remain attached to an ancestral heritage, defend a subjugated idiom, jettison an economic encumbrance, be a proud polyglot, or cleanse a shameful stigma are questions that we cannot claim to answer. Instead, we try to offer a dispassionate view of the paradoxical role of the modern Cajun family in passing on Cajun French.

Most studies that deal with the relationship between ethnicity and language transmission tend to make one of three assumptions. Either they assume, as sociolinguist Joshua Fishman does, that this relationship is a positive one, since language is a central symbol of ethnic identity, or they assume, as Richard Alba does, that the relationship is positive but weakening as ethnicity is progressively detached from objective cultural traits.[10] The third possibility revolves around an assimilationist argument: if an ethnicity is linked to material disadvantages, then group members may be discouraged from passing on characteristic traits, such as a language. The more closely connected individuals are to a disadvantaged group, the more disadvantageous the traits may be. Ironically, then, the "more ethnic" the parents, the less likely they may be to pass their language on to their children. This appears to describe the way Louisiana Cajun ethnicity is related to French language transmission.

For this investigation of the relationship between Cajun ethnicity and language transmission, we rely, as we have throughout this book, on a combination of quantitative and qualitative approaches. We once again use data from the 1990 U.S. census to look at the association between French language use of Louisiana minors and selected predictors in households with at least one French-speaking parent.[11] This should enable us to identify some of the conditions under which Francophone parents do or do not transmit the language to children. Then we employ qualitative data from historical information, interviews, and observations to provide depth of insight into the social conditions underlying and surrounding the particular type of association between Cajun ethnicity and French language transmission.

ETHNICITY AND LANGUAGE TRANSMISSION: EVIDENCE OF CENSUS DATA

We gathered data on selected characteristics that may be related to language transmission. For minors we retained sex, age, school attendance, and use of French; for households containing minors, we retained family size, one- or two-parent family, nonmetropolitan residence, median household income, one or both parents claiming Cajun ancestry, and one or both parents speaking French; and for heads of these households, we retained age, fluency in English, occupation, and educational level. We computed percentages in the three areas of Louisiana that we have identified (the non-Acadian region, the Acadian fringe, and the Acadian core) for all households containing minor children and for those in which at least one parent speaks French (see Table 6.1). The comparison of these figures rests on the assumption that children are more likely to learn French if they have at least one French-speaking parent and if they live in a heavily Cajun area where there are more Francophone households.

The descriptive data suggests that there are some interesting differences and similarities between families with French-speakers in the non-Cajun, heavily Anglophone regions of Louisiana and French-speakers in the Cajun, traditionally Francophone region. It is not surprising that Louisianians below the age of 21 are most likely to speak French in the Acadian core, where 7.3% have this language ability. This is a small percentage, but it is still three times greater than the percentage of French-speakers in the fringe and six times greater than the percentage in the rest of the state. Among households with a French-speaking parent, however, minors in all three regions show about the same probability of speaking French: the parental language is transmitted in about 17% to 18% of the cases. In the core area, in fact, the percentage of French-speaking minors is actually slightly less than in the fringe. This is extremely interesting because those in the core are not only much more likely to come into contact with French-speakers outside the home, but also more likely than those in the other regions to live in a

Table 6.1
Selected Characteristics of Minors, Household Heads, and Households in non-Acadian, Acadian Fringe, and Acadian Core Areas of Louisiana for All Families and for Families with At Least One French-Speaking Parent, 1990

	Non-Acadian	Fringe	Core
Characteristics of minors			
% speak French (all)	1.2	2.7	7.3
(French speaking parent)	*17.3*	*18.8*	*17.5*
Average Age (all)	12.0	12.0	12.0
(French speaking parent)	*12.5*	*12.3*	*12.8*
% female (all)	48.3	47.8	48.4
(French speaking parent)	*44.8*	*45.8*	*48.0*
% black (all)	44.6	38.1	28.2
(French speaking parent)	*33.8*	*13.0*	*19.4*
% in school (all)	70.4	72.3	74.3
(French speaking parent)	*67.6*	*65.1*	*67.3*
Characteristics of HH head			
Average Age (all)	41.1	40.7	40.4
(French speaking parent)	*44.5*	*42.0*	*43.0*
% fluent in English (all)	98.1	97.4	92.8
(French speaking parent)	*82.9*	*79.5*	*80.3*
Occupational level			
% prof-managerial (all)	21.5	20.7	17.9
(French speaking parent)	*27.8*	*16.7*	*13.3*
% tech-precis. craft (all)	19.6	24.6	26.8
(French speaking parent)	*23.0*	*28.4*	*29.6*
% sales-service (all)	37.0	32.2	28.5
(French speaking parent)	*26.9*	*26.0*	*26.2*
% agri-operator-laborer (all)	21.8	22.5	26.8
(French speaking parent)	*22.3*	*28.9*	*30.9*
Educational level			
% high school (all)	34.3	33.1	39.6
(French speaking parent)	*29.1*	*41.3*	*50.0*
% high school (all)	50.3	53.1	49.0
(French speaking parent)	*49.1*	*48.6*	*43.9*
% college (all)	15.4	13.8	11.0
(French speaking parent)	*21.8*	*10.0*	*6.1*

household with two French-speaking parents, rather than only one. From the outset, then, the data seem to pose a curious question: Why can't more young people in French-speaking homes in the French language center of Louisiana speak French?

The answer to that question does not seem to come from the other characteristics of minors we recorded, which do not show other significant re-

Table 6.1 (continued)

	Non-Acadian	Fringe	Core
Characteristics of family/household			
% single female head (all)	36.1	29.3	25.0
(French speaking parent)	*23.4*	*19.7*	*18.3*
% single male head	5.6	5.4	5.0
(French speaking parent)	*2.0*	*4.8*	*4.6*
Average family size	4.4	4.5	4.5
(French speaking parent)	*4.5*	*4.3*	*4.5*
$ Median HH income (all)	32,030	33,344	30,807
(French speaking parent)	*38,802*	*34,294*	*29,394*
% Ling. isolated (all)	0.6	0.5	1.4
(French speaking parent)	*2.9*	*2.1*	*3.1*
% one parent speaks French (all)	1.4	6.1	32.1
% both parents spk French (all)	0.2	1.4	12.6
(French speaking parent)	*12.4*	*23.8*	*39.4*
% one parent Cajun (all)	1.6	5.2	13.8
(French speaking parent)	*11.4*	*14.9*	*17.6*
% two parents Cajun (all)	0.3	3.2	17.9
(French speaking parent)	*3.9*	*15.2*	*30.9*
% non-metropolitan (all)	16.9	8.3	13.8
(French speaking parent)	*11.2*	*16.4*	*20.0*
Total Percent (all)	46.5	29.6	23.8
(French speaking parent)	*7.4*	*17.7*	*74.9*
N (all)	30,317	19,326	15,538
(French speaking parent)	*491*	*1,178*	*4,982*

Source: U.S. Bureau of the Census, *Census of Population and Housing, 1990. Public Micro Use Data Samples (5 %)* [Machine readable data files] (Washington, DC: Bureau of the Census, 1992).

gional differences; wherever they live and whether they have a French-speaking parent or not, their average age is 12, there are slightly more boys than girls, and more than two-thirds of them are attending school.[12] However, the characteristics of households and household heads are revealing. Outside of Acadiana, having at least one parent who speaks French tends to be associated with a relatively high parental educational and occupational level, a comparatively high household income, a greater likelihood to live in an urban area, and only one parent claiming Cajun ancestry. Within the Acadian region, though, having a French-speaking parent in the household is associated with comparatively low socioeconomic status, less education, lower income, a more rural residence, and a greater probability of having both parents claiming Cajun ancestry and speaking French. From that linguistic perspective, the same family situation, having one French-speaking parent, is associated with significantly diverging lifestyles. Before we analyze the factors at play, let us detail some of the most striking differences between French-speaking families in the Acadian region and the rest of the state. The percentages on occupational distribution provide revealing information. The closer one moves to the Acadian core, the less likely household heads are to be employed in professional or managerial occupations and the more likely they are to be employed as agricultural workers, operators, or laborers. Moreover, this trend is more marked among the French-speakers than among all Louisianians. French-speakers in the Acadian core are 8% more likely to be employed at the bottom of the prestige hierarchy than are French-speakers in the non-Acadian region. Moreover, the modal category in the non-Acadian region is that of professional and managerial occupations, whereas the modal category in the core is the lowest occupational level. Further, household heads in families with a French-speaker outside of the Acadian area are more likely than the general population in this same area to have a professional or managerial job. Household heads in families with a French-speaker in the core are less likely than the core's general population to have a high-status job and more likely to have a low-status job. This strongly suggests that many of those in French-speaking families outside of the Acadian area enjoy high-status positions, whereas inside of the Acadian area, being in a French-speaking family is associated with being in a low-status position.

We see similar trends in the educational backgrounds of household heads. Although the differences among all families in the three regions are relatively minor, those in the core are the most likely not to have finished high school and the least likely to have finished college, and those in the non-Acadian region are the least likely not to have finished high school and the most likely to have finished college. We find this same pattern among those in households with a French-speaker, but the pattern is greatly magnified. Within the non-Acadian area, further, those with an adult French-speaker in the family show higher levels of education than the population in general. Within the Acadian core, this pattern is reversed: household heads in households with a French-speaker have lower educational levels than the region's population as a whole. In education, as well as in occupation, it would appear, first, that residence in a "more Cajun" area is associated with lower socioeconomic status; second, that the socioeconomic disadvantages related to region are greater for households with a French-speaking parent than for all households; and third, that being in a household with a French-speaker is associated with comparatively high socioeconomic status outside the Cajun ethnic region and with comparatively low socioeconomic status inside the Cajun ethnic region.

A similar pattern emerges when we look at household income. Among all households, income differences were small, although those in the core showed the smallest median income. Among households with a French speaker, though, those in the Acadian fringe had a median income more than $4,000 lower than those in the non-Acadian sector, and those in the Acadian core had a median income about $5,000 lower than those in the fringe. Again, we see that, within regions, households with a French-speaker enjoyed an economic advantage in the non-Acadian part of the state and suffered an economic disadvantage in the Acadian core: outside of the Acadian areas, those with French-speakers had a median income $6,800 higher than the general median; in the core, households with French-speakers had a median income $1,400 lower than the general median.

As we saw in our discussion of the Cajun family, linguistic isolation is rare, but it does exist, and it is, of course, greatest in the ethnic core area. Having a French-speaking parent in the household is uncommon outside of the Acadian areas but common in the Acadian core, where almost one-third of the minors are found in households containing a mother or father who can speak French. Households in which both parents speak French are relatively few: even in the core Acadian area only about 13% of households with minor children have two parents who both speak French. Outside of the Acadian region, even the small number of households with one Francophone parent rarely contain a second. Even in the Acadian region, it is more common to have only one French-speaking parent than two, since only 24% of the households in the Acadian fringe with a Francophone parent contain another Francophone and only 39% of the households in the Acadian core with a French-speaker have two Francophone parents.[13]

It appears that use of French by minors is related to the region in which they live and to the socioeconomic characteristics of their parents and household. We must now determine with greater precision what factors are at play. We are looking here only at households in which at least one parent is a French-speaker to determine what characteristics increase or decrease the likelihood that French language use will be passed from one generation to the next. Again, we use logistic regression to examine predictors of French language ability on the part of people aged 5 to 18, which tells us how much more likely or less likely it is, for example, that older children will speak French or that females will speak French (see Table 6.2).[14] Among the characteristics of the minors themselves, only age shows a significant relationship with French-speaking ability. This may be interpreted as meaning either that children are more likely to pick up French as they grow older, or that it is becoming steadily less likely that the language will be transmitted, even within a generation. Since parental languages are usually passed on quite early in childhood, and since French education programs have not been successful in creating speakers, we believe that the second interpretation is the more reasonable of the two.

Among characteristics of household heads, educational level has a signif-

Table 6.2
Predictors of French-Speaking Ability among Minors in Louisiana in Households with at Least One French-Speaking Parent

	Logit Coefficient	Odds Ratio	Percentage Difference
Characteristics of minor			
Age	.050**	1.051	0.73
Sex (female)	.074	1.077	1.10
Race (black)	-.219	.804	-2.96
Enrollment in school	.172	1.188	2.65
Characteristics of household head			
Age	-.017	.983	-0.25
English fluency	-.041	.924	-1.13
Occupational level	.039	1.040	0.57
Educational level	-.045**	.956	-0.65
Characteristics of family/household			
Headed by single female	1.066**	2.905	20.75
Headed by single male	1.066**	2.904	20.74
Family size	.017	1.018	0.26
Household income	-.000	1.000	---
Linguistic isolation	1.538**	4.653	32.31
Both parents speak French	1.101**	3.006	21.56
One parent Cajun	-.096	.911	-1.32
Both parents Cajun	-.270*	.763	-3.61
Geographic Characteristics			
Non-metropolitan area	.172	1.187	2.63
Acadiana area	-.241**	.785	-3.26
N	6,651		

* $p < .05$ ** $p < .01$

icant negative association with language transmission: the better-educated the head of household is, the less likely the children will speak French. With regard to household characteristics, minors in single-parent homes are much more likely to be French-speakers than children in two-parent homes. Once again, we see the ethnic language associated with a relatively disadvantaged socioeconomic status since single-parent families are more likely to be disadvantaged.

It is not surprising that both linguistically isolated households and households in which both parents report that they speak French at home show strong positive associations with language transmission. However, the effect of parental ethnicity appears, at first, counterintuitive. Francophone households in which both parents claim Cajun ethnicity are significantly less likely to transmit French to young people than Francophone households in which neither parent claims Cajun ethnicity. This suggests that even though Cajuns speak French much more than non-Cajuns, French-speaking Cajun parents pass on the language less often than French-speaking non-Cajuns do. The influence of region is also striking. Each of the three regions, from the non-Acadian region to the Acadian core, is associated with a 3% decline in the probability of language transmission. The more Cajun the area, the less likely it is that French speakers will pass the language on to their children. In terms of both parental ethnic identification and geographic ethnic concentration then, Cajun ethnicity is negatively related to French language transmission.

To address this perplexing finding in more detail, we look now at predictors of language transmission within each of the three regions we have identified. Although the analysis shows that some variables, such as family size, age, and education have a limited impact, the effects of parental ethnicity and linguistic abilities clearly appear as the most constant and strongest (see Tables 6.3, 6.4, and 6.5). As for language, statistical analysis and common sense agree: children living in linguistic isolation (that is with no parents speaking English well) and those living with two French-speaking parents are significantly more likely to speak French. However, a paradoxical finding emerges from the analysis of the influence of Cajun ethnicity: coming from a family with one or two Cajun parents and living in an Acadian region are negatively related to French language transmission. In addition, the negative relationship of coming from a family with two Cajun parents with French transmission is clearest in the Acadian core. This negative association is found in the non-Acadian part of Louisiana, where having one parent claiming Cajun ancestry significantly decreases the likelihood that a child will speak French. Those with one Cajun parent are 12 percentage points less likely to speak the language than those in Francophone homes with no Cajun parents.

In the Acadian core, children with at least one Cajun parent are markedly less likely to speak French than children with non-Cajun parents, and children with two Cajun parents are the least likely of all to have French language abilities. In addition, it appears that the negative effect of this parental ethnic ancestry is actually greater in the ethnic core than it is in the ethnic fringe: in the fringe, children with two Cajun parents were just over 2 percentage points less likely to speak French, but in the core, children with two Cajun parents were close to 4 percentage points less likely to speak French.

We can summarize our major findings from the census data as follows.

Table 6.3
Predictors of French-Speaking Ability among Minors in Louisiana Outside of Acadiana in Households with at Least One French-Speaking Parent

	Logit Coefficient	Odds Ratio	Percentage Difference
Characteristics of minor			
Age	.017	1.017	0.23
Sex (female)	.502	1.653	8.38
Race (black)	-.328	.721	-4.20
Enrollment in school	.165	1.179	2.47
Characteristics of household head			
Age	.015	1.015	0.20
English fluency	-.125	.883	-1.72
Occupational level	.116	1.123	1.71
Educational level	-.046	.955	-0.66
Characteristics of family/household			
Headed by single female	.510	1.666	8.53
Headed by single male	.838	2.312	15.28
Family size	.324**	1.383	5.12
Household income	-.000	1.000	---
Linguistic isolation	1.675**	5.337	35.43
Both parents speak French	.580	1.786	9.88
One parent Cajun	-1.269*	.281	-11.75
Both parents Cajun	-6.701	.001	-17.28
Geographic Characteristics			
Non-metropolitan area	.907*	2.477	16.81
N	491		

* $p < .05$ ** $p < .01$

First, although most French speakers are found in the Acadian area, the ability to speak the language has different implications in different places; outside of Acadiana, this ability is associated with high socioeconomic status; inside, it is linked with low socioeconomic status. Second, controlling for parents' language use, living in an ethnic area and coming from an ethnic family apparently lessens the likelihood of receiving the language that is closely connected to the ethnicity. Third, this mechanism appears to be stronger at the core of the Acadian region.

Table 6.4
Predictors of French-Speaking Ability among Minors in the Acadian Fringe in Households with at Least One French-Speaking Parent

	Logit Coefficient	Odds Ratio	Percentage Difference
Characteristics of minor			
Age	.042**	1.043	0.62
Sex (female)	.468*	1.597	8.15
Race (black)	.479	1.615	8.37
Enrollment in school	.403	1.497	6.90
Characteristics of household head			
Age	-.002	.998	-0.07
English fluency	.051	1.053	0.77
Occupational level	.080	1.083	1.21
Educational level	.063	1.065	0.94
Characteristics of family/household			
Headed by single female	1.269**	3.559	26.32
Headed by single male	1.006*	2.735	19.92
Family size	.039	1.040	0.57
Household income	-.000	1.000	---
Linguistic isolation	1.885**	6.586	41.54
Both parents speak French	.919**	2.507	17.87
One parent Cajun	.290	1.336	4.78
Both parents Cajun	-.161	.851	-2.37
Geographic Characteristics			
Non-metropolitan area	.732**	2.078	13.63
N	1,178		

* $p < .05$ ** $p < .01$

Our analysis suggests that there is a curiously negative relationship between ethnicity and language use. To some extent, Cajuns appear to be fitting an assimilationist pattern, one in which members of an ethnic minority and their descendants gradually shed disadvantageous ethnic traits and move out of areas of early settlement. The processes at play in the evolution of Cajun ethnicity do not, however, perfectly fit in an assimilationist explanation. Acadians arrived in Southwestern Louisiana and Cajuns

Table 6.5
Predictors of French-Speaking Ability among Minors in the Acadian Core in Households with at Least One French-Speaking Parent

	Logit Coefficient	Odds Ratio	Percentage Difference
Characteristics of minor			
Age	.063**	1.065	0.71
Sex (female)	-.042	.959	-0.60
Race (black)	-.432**	.649	-5.41
Enrollment in school	.122	1.130	1.83
Characteristics of household head			
Age	-.032**	.969	-0.46
English fluency	.051	1.052	0.74
Occupational level	.021	1.021	0.29
Educational level	-.076**	.927	-1.08
Characteristics of family/household			
Headed by single female	.986**	2.681	18.74
Headed by single male	1.020**	2.772	19.51
Family size	-.031	.969	-0.46
Household income	-.000*	1.000	----
Linguistic isolation	1.493**	4.450	31.04
Both parents speak French	1.149**	3.156	22.59
One parent Cajun	-.145	.865	-2.00
Both parents Cajun	-.287*	.751	-3.56
Geographic Characteristics			
Non-metropolitan area	-.027	.973	-0.40
N	4,982		

* $p < .05$ ** $p < .01$

stayed there. Moreover, if Cajuns were trying to jettison ethnic markers, they would not claim their Cajunness in increasingly visible and powerful ways. The paradox thus remains: why claim ancestry and apparently refuse to transmit its most powerful agent? To address this question, we will now present contemporary qualitative evidence regarding language and Cajun ethnicity.

CAJUN AS A CONTINUING PROBLEMATIC ETHNICITY: CONTEMPORARY QUALITATIVE EVIDENCE

We have seen how from its inception the Cajun label was problematic. In some measure, Cajun ethnicity continues to be problematic; clearly, after three decades of Cajun renaissance, Cajunness is no longer universally viewed by Cajuns and non-Cajuns alike as a shameful condition. The wave of ethnic pride over Southwestern Louisiana has eroded most signs of negative ascription. However, we suggest that some elements of stigma, coexisting with pride, persist in Cajun ethnicity.

Cajun activists point to problematic outcomes of the wave of renewed pride and acceptance. One, as we have seen earlier, is the construction of a new stereotype of Cajuns broadcast in print and films. The stereotype formed in the nineteenth century portrayed the Cajun as the alien brute of the bayou, unaffected by time and progress, wallowing complacently in illiteracy and rural backwardness. The current, popularized version of this stereotype is that of a hedonist whose ancestral instincts require a spicy regimen of dancing, drinking, crawfishing, brawling, and occasional lawbreaking to make the bland modern world of *les Américains* more palatable. If some stereotypical aspects appear to be fitting larger cultural aspirations shared by society at large (valuing of tradition, sense of community, harmony with nature), other ascribed traits such as the consumption of alcohol, caffeine, and fatty food, a relaxed lifestyle, and some ethnic particularism contribute to isolating Cajuns from a perceived and desirable mainstream. The emphasis on joie de vivre (joy of living) has been a powerful tool for the local tourism industry but it has been blamed by some for having not only "undermined the dignity of the people, but also scared off some of the potential new industry that is sorely needed in Louisiana today."[15]

Another contested outcome is the proliferation of Cajun humor. Cajuns have a long tradition of folktales and jokes told in French by raconteurs. This practice is now waning; the discontinuity in the transmission of French has diminished the passing on of oral material, and the Americanization of community and family life has limited the opportunities for telling and listening to tall tales. Cajun humor now mostly refers to humor about Cajuns. They have long been the subject of jokes by outsiders. From the 1920s on, Cajun dialect, alleged simplemindedness, and bizarre ways have been portrayed in comedy acts by, among others, Walter Coquille, the caricaturesque mayor of fictitious Bayou Pom Pom, and Justin Wilson, host of a popular cooking show televised nationwide in the 1970s. Newspaper columns and joke books have also carried the tradition of Boudreaux and Thibodeaux, two fictional characters, simple but wily, struggling in heavily accented English to reconcile their immutable ways with the demands of modernity.[16]

Cajun humor has adapted to the changes brought by increased ethnic awareness. There are claims that the "old brand of Cajun humor . . . is becoming passé" and that a new breed of humorists are now telling clean stories typifying the "happy, open, good-hearted nature of the Cajun people." A cursory examination of recent publications and performances suggests, however, that "the exaggerated Cajun accent, silly-looking costumes [and] punch line that belittled the Cajun people" have not been swept away by political correctness and still garner laughs and sales.[17] Still they are coming under greater scrutiny. Press articles about the death of humorist Justin Wilson in 2001 mentioned the negative reactions generated by his brand of Cajun humor.[18] The tolerance of Cajuns is also tested, as this account by a Mr. Boudreaux illustrates:

> What broke the camel's back was an incident that happened at the Jean Lafitte Prairie Cajun National Historic Park in Eunice. As my family and I walked in, the park ranger was playing Cajun music to locals and tourists. When the music stopped, the ranger asked us to introduce ourselves and asked us where we were from. With the mention of Boudreaux, everyone, led by the ranger, burst out laughing as if the mere name was a national joke. . . . It is time to put this type of "joke" in the trash heap. Cajun humor is boundless; adding jokes about the good surnames of Boudreaux and Thibodeaux makes Cajun humor tasteless.

Another development is also taking place. Jokes are now told by insiders who "are more apt to have their audience laugh with Cajuns than at them." Cajun humor has fully entered the realm of commercialism as a commodity. Books and audio- and videocassettes by humorists claiming a Cajun heritage (Dave Petitjean, Ralph Begnaud, J.J. Reneaux) are prominently displayed on shelves dedicated to the local culture in Louisiana bookstores. Television shows, appearances in comedy clubs, commercials, and at sports and promotional events, as well as joke-telling contests, have increased the visibility of Cajun humor.

Fianlly, the continued use of the derogative term "coonass" in speech and on bumper stickers, promotional items, and souvenirs attests to a continuously stigmatized identity. "Me, I'm a coonass," "We're all coonass around here" are comments frequently heard in Southwestern Louisiana. It is used as a derogative by non-Cajuns, and by Cajuns as "a term of endearment much in the same way that African-Americans haved used the word 'nigger' among themselves to try to disarm that hurtful word." The insiders' use of the ethnic slur, even "disarmed," mixing pride and defensiveness,[19] is a fitting illustration of the continued general ambivalence of insiders and outsiders alike toward Cajun ethnicity.

Nowhere is it more evident than in a persistently stigmatized view of Cajun French language among non-Cajuns and Cajuns. Studies by linguists suggest that Cajun French occupies a position lower than English on a status scale. Condon and Pittman reported in 1992 that their sample of 258 Southwestern Louisiana residents consistently rated standard English higher than Cajun French and Cajun English in terms of general knowledge, reliability, honesty, friendliness, and attractiveness; the contrast was greatest among the 21–39 age group. In a study of linguistic attitudes toward varieties of French, other researchers qualified their finding of a new positive attitude toward Cajun French with several remarks. Whereas Cajun French received the highest support as the best variety for Louisiana (56% of respondents) as an almost-equal to standard French (67%), a significant proportion of the sample (30%) rated Cajun French as an inferior variety of French; also, the authors noted that "the continued credibility of Standard French as the most acceptable language of instruction [and] the perception that Cajun French is a mixture of languages can be problematic" for the maintenance of Cajun French.[20]

Among Cajuns the persistence of a stigmatized view of their variety of French is expressed in two ways. One relates to the perceived inferiority of Cajun French to French "from France": for many, Cajun French is "bad French." Daily informal contacts between a French-born co-author and Cajuns quasi-systematically elicit self-deprecating statements on Louisiana French; "You speak good French, I speak broken French" is a typical comment frequently volunteered. "I can speak real French but I am chagrined because she wants me to speak Cajun," said an elderly Cajun woman from Iberia Parish, recalling a previous interview.

Also, some French-speaking Cajuns continue to reluctantly acknowledge their bilingualism to outsiders. CODOFIL officials had argued that the sharp decrease in the number of French-speakers noted between 1970 and 1980 was in part caused by the concealment by Cajuns of their French-speaking abilities. Indeed in the course of fieldwork in the 1980s, we met and dealt with many people whose bilingual abilities could mostly be identified through nonlinguistic communication. In stores and in crowds, people would volunteer information in English after hearing a request made in French; others would turn their heads and listen in on a French conversation between two strangers. One of the authors worked in English with a Cajun professional in his 40s over a period of several months before he revealed a significant mastery of French. Similar reactions have recently been noted by other researchers and among Acadiana Creoles.[21] Elderly and middle-aged Cajuns typically offer a continued fear of ridicule and reprisal as reasons for such a behavior. "We were beaten in school if we were caught speaking French" is a leitmotiv likely to appear in any discussion of French in Louisiana. Punishments were indeed meted and their long-term consequences are undeniable although difficult to precisely assess. For instance, the claim is brought forth by individuals too young to have been subjected to corporal punishment outlawed for more than thirty years in Louisiana schools and by native English-speaking Cajuns who arguably would not have the inclination or ability to speak the forbidden idiom.

An informal but quite systematic effort by one of the authors over many years to determine if and under what circumstances informants had themselves been punished frequently resulted in vague noncommittal answers such as "No, not me, but my grandfather was" or references to generic disciplinarian measures like "The teacher made you kneel down on gravel if he caught you speaking French. That hurt!"; a couple of informants also acknowledged that they were punished less for speaking French than for misbehaving. Men tend to make the argument much more frequently than women. This gender difference suggests that boys may have been more likely to speak French—and be caught—than girls, although there were and still are virtually no difference in language abilities between the sexes. Regardless of whether individual Cajuns have faced punishment for using the ancestral language, though, French language use is still commonly portrayed as a cause of chastisement.

EVIDENCE ON THE RESISTANCE TO LANGUAGE TRANSMISSION IN THE CAJUN CORE

The desire to protect their children from the embarassment brought by Cajun ethnicity and French language is the reason universally mentioned by middle-aged and elderly Cajuns for not transmitting their cultural heritage. This trend did not end with the ethnic revival of the 1970s. Commented a Cajun man in his 30s in 1991:

> I am from Bayou Lafourche with a French-speaking background. My parents' first language was French and I did not speak a word of French until I was 22 years old. My parents never wanted me to learn French. . . . My mother did not want me to become a fisherman, a trapper, but wanted me to become a respectable, wealthy man.[22]

Regardless of the linguistic abilities of Cajun parents, their attitude toward French was pivotal in shaping their children's view of and contact with French. Although much attention is given to cases in which transmission occurred,[23] there is little documentation on the more numerous cases in which it did not. However, in hundreds of contacts over a decade, monolingual Cajun young adults showed a limited and passive comprehension of French, and expressed regrets—and an understanding—of their parents' decision; also, many indicated a significant but insufficient role of grandparents in attempts to acquire French.

Dwayne Meaux, the oil-field worker we quoted earlier, clearly shows the ambivalence of many working-class Cajuns toward their own linguistic heritage:

[My grandparents] spoke no English at all. My grandmother didn't even know how to pronounce her name. Her name was Iris Richard. Iris Richard (*French pronunciation*). My mother's mother. She said that when she went for first grade, first day of school, everybody had to say their name. She said it in French and they said: "Oh no, you can't speak French, you speak English. In school you have to speak English." From that point on she said, if you spoke French they would punish you in some sort of way. You had to learn the English language.

[My parents] speak fluent French, Cajun French. They would speak then when they didn't want us to know what they were talking about. . . . "What you're saying?" "Oh don't worry about it!" So we never really learned French. That's how it was with the kids our age. All my friends' parents, everybody spoke French. But when it came down to teaching the next generation, which was us, it didn't get passed on. It's a shame. I wish I did speak French. I do know some people that are my age that do speak French. And you got all these other cultures that came to the United States recently, the Asian people and all, they will keep their language and that's great. I wish we'd have kept our French language.

Despite his own regret about not learning French, Meaux shows a different attitude toward his son's efforts to learn French, an attitude rooted in desires for upward mobility:

[W]hen he came with his schedule, his plan for the next semester, he said, "I'm'a take French." I said, "Why do you take that? Why don't you take a computer class?" He said, "No, Dad, I need to take French 1 and I need two languages." "Why do you need that? You need to take something you can use around here." French is a language I grew up around but I was never taught it. It was something that was used when my grandmother was a child. She couldn't speak English but when she went to school they wouldn't allow her to speak French. She had to learn English. So I'm telling my boy: "Why don't you do something that's gonna help you in the work life when you get out of school?" He said, "No, Daddy. They have a new program coming up that's called TOPS. See, you have to have two languages." "All right, all right, waste of your time!" He stuck it out, he took his two French classes, did all his other stuff, kept his grade point average good, he ended up with 3.3. . . . I was the hard-headed one but sure enough it's working out fine.

One of the most interesting aspects of Meaux's family language history concerns the source of support for reviving French among the young. His son was not encouraged to study the language by parents, but by the demands of official programs. This suggests that we should give careful attention to the role of schooling and formal education in encouraging or discouraging the French language. Historian Carl Brasseaux has noted the traditional resistance of Cajuns to formal schooling. Brasseaux points out that schools conflicted with the rhythm of economic production in a farm economy, they were costly, and English education was clearly viewed as a powerful mechanism of acculturation. French education was largely bypassed in the development of Louisiana's educational system in the twentieth century. The few Louisiana French initiatives in the 1950s were taken outside of the Acadian Area, in Alexandria and New Orleans.[24]

The French education program launched in Acadian Louisiana in the 1970s provides an interesting illustration of the obstacles to the perpetuation of Cajun French. This ambitious program was marred by problems from the start. One was the lack of cooperation between an ethnically conscious socioeconomic elite and a largely apathetic Cajun public. Although many Cajuns expressed the same nostalgic attachment to French that Meaux did, they also tended to place a great deal of importance on economic opportunities for children in an English-speaking America. Early promoters of the movement consisted of professionals, educators, elected officials, and civic-minded businessmen whose involvement rested on a combination of sense of personal loss, humanistic concern for a vanishing culture, political calculation, and hopes for economic development. For their part, in 1968, most Cajuns learned from press and television reports that the battle to save their heritage had started and that the battleground was the elementary school in their district. The swell of ethnic support hoped for by the movement's leaders, mirroring that generated by civil rights activists, feminists, or opponents to the Vietnam War, failed to materialize. Drawing, depending on their age, from the experience or tales of forced acculturation in the classroom, reactions by Cajuns ranged from benevolent passiveness to heated condemnation.

Middle-class, professional Cajuns, who are often more likely than their working-class co-ethnics to be detached from ethnic roots, are often precisely the ones who are most likely to support efforts to perpetuate French through formal education. Blaine Landry, an actor and high school acting teacher, offered an interesting contrast to Meaux's ambivalence toward the study of French by children:

> [I have] three children, eleven, nine, and four, two girls and a boy. . . . They are in the French Immersion program, the oldest two. I felt it was something that would help them in the long run. The acquisition of the French language for me is and has been a very difficult road, process, for me. . . . We read research that children under a certain age are more apt. It's not like an adult trying to learn the language. So that was something that eased my mind. And true to form, they're doing beautifully, they're reading, writing, speaking. It seems like it's come much easier to them than to me. I've taken classes at the university in French and it's like banging a head against the wall. . . . I felt that something was taken away from me as a kid. Because it was so close to me, my grandparents, my parents, my brother—even they have this language. I felt there was something that was taken away from me, and the older I got the more upset I became about that. I felt like it was something that was yanked. It was a part of my heritage that should have been a given and it wasn't.[25]

In addition to the estrangement of the French movement's cadres from the grass roots, ideological differences about the variety of French to be promoted compounded the difficulty of the task at hand. Not only was teaching French in the schools to save it a challenging proposition, but the kind of French to be taught and by whom became points of contention. As a matter of cultural policy and political expediency, the movement's official and pivotal organization, CODOFIL, had opted to teach basic standard French. Its founder and powerful chairman, former congressman and Lafayette attorney James Domengeaux, justified his choice by pointing out to the mostly oral and dialectal nature of Cajun French and the necessary reliance on imported foreign teachers, given the shortage of qualified local personnel. "Do you teach *joual* in Quebec? Do we teach hillbilly English in America? No," he said adamantly. Since Cajun French, a variation "that gives flavor and zest to basic international French," had "no literature . . . , no grammar . . . , no formality," only standard French could be taught and by native speakers. This position and its chaotic implementation during the 1970s bothered many Cajuns and angered a small group of activists. Some parents criticized the discrepancy between their French and the one taught to their children: "The French they teach in school is not the French we speak," remarked informants; they complained that they could not properly converse with their children or grandchildren because of the different words, expressions, and accents imposed on the youngsters by the state-sponsored program. French-speaking young adults of Cajun extraction also routinely report how they are chided by their relatives for their "different French" when they return home from out-of-state graduate programs or visits in the Francophone world. However, the strongest reactions came mostly from ethnic-minded young Cajun intellectuals. They argued with what they called CODOFIL's top-heavy approach, its standard French imperialism, narrow focus on formal education, and general disdain of genuine Cajun culture. On some occasions, such as the release of an evaluation report on the program, the publishing of a Cajun French textbook or Cajun poetry, epic but civil confrontations erupted between both sides.[26]

Subsequently, the statewide implementation of the French education program in elementary schools in the 1970s was met by various reactions in the Cajun region. In 1974–75, most Acadiana parishes participated except parishes on the fringe (Ascension, Assumption, Cameron, West Baton Rouge). However, rates of participation of eligible students varied greatly in Acadian parishes (from 55% to 2%), incidently on the same scale as in non-Acadian parishes (61% to 3%). The highest rates were found in parishes on the fringe (Avoyelles, 55%; St James, 48%) but much lower rates were reported by parishes in or near the core (Iberia, 13%; Jefferson Davis, 11%; Iberville, 10%; Calcasieu, 2%); some core parishes reported medium-range participation (St Martin, 33%; Lafourche, Vermilion, 31%; Acadia, 28%; Lafayette, 21%), and others showed low levels (Evangeline, 9%; Saint Landry and Terrebonne, 8%).[27] It is difficult to extrapolate the meaning of the data that bear the impact of local circumstances such as school districts' financial situations and dispositions of educators as much as that of popular attitudes toward Cajun ethnicity. The reasons offered by opponents to the program typically revolved around the additional financial charge, the lack of popular support, and resistance to the introduction of standard French. However, the vicissitudes of the state-sponsored French program in some Acadian parishes where it was curtailed, interrupted, or dropped further confirm the lukewarm and ambivalent support for the ethnic endeavor in the concerned region.

This development, largely unexpected by the French movement's leaders, left many activists puzzled and indignant; some condemned the education system:

> It's a shame that with all the excitement and enthusiasm to preserve our second language, nothing or almost nothing is done to teach it in public schools of some parishes which are the hubs of the French language. . . . Here in Mamou High, we have a lot of students who would like to study French but they are told that some other courses come first; because of this, there was never a good French class in Mamou despite the presence of four qualified French teachers. Funny, no?

Others found fault with the apathy of Cajun parents; commented an activist in a 1981 interview:

> We had French programs created but when a program is terminated in a school or a parish, there is no immediate reaction. If some noise is made, the handful of people associated with CODOFIL are responsible, like in Vermilion Parish; [the French program] was stopped in many French-speaking towns but nobody said anything. Now Vermilion Parish has said the program would be terminated in all schools. . . . I would like the parents to say: "but we want our children to learn French."

It would be erroneous to generalize these developments and to qualify the reactions of Cajuns to French education as overwhelmingly antagonistic. In many school districts, the program was calmly and consistently implemented and managed with steady—if silent—support from local educators, parents, and civic leaders. By the 1990s, French classes in elementary schools had become an unquestioned fixture of the curriculum and gathered wide support, although their pedagogical achievement remain quite limited.[28]

Several factors can explain the gradual abatement of the resistance to French programs. Quite pragmatically, after decades of implementation and continued state funding, people became used to them. By the mid-1980s, parents and educators acknowledged the value that second-language programs added to an otherwise rather dismal education system. Indeed, second-language education is one, if not the, area in which Louisiana is not near its usual bottom in national performance rankings. From a cultural standpoint, the controversy about "teaching the problem language," as one participant labeled it, was resolved. For Cajun activists from both camps, the ongoing debate over the stigmatization of Cajun French represents an obstacle to French education endeavors in general. As one musician wrote in 1981, "There is far too much dispute and energy lost over whether the French taught in our Louisiana schools should be Standard French or Cajun French. . . . Will we teach Cajun French of 1980 which is bordering on half slang, half English, or will we go back to the better French spoken by our grandparents?" To which a Cajun female professor responded, "We must slowly make Cajuns understand that [Cajun French] is a language, that it exists, that it is French. It becomes tiring to hear Cajuns say 'Yes I speak Cajun but it's not the real French, the good French."

Gradually, the early view that the forceful implantation of standard French in elementary schools reinforced the stigmatization of Cajun French took a more ecumenical tack. As expressed by one Cajun educator, the exposure of Cajuns to full-fledged French-speakers could be beneficial:

> The fact that people can communicate in Cajun French with outsiders helps. The [foreign] French teachers here do much more outside than inside the classroom because they live with a family, they are invited for supper here and there, they go fishing here and there. They learn from Louisianians and Louisianians learn from them.

On another front, a pedagogical consensus developed. Academic formalists warmed up to the ethnic sentiment expressed by the grass roots and agreed to Louisiana French words and expressions in lesson plans; for their part, activists pragmatically acquiesced to some measure of standardization and accepted standard French as a useful basis to teach the language to English-speaking students. Its implementation was facilitated by the formalization of Louisiana-based pedagogical alternatives and the decreasing involvement of foreign teaching personnel, and the successful implantation of French immersion programs. The fact that, by the 1990s, energies were channeled in another direction also helped. Drawing from the Canadian experience of teaching all subject matters in the second language, thus "immersing" students in it, Louisiana educators developed French-immersion programs. More demanding but potentially more successful than traditional foreign language methods, these programs offered the long-delayed promise of creating new French-speakers. Still in its relative infancy and not yet analyzed, interestingly, this recent educational venture displays characteristics similar to previous endeavors: it started in the fringe (Lake Charles, 1983) where it is relatively more developed (forty-five classes in Calcasieu, Assumption, and Orleans for 1996–97) than in the core (twenty-nine classes in Lafayette, Saint Martin, Saint Landry, and Acadia). Its curriculum is based on standard French and its personnel is mostly composed of foreign teachers from Belgium, France, and Canada. Yet, signaling a continuous evolution of attitudes, the launching of French-immersion programs was met by firm support despite the greater demands placed on students, parents, and school administrators.

Overall, the effect of the French language programs over the past thirty years has been mixed. The stated intent of creating speakers has not been met, and the scope of immersion programs, several hundred students, appears too limited to have a measurable effect despite notable results. However, the derived effects of the educational policy are undeniable and wide-ranging. It pulled participants and opponents into the ethnic renaissance movement, creating a synergy of debate and cooperation. It also widely publicized Lousiana ethnic issues more than CODOFIL's media savvy could have ever achieved. From a social movement perspective, these are valued resources. Moreover, the educational debate bluntly posed the fundamental question of the relevance of French in modern Louisiana society: why speak it? CODOFIL argued for an instrumental use of French as an asset to Louisiana's prestige and economy, and activists emphasized the continuation of a cultural heritage and maintenance of ethnic particularity. The compromise between factions, the popular acceptance that French education gained over time, and the development of new pedagogical approaches suggest that the answer currently pulls from both positions.

Nevertheless the language transmission issue remains problematic. Our analysis clearly shows that what impedes it is the combination of Cajun ancestry and the relatively average socioeconomic status of Cajuns. In the non-Acadian part of the state where French is not connected to ancestry or working-class status, children are more likely to acquire it than in the Acadian southwest.

LANGUAGE, CLASS, AND CHANGING CAJUN ETHNICITY

Language is a central symbol and expression of collective identity. Collective identities, though, are rarely unidimensional. They involve internal contradictions and inconsistencies. Being Cajun, for example, can be at once a source of pride and a socioeconomic stigma for people in Southwestern Louisiana. We have shown here that contrary to the commonsensical assumption of a positive relationship between claims of Cajun identity and transmission of Louisiana French, parents who live in Cajun areas and identify themselves as Cajuns may be less inclined to pass on French language abilities than non-Cajun parents or parents in non-Cajun areas. This situation can be explained by the continued effect of the stigma traditionally attached to Louisiana French and Cajun identity and the different position that Cajuns occupy in Louisiana's socioeconomic structure. We have seen, in the discussion of qualitative data, the profound ambivalence regarding language and ethnicity of those who identify most strongly with the ethnic group. Although the pride produces public celebrations of ethnicity, the stigma and the disadvantage result, in the privacy of Cajuns' homes, in a turning away from the pivotal marker of that ethnicity. However, the shunning of French declines as social class rises. Both the use and transmission of French are thus matters of negotiation and manipulation. Nevertheless, the choice is not wholly an individualistic decision because it is framed by the socioeconomic variables we have identified. They reveal that family and socioeconomic factors are reliable predictors of whether that parents do or do not transmit French to their children. The adaptation of Cajuns to the new economic circumstances that emerged during the twentieth century framed their ethnic self-definition and behavior as well their choice and ability to transmit them to their children.

So far we had demontrated how Cajuns had historically accepted symbols and behaviors imposed on them by outsiders only to, recently, reinterpret them and make them acceptable. However, individual Cajuns played little or no role in the genesis and development of these social movements initiated and propelled by powerful social forces. The label and representations originated from elite groups and were disseminated by popular media; the emergence of English as the idiom of social life and the economic processes that changed people's lives in Louisiana were not the Cajuns' doing. As a group, Cajuns adopted, reworked, and adapted to these new circumstances.

Our analysis of economic, marital, and linguistic strategies allowed us to examine individuals' behaviors, how real people acted. After all, groups do not speak, marry, have children, and report to work: people do. This investigation reveals that the social processes mentioned above had different effects on people, depending on their socioeconomic position, a social location itself largely defined by the position of people in production processes. We will now consider a dimension increasingly important in determining who people are in modern economies: consumption.

NOTES

1. In statistical terms, we can express the relationship between French language use and Cajun ethnicity as "r = 915." The "r" statistic describes the extent to which one variable can be used to predict another. If this statistic is squared, it describes the percentage of overlap between the two variables. Thus, by knowing whether a Louisianian is a Cajun, we should be able to predict whether or not that person speaks French with 84% accuracy (.915 × .915).

2. Frederick L. Olmsted, *A Journey in the Seaboard Slave States*, 2 vols. (New York: Dix, Edwards and Co., 1856); Alfred Rodolph Waud, "Acadians in Louisiana" (1866), reprinted in Timothy Reilly, "Early Acadiana Through Anglo-American Eyes (Part 2)," *Attakapas Gazette* 12 (1977):1, 3–20; Albert Rhodes, "The Louisiana Creoles," *Galaxy* 16 (1873):252–260; R.L. Daniels, "The Acadians of Louisiana," *Scribner's Monthly* 19 (1879–1880):383–392; W.H. Sparks, *The Memories of Fifty Years*, 4th ed. (Philadelphia: E. Claxton & Company, 1882).

3. Alcée Fortier, *Louisiana Studies; Literature, Customs and Dialects; History and*

Education (New Orleans: F.F. Hansell and Bro., 1894); Marguerite Roman, "Les Acadiens au XXème siècle," *Comptes Rendus de l'Athénée Louisianais*, Mai (1924): 12–23; Ralph Graves, "Louisiana, Land of Perpetual Romance," *National Geographic* 57(4) (1930):393–482.

4. David Marcantel, "Statut légal du français en Louisiane," *Parlements et Francophonie* 54 (1984):34–43; Jacques Henry, "L'enseignement du français en Louisiane: L'effort continue," *Parlements et Francophonie* 60 (1986):98–110; Rodrigue Landry, Réal Allard & Jacques Henry, "French in South Louisiana: Towards Language Loss," *Journal of Multilingual and Multicultural Development* 17(5)(1996): 442–468.

5. Lawrence Estaville, in "The Louisiana French Language in the Nineteenth Century," *Southeastern Geographer* 30(2)(1990):107–120, argues that "the collapse of the Louisiana French resistance to Anglicization generally and to the learning of English in particular" started in earnest during the last half of the nineteenth century, although Louisiana French had not "forsaken their native tongue altogether."

6. Authors' interview, February 1, 2001.

7. Authors' interview, February 11, 2001.

8. Larbi Oukada, "The Territory and Population of French-speaking Louisiana," *Revue de Louisiane/Louisiana Review* 7(1)(1978):5–34; U.S. Bureau of the Census, *Census of Population—1970, vol 1. Characteristics of the Population, Part 20—Louisiana.* (Washington DC: Bureau of the Census, 1973). Although the comparability of census figures between 1940 and 1990 is limited because of changes in questionnaires, target population, and coding, their interpretation is unambiguous: French has been and remains overwhelmingly spoken by white people claiming Acadian descent living in Southwestern Louisiana, and is declining in use.

9. Francis Debyser, Jan Lobelle, André Paquette, Robert Paris & Lawrence Richard, *1978 Evaluation of Louisiana Statewide CODOFIL French Program* (Lafayette, LA: CODOFIL, 1978); Consulat Général de France, *La Question du Français en Louisiane* (New Orleans: French Consulate, 1979); Pierre Thibaud, "1972–1974: Deux années de coopération à Mamou (Louisiane)," in Gerald Gold (ed.), *The Role of France, Quebec and Belgium in the Revival of French in Louisiana Schools*, edited by Gerald Gold. (Toronto: Projet Louisiane 7, York University, 1979), 60–81; Board of Regents, *Report on the Commission on French as a Second Language* (Baton Rouge: Board of Regents, 1983); Maurice Girard, "La survie passe par l'immersion," *Journal de Québec*, 15 avril 1991.

10. Joshua Fishman, *Language Loyalty in the United States* (The Hague: Mouton & Co, 1966); Joshua Fishman, "Language and Ethnicity" in H. Giles (ed.), *Language, Ethnicity and Intergroup Relations*, (London: Academic Press, 1977), 15–57 Joshua Fishman, "What Is Reversing Language Shift (RLS) and How Can It Succeed?," *Journal of Multilingual and Multicultural Development* 11(1–2)(1990):5–36; Richard Alba, *Ethnic Identity: The Transformation of White America.* (New Haven: Yale University Press, 1990).

11. To accomplish the quantitative portion of our study, we arranged the PUMS data into a rectangular data set, in which census data for children is attached to the data for householders and spouses of householders in each household. Our dependent variable was whether or not children spoke French at home. Since this was a dichotomous variable, coded as "0" for not speaking French and as "1" for speaking it, we employed logistic regression as a means of statistical analysis. Our independent

variables included indicators of characteristics of the minors themselves, of household heads, and of the families. We also included two geographical variables. One of these indicated the extent to which young people lived in a Cajun ethnic area of the state. We discuss the designation of ethnic regions below. The second geographical variable was whether the minors lived in a metropolitan or nonmetropolitan area, a rough measure of rural residence. For a full description of all variables, readers are referred to the technical documentation of the 1990 Public Use Microdata Samples published by the U.S. Bureau of the Census, *Census of Population and Housing, 1990. Public Micro Use Data Samples. Technical Documentation* (Washington, DC: Bureau of the Census, 1992).

12. We note that the Acadian core has the smallest percentage of blacks, among all households, whereas the fringe has the smallest percentage of blacks in households with a French-speaking parent. Moreover, smaller percentages of young people in French households are black than in all households. This is understandable when we consider that Cajuns are the primary French-speakers in contemporary Louisiana, and Cajun is almost exclusively an ethnic identity of whites. The core probably contains more blacks than the fringe among those in French speaking families because the relatively small number of Creoles, or French-speaking blacks (Carl L. Bankston III & Jacques Henry, "The Socioeconomic Position of the Louisiana Creoles: An Examination of Racial and Ethnic Stratification," *Social Thought and Research* 21(1998):253–277, are found primarily in the core Cajun area.

13. Other variables are of little help in explaining regional differences. For instance, French-speaking parents are uniformly slightly older and less fluent in English than other household heads. Similarly, Francophone families are less likely to be a one-parent family than other Louisiana families overall.

14. As a reminder, the asterisks indicate our degree of confidence in generalizing from this sample to all of Louisianians. One asterisk indicates that the relationship is strong enough that we should find it in 95% of all random samples we would take from the Louisiana population. Two asterisks indicate that the relationship is strong enough that we should find it in 99% of all random samples.

15. Trent Angers, *The Truth About the Cajuns* (Lafayette, LA: Acadian House Publishing, 1990), 8.

16. Barry J. Ancelet, *Cajun and Creole Folktales: The French Oral Tradition of South Louisiana* (New York: Garland, 1994); Howard Jacobs, "Cajun Laugh-in," *Acadiana Profile* 3(2) (1971).

17. Angers, *The Truth About the Cajuns*, 83–86.

18. "Justin Wilson, 87, Cajun Chef and Humorist," *New York Times*, September 7, 2001; Bob Anderson, "Farewell to a Legend," *Baton Rouge Morning Advocate*, September 7, 2001.

19. Barry J. Ancelet, "Ragin' Cajuns: What's in a Name?" (Unpublished paper on file with Jacques Henry, 1996).

20. Sylvie Dubois, W. Gautreau, H. Margot, M. Mélançon, & T. Veler, "The Quality of French Spoken in Louisiana: Linguistic Attitudes Towards the Varieties of French in Cajun Communities," *SECOL Review* 19(2)(1995):126–150.

21. Becky Brown, "The Social Consequences of Writing Louisiana French," *Language in Society* 22(1993):67–101; Sara LeMenestrel, *La voie des Cadiens: Tourisme et identité en Louisiane* (Paris: Belin, 1999). Although the fact that a co-author is of French birth had an undeniable effect on the linguistic behavior of Cajun French-

speakers, the effect could also be positive. In many cases, Cajuns would express, in French or English, interest and curiosity about the presence of a fluent French-speaker in their midst. Also, we frequently witnessed situations where Cajun speakers would query or chide one another about their French-speaking abilities.

22. Cited in Alain Guillermou & Jeanne Ogée, *En Lutte pour l'Avenir du Français* (Paris: Biennale de la langue française, 1993), 462.

23. Jacques Henry, "Le français nouveau arrive?" *LA Gazette de Louisiane* 1(3) (1990):1–5; Katrina Huggs, "The Roots of the Language," *Times of Acadiana*, October 10, 1990).

24. Jacques Henry, "L'enseignement du français en Louisiane: L'effort continue," *Parlements et Francophonie* 60 (1986):98–110.

25. Authors' interview, March 2001.

26. Barry J. Ancelet, "A Perspective on Teaching the 'Problem Language' in Louisiana," *French Review* 61(3)(1989):345–356; Henry, "Le français nouveau arrive?"

27. Louisiana State Department of Education, *CODOFIL French Program 1974–1975* (Baton Rouge: Louisiana State Department of Education, 1974).

28. Henry, "Le français nouveau arrive?"

CHAPTER 7

Festivals of Ethnicity: Cajuns in a Consumer Economy

To this point, we have concentrated on the position of Cajuns in Louisiana's economy of production. Modern-day Americans are not just producers, though; they are also consumers. In fact, styles of consumption may influence expressions of contemporary American culture even more than means of production. Economists were keen to this development early on. In the 1930s, John Maynard Keynes advocated an economic policy centered around consumption as the driving force. In 1958, John Kenneth Galbraith observed that techniques of production in the economies of the West had outstripped distribution, resulting in an unprecedented quantity of goods available for consumption, even though the buying power of individuals might lag far behind this productive capacity.[1] At the same time mass-produced commodities became a more prominent part of the social landscape, the geographic and social mobility of the late-twentieth century tended to loosen many ascriptive social ties so that the role of individual choice in group affiliations became even greater than it had been earlier.[2] Even religious affiliation became less a matter of ascriptive connections to others and more a matter of a voluntary choice among institutions competing for adherents in the manner of producers competing in a market for customers.[3]

As a consequence of these changes in American society and economy, social organization, behavior, and expectations have come to be based increasingly on the consumption of mass-produced commodities. Although the word "consumerism" may have a number of different uses, one of the most prevalent refers to the organization of social activities and individual beliefs and behaviors around the consumption of products. Referring to this sense of the word, Bocock has remarked, "Consumption [has] become established as the characteristic socio-cultural activity par excellence of late twentieth-century post-modern capitalism. . . . Consumption is a, or even the, major characteristic of postmodernity."[4] The growing scholarship on the commodification of modern societies and cultures has certainly contributed to expose the processes and forces at hand in greater depth and detail than Marx's writings on labor as commodity or Thornstein Veblen's analysis of consumption among the "leisure class" as a way to assert social status. Pierre Bourdieu, among other social scientists, has placed the consumption of cultural and symbolic goods such as artworks, language, fashion, or cuisine at the center of his analysis of modern society.[5] Other authors have also predictably seen consumerism as a central characteristic of the contemporary American scene.[6]

One of the findings of this school of thought is that the marketing of goods in a consumer-oriented society tends to become the marketing of social identities.[7] Consumers are categories of people based not on their relations to each other, but on their relations to classes of chosen products. In a consumer society, individuals tend to define themselves in terms of what they buy, rather than in terms of their primary groups or economic or political interest groups.[8] One observer has noted that "commodities convey the social attributes of the group and individual (i.e., clothes, musical recordings, personal adornments, etc.) as well as providing sites of socialization (shopping mall)."[9] Since they are means of defining people, in their own eyes as well as in the eyes of others, commodities are rich in symbolism. The choice of a sport utility vehicle or a compact disc is not simply a choice of an object, but a choice of an identity. Americans, maybe more than other Westerners, define themselves through the purchase of symbolically rich commodities. Sites devoted to consumption, such as fast-food outlets, retail centers, shopping malls, museums, and amusement parks have become central to this identity quest. George Ritzer has evoked the almost sacred character many of these sites seem to have in his term "cathedrals of consumption." [10]

Another phenomenon noted by the analysis of modern societies in terms of consumption is the transformation of social identities and processes into products themselves. A growing scholarship addresses issues in the the commodification of power, health, the female body, knowledge, difference, religion, culture, and the natural environment by states, medical institutions, advertising, and the tourism industry.[11] It is not surprising that ethnic identities have also been affected by commodification both for consumption by others and for self-identification.[12]

Given the growing influence of consumerism in American life, we suggest that much of contemporary ethnicity, including Cajun ethnicity, can be understood as a form of consumption. The ethnic identification is based less on social ties to other group members and distinctive cultural and linguistic characteristics than it is on the choice of products that express a self-ascription to ancestral social ties, culture, and language; it is the argument of symbolic activity reviewed in our introduction. However, the commodities themselves are constructed. One strategy of construction consists of utilizing references to an imagined earlier set of social relations or a desired situation as building blocks. Since contemporary Cajuns participate in the economy as consumers as well as producers, we suggest that the ways in which their ethnic identity is expressed, by the Cajuns themselves and by outsiders, tend to take forms that are familiar to consumer society. Images of Cajun identity are based on an idealized past. As we have discussed in Chapter 2, contemporary Cajuns share the idealized images of their group held by other Americans. These images take shape in the present, though. They therefore tend to be realized as marketed goods. The commodification of Louisiana ethnic identity may be clearest in the recent reappraisal of Cajun cuisine and music and in the ethnic festivals that have become popular throughout Cajun country.

FESTIVALS AND ETHNIC TOURISM IN ACADIANA

The commodification of Cajun cultural products in recent years has received various explanations. On the basis of ethnographic data collected in a small village, Esman proposes that tourism encourages Cajuns to act out their culture both for commercial gain and cultural preservation.[13] In disagreement, Trépanier views the commodification of Cajun culture as an indicator of its incorporation into American culture. Trépanier believes that with commodification Cajun culture has become unauthentic, a sheer commercial attraction devoid of meaning, and that this evolution signals its impending demise.[14] A noted and involved folklorist, Barry Ancelet argues in favor of cultural tourism, a measured exploitation of cultural resources informed and controlled by scholars.[15]

In a study that is by far the most comprehensive work on the matter, Sara LeMenestrel offers to reconcile the various approaches by studying the interaction of identity construction and tourism.[16] Drawing from extensive fieldwork in four communities and their festivals, she notes that festivals reinforce social bonds, contribute to the economy, and foster identity construction in a dual mechanism. Two concepts of culture coexist: one as a commodity and one as heritage. Cajun culture, rehabilitated and a unique resource in a rarified Louisiana economy, is valued and promoted by insiders who can use it to shore up ethnic awareness. Popular and consumed by others, a commodified Cajun culture signals the acceptance of the group by outsiders and its integration to the American society, again reinforcing a positive ethnic identification.

In our view, LeMenestrel's sophisticated view of the dialogue between tradition and tourism can help correct simple, one-sided interpretations. Esman's claim that tourism perpetuates ethnic behavior, such as speaking French for the contentment of visitors, is doubtful, considering the value of efficient communication for commercial transaction and the limited and stereotyped use of the language often reduced to "*Bonjour! Comment ça va?*"[17] Trépanier's condemnation of nonauthenticity assumes a static and now largely rejected view of culture as frozen tradition threatened by change. Ancelet's hope for a measured, carefully tended commercialization of his own culture is in part embodied in recent creations such as Festivals Acadiens (which he helped create in 1974), the best-known of the festivals. However, numerous other endeavors suggest that entrepreneurs have the upper hand over academics and preservationists when cultural items are marketed. There is a proliferation of "Cajun" restaurants and boat tours, complete with alligator calling and ethnic joke telling. Interestingly, in another work Ancelet comments on the adaptability of Cajun culture and acknowledges that today's commercial Cajun culture often bears little resemblance to the old folkways.[18] However, he views the modernization as only a superficial transformation to "appeal to the sophisticated tastes of a mostly urban population."

The explanation of Cajun ethnic expressions that we offer here attempts to avoid judging cultural expressions as "authentic" or "inauthentic." Seeing cultural commodities as preservation, moreover, ignores the transformation of the nature of ethnicity in contemporary America. The increasing body of research on the issues of globalization and commodification of ethnicity in the form of touristic endeavors, museum exhibits, or staged events has surveyed the political economy of culture. In this perspective, one is either a tourist, a "touree," or an intermediary, to borrow van den Berghe's terminology, and no aspect of ethnicity, as culture or identity, can theoretically escape commodification.[19]

Therefore, we seek to look at the development of the Cajun festival, foodways, and musical expression as part of the changing meaning of ethnic identification in the United States. As in the rest of the United States, relatively few people in contemporary Louisiana are engaged in small-scale agriculture, hunting, trapping, and fishing (see Table 3.2). Among people who refer to themselves as Cajuns, employment in the oil industry, factories, and service activities are especially common. Like other working-class and middle-class Americans, the Southwestern Louisianian of today is much more likely to buy dinner at the Super Kmart than to trap it in the bayou. However, the past, our evidence indicates, continues to be relevant. Many Southwestern Louisianians draw on images of an agricultural past to make sense of a post-industrial or late-industrial present. They express and experience these images of the past as items of consumption in a marketplace because they are fitting a subjectively primordial social identity into contemporary forms of social organization.

THE MAKING OF CAJUN CUISINE AND THE NEW BEAT OF CAJUN MUSIC

We pointed out earlier that Acadians and Cajuns have long been associated with particular foodways and that they have been described as fond of song and dance. This propensity to enjoy such earthly delights was mostly frowned upon by upper-class Creoles and Americans, who viewed it as rural backwardness or wasteful habits. How things have changed! Cajun foodways and musical talents are now labeled cuisine and genuine American folk music. Outsiders flock to taste the food and enjoy the music, whereas, insiders revel in this revaluation and keep on cooking and playing.

Historically, brief reports on the Cajun diet usually focused on its adequacy in terms of quantity and quality. Acadians had enough to eat, grew and caught most of their food, and appeared to thoroughly enjoy its consumption. Descriptions of Cajuns' daily and ceremonial fare include such dishes as gumbo (a flour-based, thick soup), sweet potatoes, pancakes, molasses, oysters, bacon, eggs, rice, red beans, cornmeal, fish, milk, and the ever present coffee.[20] Corn bread, potatoes, beans, peas, fresh and salted meat and fish, and game were the mainstay of a mundane and monotonous diet.[21] Comments about crawfish as a delicacy start to appear after World War II with mentions of Cajun food as a culinary item. The accommodations of local products had fed Cajuns for decades without fanfare, but by the 1970s these were elevated to the rank of a unique cuisine to be sampled by the world at large.

Indicators of the current popularity of Cajun foodways are easy to find. Indeed, listings of restaurants and restaurant menus nationwide are more than likely to include an establishment or a dish labeled Cajun or inspired by an idea of Cajunness. Like numerous other adventurous eaters, we have sampled Cajun blackened whitefish in Michigan, Cajun enchiladas in Texas, and a variety of seafood gumbos from Virginia to California, not to mention locales abroad. It is also extremely probable that a trip to any supermarket in North America will allow the curious shopper to find a host of Cajun sauces and spices in the ethnic food section. Cookbooks with a global perspective, as well as cooking columns in newspapers and on the Internet, are also likely to include a Cajun recipe. Unsurprisingly, Southwestern Louisiana is home to many eateries catering to the Cajun taste. The telephone directory of Lafayette contains expected advertisements such as "Miss Helen's Cajun Seafood Restaurant" serving "Cajun Seafood At It's [*sic*] Finest," "Enola Prudhomme's Cajun Café," "Randol's Restaurant and Cajun Dancehall," and "Don's Seafood Hut," which has been "Serving Cajun Cuisine Since 1934." Less mainstream are establishments claiming to be "The Italian Restaurant with a Cajun Flair," or that serve "Creative Cajun" or "New Acadian" cuisine.

One of the reasons for this wide availability is that Cajun sells. Food processors and marketers have been on to this since the 1980s, after noticing that just adding the Cajun label to a product elicited spectacular response from consumers.[22] Although the commodification of Cajun cuisine is a social phenomenon with structural factors at play, the prominent role of an individual must be acknowledged. Chef Paul Prudhomme is credited by many to be the prime initiator of the ongoing Cajun cooking craze; his personality, business acumen, media shrewdness, and culinary imagination have made great contributions to the popularization of Cajun fare. In particular, the blackened redfish dish he serendipitously concocted one day launched such a run on the species that only a two-year legislative ban on catch in the Gulf of Mexico could protect it from complete extinction. The saga of Prudhomme as a Cajun chef is exemplary in other, paradoxical, ways. Adept at saltwater fishing, Cajuns typically boiled fish in gumbos and courtbouillons. The "blackening," a technique by which the fish is quickly broiled over high heat, requires a frying pan and a kitchen oven, both of which were scarce items in traditional Acadian kitchens. This Prudhomme creation is as Acadian as french fries are Gallic. Also, hailing from Saint Landry parish in the core of Cajun country, Chef Paul made his mark as a restaurateur in New Orleans, which, for all its cosmopolitan flair and cultural proximity, has no association with Cajunness. Finally, the generous use of butter and cream in the original nondiet versions of Prudhomme's cuisine is at odds with traditional and contemporary Cajun fare, which is notable for its shunning of dairy products. Nevertheless, even considering the addition of ingredients, the invention of techniques and the nonethnic basis of success, it is impossible to reasonably argue that Prudhomme's cuisine is not in any sense Cajun. So what is Cajun food made of nowadays?

In detailed examinations of Cajun foodways, anthropologists have recently compiled lists of what goes into food contemporary Cajuns eat: meat (pork, beef, chicken, and turkey are mostly bought), fish (freshwater and saltwater species, mostly caught), shellfish (crawfish, shrimp, oysters, mostly bought), game (duck, deer, rabbit), grain (always rice, some flour), some vegetables (okra, corn, tomatoes, mustard greens, cabbage) and seasoning vegetables and herbs, mostly onions and red peppers. These ingredients are combined into traditional Cajun dishes such as gumbos, fricassées, etouffées, sauces piquantes, jambalayas, boudin and sausages, and stuffed vegetables. They illustrate the "aesthetics" of Cajun cuisine that make a particular food Cajun more than the kind or origin of the components: strong flavors emanating from tasty ingredients and use of spices, a systematic combination of ingredients, and a long cooking time.[23] Given these requirements, an Inuit could muster a decent Cajun gumbo in Nunavut, providing the availability of flour, oil, rice, onions, bell pepper, celery (the frozen kind will do), spices, and any kind of meat or seafood, whereas a tenth-generation Broussard serving a bland crawfish bisque over pasta will make the startled guests wonder about the ancestry or sanity of their host.

The examination of food logs maintained by senior and high school respondents throughout Southwestern Louisiana reveals a diversified diet.[24] In addition to Cajun dishes, nonethnic food is popular. Staples of American food are widely consumed: hamburgers and french fries by 80% of teenagers and 40% of seniors, pizza (57% of teenagers), and hot dogs (49% of teens, 31% of seniors). Mainstays of a Southern diet are also common: fried chicken, biscuits, and watermelon are favored by a majority of respondents, and grits remain a favorite of 60% of seniors, making it the second-most-consumed item after rice.

The diversity and adaptiveness of Cajun food are apparent both in the assimilation of various cultural influences and its coexistence with other culinary traditions. Cajun food is anything but traditionally Acadian, and Cajuns consume many nonethnic items. The combination of "French, Acadian, Spanish, German, Anglo-American, Afro-Caribbean, and Native American influences"[25] is a trait most noted of Cajun cooking, as well as its reliance on the gamut of resources available in the environment. Local humor emphasizes the propensity of Cajuns to cook anything that moves and the supposed consequent risk of taking one on a visit to a zoo. Although squirrels, alligators, and turtles are occasionally consumed, however, chicken, rice and gravy, steaks, pork chops, and sandwiches are much more common.

Finally, beyond the culinary dimension, a central characteristic of Cajun food is its socializing function. How people cook and eat is as revealing as what they eat. Among the practices most noted are the communal participation in animal butchering (the *boucherie* organized with the neighborhood or extended kin), celebratory consumption in the form of crawfish boils, community gumbos, ethnic (*cochon de lait*) and nonethnic barbecues, and the involvement of men in mostly ceremonial cooking. Such food events "help express and validate Cajun environmental competence" and sociability.[26] These events also have "definite performance aspects" in which at home or in festivals, dining guests observe and comment on the cook's skills.[27] Overall, Cajun foodways appear as a flexible ethnic symbol. Acceptance of the food, and dexterity at preparing and consuming it identify insiders and outsiders. Cajuns usually inform their occasional guest about the potency of some added spices and are usually helpful in demonstrating the efficient technique of peeling a steaming crawfish. However, the transformation of Cajun ways such as the increased purchasing of products and the utilization of modern amenities such as microwave ovens, and the acceptance and reproduction of Cajun food by nonethnics have contributed to lessen the role of cultural skills in using food to establish group membership. The Cajun restaurants and the widely marketed sauces and spices tend to make Cajun food more and more something that is bought, rather than caught and prepared.

The other pillar of the Cajun joie de vivre, Cajun music, has emerged in the past decades as an original and celebrated form of American folk music.

Following a process similar to the emergence of Cajun cuisine, today this music involves neither strict adherence to an ancestral tradition nor the invention of a new form. Instead, it is best understood as the reassessment of a set of diversified contributions. The history and content of Cajun music have been the subjects of excellent treatments by other authors,[28] so a brief account will suffice. Traditionally rooted in the French folksinging tradition and fed by musical tributaries of neighboring cultures (blues, Scotch-Irish, Anglo-American folk), Cajun music per se emerged as a recognized form in the 1930s. Recordings by commercial companies or by folklorists John and Alan Lomax for the Library of Congress allowed the documentation of a local and largely domestic musical style. This style, however, arose out of a variety of sources with roots in earlier centuries. Ballads, two-steps, waltzes, and drinking songs sung and played at first by amateur musicians on fiddle, and later with an accompaniment of guitar and diatonic accordion became available in a stable format to a larger audience. Ironically, the development of modern means of recording and performing threatened Cajun music at the same time that it created it as a single form out of these diverse beginnings. The arrival of electricity, radio, and record players in country homes and the development of modern means of transportation allowed for the penetration of nonethnic American music in Cajun Louisiana. Country, swing, and later, rock and roll competed with Cajun music for audiences and popularity. Despite integrating these influences by translating popular songs in French and adding modern instruments (drums, bass, pedal-steel guitars) to sound up to date, and steadily entertaining a faithful audience in local dance halls, Cajun music was losing out. The cultural revival of the 1970s brought a drastic change.

Although Cajun music and its performers have not reached the peak of adulation occupied by pop stars and great composers, the unique musical format originating from Southwestern Louisiana is now widely considered as a wholesome, valued part of the American music scene. Prominent Cajun musicians are signed by major record companies, accompany well-known pop and country stars, are favorably featured in the national media from the *New York Times* to *Rolling Stone*, perform on prestigious stages, and receive peer recognition such as the Grammys awarded by the recording industry. Cajun music also has an international status. It is known not only in French-speaking countries, but also in countries such as England and Norway where local bands emulate the sound of their distant idols. In its homeland, Cajun music is triumphant. Dozens of bands perform regularly in festivals, restaurants, and private functions, and their recordings are heavily played on local radio stations. The sounds once dismissed as "chanky chank" are now routinely used in advertising campaigns and seriously studied by aficionados of all stripes.

As we have seen with the emergence of Cajun cuisine, the current status of Cajun music owes much to structural and extraneous factors. The revaluation of American folk music, the white ethnic revival, and the growth of a leisure culture have contributed to the music's popularity. However, a group of events and performers have been described as central to the transformation of potentialities into realities. The invitation of a group of traditional Cajun musicians to the prestigious Newport Folk Festival in 1964, where they received an unexpectedly warm response, and the surprising success of a Tribute to Cajun Music organized in Lafayette in 1974 represent the bookends of the national and local process of reappraisal of Cajun music. It prompted young aspiring musicians to trek to the old masters' houses to learn their technique and draw from their spirit. Dennis McGee, Dewey Balfa, Nathan Abshire, and other individuals who were fine instrumentalists but unassuming amateur musicians became the teachers of a class of ethnically conscious professional performers. Each in their own way, Zachary Richard, Beausoleil's Michael Doucet, Steve Riley, and Wayne Toups built on the traditional repertoire and sound of fiddle and accordion. The integration of rock and roll, bluesy syncopated zydeco, and virtuoso technique resulted in the modern sound of Cajun music. All of these moves were resisted at first by traditionalists but quickly embraced by a growing audience.

In sum, the recent developments noted in Cajun cuisine and music are among the most visible examples of the transformation of particular cultural activities into marketable commodities. They involve a dialogue between tradition and modernity as well as between Cajuns and outsiders. Interestingly, both parallel evolutions converge in festivals and ethnic tourism endeavors. Festivals and tourism have, we argue, become an important part of modern ideas of Cajun ethnicity. We turn, now, to a closer look at these regional displays.

ORIGINS AND DEVELOPMENT OF CAJUN FESTIVALS

Just as modern-day Disneyland emerged from the older models of the World's Fair and the amusement park,[29] contemporary festivals in Louisiana have historical precursors in parish (county) and state fairs, as well as in the seasonal celebrations of rural people. The fairs were designed to meet the needs of an agricultural economy. State involvement with fairs began in 1861, when the Louisiana legislature established the Mechanics and Agricultural Fair Association.[30] In 1877, the state held its first fair, which became known in 1905 as the Louisiana State Fair. In the late nineteenth century, also, farmers began to form farmers' institutes, "sessions in which farmers met to hear lectures on solving their problems."[31] In 1897, these farmers' institutes formally established the Louisiana Farmer's Institute, which helped to create six parish fairs the following year. By 1902, there were sixteen parish fairs. Louisiana's largest parish fair, the Washington Parish Fair, began in 1903. It is worth noting that this largest fair has moved away from agricultural exposition as a chief purpose in recent years, and toward the reconstruction or construction of ancestral heritage. During the 1980s, old residences, a blacksmith shop, and a general store were moved to the fairgrounds from scattered sites and restored as a museum village of the parish's founding families (a village that never, in fact, existed until the restoration).[32]

Festivals in Southwestern Louisiana, as opposed to state and rural fairs, began to appear toward the middle of the twentieth century. The oldest one, the National Rice Festival, took place in Crowley in 1937, a successor to the original Rice Carnival, which had a short run a decade earlier. Other festivals were later organized such as the blessing of shrimp fleets (1930s), Yambilee Festival (1946), and the Dairy Festival (1949).[33] The growth remained limited: by 1965, there were twenty-one festivals in Acadiana.[34]

In several ways, the festivals that were established from the 1930s through the 1960s were heirs to the traditional celebrations of agricultural societies. They were dedicated to the main local agricultural product (shrimp, crawfish, cattle, sugarcane, cotton, or oranges). They mostly took place during September and October to coincide with the end of the harvest season or the beginning of the fishing or planting season. Finally, although early Louisiana festivals were secular affairs, they typically included a mass or a blessing by the local clergy. In all, they contributed with Catholic holidays (Easter, All Saints Day, Christmas) and secular patriotic celebrations to form the cycle of community activities.

Efforts to revitalize Louisiana's French culture in the 1970s coincided with a significant increase in the number of festivals and change of their meaning. There were 36 festivals in Acadiana by 1977, 88 in 1985, close to 300 in 1993, and 240 in 1998. Most of the festivals in existence today were established after 1968. Explanations of this phenomenon, also noted statewide, rely on two main factors: ethnic revival and economic diversification. Whereas early festivals had only implicit ethnic connotations, recent festivals have made the Cajun connection explicit: 34% of festivals in Acadiana in 1993 had an ethnic marker in their name (for example, Lagniappe on the Bayou, Festivals Acadiens, South Lafourche Cajun Festival).[35] In 1998, 19% had an ethnic marker, but the ratio increases to 40% if the 60 different celebrations of Mardi Gras are included.[36]

The creation of Festival Acadiens, in 1974, was a particularly important point in ethnic festival history in Louisiana. This was a conscientious and self-conscious attempt to maintain Cajun music as a living tradition. Many individuals were active in organizing this yearly event, but its most active proponent and most tireless supporter was Dr. Barry Jean Ancelet, a professor of French at the University of Southwestern Louisiana (renamed the University of Louisiana at Lafayette in the fall of 1999), who later earned a doctorate at a French university. In various accounts,[37] Ancelet reported that he had discovered his own sense of heritage while abroad in the French-speaking world, a significant fact when thinking about the meaning of contemporary ethnic festivals. The role played by the dislocation, the separation from group membership stimulating the search for the historical roots of ethnicity, has been similarly reported by other Cajun activists of this period.

Festivals are dedicated to major topics in Cajun culture, particularly foodways and music. In 1998, 17 of 46 festivals were dedicated to products from the environment (wildlife, oysters, crawfish, frogs, peppers), and crops (sugarcane, rice, cotton, herbs), and 14 were dedicated to processed products (gumbo, boudin, sauce piquante) with an emphasis on pork products (*cochon de lait*, cracklin, *grande boucherie, viande boucanee*) and seafood. The remaining third are mostly dedicated to Cajun music (Festival de Musique Acadienne, Accordion Festival). In 1999, the state of Louisiana dedicated its 300th anniversary year—and a special brochure—to the FrancoFête, a yearlong celebration of its French heritage with an emphasis on Acadians who met by the thousands at the Congres Mondial.[38]

From the inception of the ethnic revitalization movement, ethnic claims were connected to economic pursuits. The 1968 legislative act establishing the Council for the Development of French in Louisiana instructed the state agency to develop actions for the "cultural, economic and tourist benefit of the State." Largely successful, CODOFIL officials repeatedly emphasized their ability to bring dignitaries and paying visitors to Louisiana as well as the free worldwide publicity their endeavor generated to justify their mission and to request state funds. The state and local municipalities also strived to capitalize on the promotion of an ethnic image. In addition to festivals, twinning with foreign cities mostly from the French-speaking world, close cooperation of local officials with cultural associations, and renovation and building of local attractions (commemorative parks, theaters, museums) became major tools of economic development.

At the state level, the economic downturn brought about by the oil crisis of the mid-1980s triggered a renewed interest in tourism as an alternate industry. A Louisiana Office of Tourism had been established in 1977 but really became active by the 1990s with increased funding and the launching of coordinated programs (tax-free shopping for foreign visitors, nationwide advertising campaigns, division of the state into five specific zones). Although claims of the economic effect of tourism are inherently difficult to gauge (tourism is not listed as an industry, and anyone traveling 100 miles for at least one day is considered a visitor) and tend to be inflated by interested parties, tourism appears as a significant industry: it is estimated that more than 20 million visitors spent $6 billion, filling 97,000 jobs and generating $765 million in taxes in 1994.[39]

Food and music have been central to the tourist business of Cajun country. These two cultural expressions make up 64% and 46%, respectively, of local attractions, compared with 20% and 14% in the rest of the United States.[40] The dishes popularized by Paul Prudhomme and others and the varieties of folk music brought together and broadcast by the mass media now virtually define "Cajun" for the American public at large. Following the long-established pattern of dialogue between outsiders and insiders, the food, music, and related entertainments also became critical to the self-images of the Cajuns themselves.

FESTIVALS AS EXPRESSIONS OF ETHNIC GROUP MEMBERSHIP

The *Encyclopedia of Cajun Culture* says of festivals in Southwestern Louisiana: "Attracting both locals and tourists, festivals are an important part of Cajun life, and occur throughout the year in Acadiana. Most of these feature Cajun food and music, as well as arts and crafts."[41] As we have seen, however, this "important part of Cajun life" is a fairly recent addition to the social landscape of southern Louisiana. Nevertheless, data from a survey conducted by the Council on the Development of French in Louisiana (CODOFIL) support the contention that these events are widely attended in this part of the state. In Table 7.1, we present reported attendance at mostly Cajun-themed festivals[42] by claims of Cajun or Acadian ethnicity and by age. We report attendance at these festivals with and without the Festivals Acadiens in Lafayette, since this is the best-known of the festivals, attracting the largest non-Cajun tourist audience.

Three interesting facts appear in the data on all festivals. First, in the two younger age groups (under 40 years and 40 to 49), those who classified themselves as Cajuns were more likely than those who classify themselves otherwise to have attended a festival. More than one-fourth of the Cajuns aged 39 or younger had attended at least one festival, compared with less than 19% of non-Cajuns of comparable age. In addition, 8% of these young Cajuns had attended two or more festivals, compared with just more than 1% of the young non-Cajuns. In the middle-age group, more than 18% of Cajuns had attended a festival, compared with less than 13% of middle-age non-Cajuns. Second, festival attendance is linked to age as well as ethnicity. The younger people in both ethnic categories were more likely than older people to have participated in these events. Multiple festival attendance, moreover, occurred primarily among young Cajuns. Of the 22 people who had attended two or more festivals, 17 (77%) were Cajuns and 13 (59%) were young Cajuns. Third, participation in an ethnically themed festival is fairly common in Southwestern Louisiana. More than 14% of all those in this random survey said they had been to one of these events. If we take into consideration the fact that older people tend not to take part in these activities, it seems to be even more common. If this random survey is representative of the population, it appears that nearly one out of every five people under 50 and between one out of every four and one out of every five people under 30 in Southwestern Louisiana has been to a festival ded-

Table 7.1
Attendance at Cajun-Themed Festivals, at Festivals Acadiens, and at All Cajun-Themed Festivals Except Festivals Acadiens, by Age, 1989

	Cajuns			Non-Cajuns		
	<40	40-49	50+	<40	40-49	50+
All festivals						
No attendance	74.2	81.6	94.6	81.2	87.2	94.8
Attended one festival	17.8	16.7	3.6	17.6	11.7	5.2
Attended two festivals	6.7	1.8	0.9	1.2	1.1	0.0
Attended three festivals	0.6	0.0	0.9	0.0	0.0	0.0
Attended 4 or more	0.6	0.0	0.0	0.0	0.0	0.0
Festivals Acadiens						
No attendance	91.4	93.9	98.2	87.2	93.1	96.9
Attended	8.6	6.1	1.8	12.8	6.9	3.1
All festivals but Festivals Acadiens						
No attendance	80.4	86.8	95.5	92.8	93.1	97.9
Attended one festival	13.5	12.3	3.6	7.2	6.9	2.1
Attended two festivals	5.5	0.9	0.0	0.0	0.0	0.0
Attended three festivals	0.0	0.0	0.9	0.0	0.0	0.0
Attended 4 or more	0.6	0.0	0.0	0.0	0.0	0.0
Totals (N)	163	114	112	250	188	193

Source: CODOFIL Survey, 1989.

icated to the celebration of Cajun ethnicity. Once again, we see that age is closely connected to the ways in which people express ethnicity.

Analysis of the attendance at the Festivals Acadiens, show that the non-Cajuns were more likely than those who labeled themselves as Cajuns to have attended. Further, this was the festival in which most of the non-Cajun participants had taken part. It would appear that the very success of the festival has led it to appeal chiefly to an audience outside the group it represents and whose name it bears. This wide popular appeal is interesting because Festivals Acadiens features music, cultural activities, and foods that are virtually exclusively devoted to the celebration of Cajun ethnicity. We suggest that ethnicity as a commodity blurs the line between "authenticity" and "inauthenticity." Although ethnicity can be marketed to ethnic group members, it may be most successful when the feeling of participation in an ethnic heritage can be sold to the larger public. The more apparently authentic this heritage claims to be, the greater its marketability.

Once we remove Festivals Acadiens from the analysis, the association of Cajun-themed festival attendance with self-described Cajun ethnicity becomes evident, particularly among the young people. Indeed, one out of every five younger Cajuns had participated in one of the festivals other than Festivals Acadiens. The association of youth, particularly Cajun youth, with festival attendance is interesting in the light of data on language. As we have discussed in the previous chapter, French language ability, the chief objective cultural marker, is in a state of rapid decline. The young people are the least likely to bear the linguistic marker of their ethnicity, but the most likely to enjoy ethnically themed festivals. Ethnic expression through festival attendance, moreover, is as accessible to nonmembers as it is to ethnic group members.

Table 7.2 gives selected characteristics of festival attendants and nonattendants. There is no clear linkage between parish residence and festival attendance, except that attendants are most likely to reside in Lafayette, particularly when Festivals Acadiens is included in the analysis. Whites are much more likely to participate in these events than blacks are, even considering the fact that whites constitute the majority of the population. Again, festival attendants are generally younger than the nonattendants.

Perhaps the most interesting results in Table 7.2 are the findings on occupation. People with professional, technical, and managerial jobs are proportionately the most likely to attend festivals, among both Cajuns and non-Cajuns. Those in working-class types of jobs make up the majority of the population, particularly among the Cajuns, and therefore most of the festival-goers are working class. There were very few people in agricultural activities in our sample and none of them had been to a Cajun-themed festival. The prominence of working-class occupations among the Cajuns supports the argument that we have been making throughout this book that contemporary Cajuns have disproportionately become the blue-collar workers of Southwestern Louisiana. However, even though Cajuns continue to occupy a definable socioeconomic position, this position has been changing both for individuals and groups, a development that has prompted a need to redefine identity.

As we have discussed above, festivals emerged as a vehicle of ethnic expression in recent history, when Acadiana had changed from a rural, farming, and fishing society to a modern industrial, retail, and service economy. This ecological shift, we suggest, dislocated the population from its older identities and social ties and created a desire to reconstruct identities by reconnecting with a rapidly disappearing past. Here, we see that those who were most uprooted, the professional classes, were the most likely to visit the places where ethnic identity is marketed.

Table 7.2
Selected Characteristics of Attendants and Nonattendants at All Cajun-Themed Festivals and at All Except Festivals Acadiens, 1989

	All Festivals		All Except Festivals Acadiens	
	Attendants	Non-Attendants	Attendants	Non-Attendant
Parish of Residence (%)				
Acadia (rural)	6.7	13.0	9.2	12.3
Evangeline (rural)	10.7	5.8	18.4	5.4
Iberia (urban-rural)	10.0	12.5	9.2	12.4
Lafayette (urban)	44.7	19.8	23.5	23.0
St. Landry (rural)	4.7	18.0	6.9	16.8
St. Martin (rural)	14.0	6.6	19.5	6.5
St. Mary (urban-rural)	5.3	13.1	8.0	12.3
Vermilion (rural)	3.4	11.2	5.7	10.6
Race				
White	91.9	82.3	94.1	82.7
Black	6.8	17.0	5.9	16.4
Median Age	36	47	36	45
Occupation				
Professional, technical, managerial, higher sales	29.3	20.8	25.3	21.8
Cajuns only	26.1	16.6	21.2	17.8
Lower clerical & sales, crafts, operatives, laborers	55.3	56.0	60.9	55.4
Cajuns only	62.3	63.8	67.3	62.9
Agriculture	0.0	1.0	0.0	1.0
Cajuns only	0.0	0.6	0.0	0.6
Other	15.3	22.2	13.8	21.9
Cajuns only	11.6	19.1	11.5	18.7
N	150	869	87	932
Cajuns only	69	320	52	337

Source: CODOFIL Survey, 1989.

FESTIVALS AND THE COMMODIFICATION OF TIME, SPACE, AND HISTORY

Festivals are by definition spectacles, staged public events. People in all types of economies have their periodic public celebrations. However, the pervasiveness of the spectacle is a consequence of the post-industrial capacity for reproducing human experience as a marketable commodity in a temporally and geographically delineated setting.

Agricultural societies are strongly influenced by the rhythm of planting and harvesting, with the harvest typically the chief occasion for celebration. As Figure 7.1 indicates, fall, the time of harvest, continues to be a popular season for festivals. The greatest number of festivals in 1998 fell in February, because so many of these ethnic-themed festivals were associated with Mardi Gras, which came in February in that year. However, five Cajun-themed festivals were held in September and six in October, the harvest months in Louisiana. It will also be noted, though, that no months are without festivals. This is because the timing is driven less by any agricultural or religious calendar than by marketing calculations. In interviews with festival officials and in the course of participation in festival organization, the organizers continually stressed the need to spread the events over the course of a year to avoid competing with one another for attendants and account for the region's hot summer weather.

A second important point about the timing of festivals concerns their placement in the week. All of these, without exception, are weekend events. Some may start on Thursday afternoons, but they are timed around the modern workweek, with the main events scheduled Friday evening through Sunday afternoon. This may seem obvious: of course, one might object, who could attend a festival on Monday morning? The very assumption that this is an obvious time to hold spectacles, when examined, suggests how deeply the modern workweek has sunk its framework into the organization of time. The weekend is the time for social events, for the shopping mall, for trips to Disney World. It is also the time for spectacles of ethnicity.

If Cajun festivals resemble other commodified entertainments in their temporal organization, they also display commodification in their arrangement of space. All festivals are held in open spaces, usually in parks and downtown areas. Festivals Acadiens, for example, is held in the central park of Lafayette, Girard Park. Very few actually charge admission fees. The Crawfish Festival in Breaux Bridge is notable because it recently started to charge an admission fee to control the impact of large crowds (more than 100,000) on a small town. Most of these are manifestly free events, not commercial endeavors. However, the intentionally noncommercial character of the festivals makes the predominance of commercial activities at them all the more interesting.

The center of the festivals is generally a stage, providing free music for all

Figure 7.1
Number of Cajun-Themed Festivals Per Month, 1998

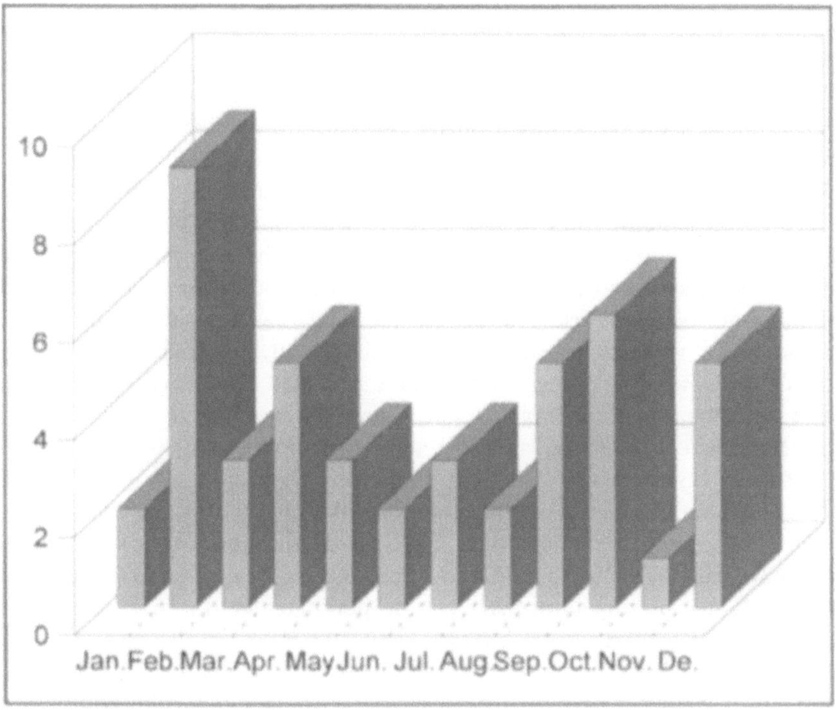

Source: Louisiana Office of Tourism, *Louisiana Fairs and Festivals* (Baton Rouge, LA: Louisiana Office of Tourism, 1998).

the attendants. At the Festivals Acadiens, music is provided either by zydeco bands or by groups that provide some variant of traditional Cajun folk music. A number of the other festivals, particularly those outside of the Lafayette area, present the "Cajun country music" that blends local strains of music and characteristic Louisiana instruments such as the accordion with electric guitars and the rhythms of contemporary popular country music. Around the stage, the festival grounds are organized as temporary shopping malls, with booths under small tents.

Two kinds of activities predominate in the booths: the sale of putatively ethnic foods and the sale of arts and crafts items. All of the booths that we have visited readily accept credit cards.[43] The foods include dishes such as jambalaya, stuffed breads, and crawfish and alligator dishes, all prepared by local merchants. These foods may vary in their quality and in the degree to which they would have been familiar to inhabitants of Southwestern Louisiana in the late nineteenth or early twentieth centuries. Nevertheless, we are not interested in evaluating the historical authenticity of foodstuffs or in acting as culinary critics. The important point is that all of these foods have explicit associations with Cajun ethnicity; those who eat them are consuming ethnicity by ingesting ethnic products.

The arts and crafts items are also symbolically rich. Paintings, carvings, decorated aprons, T-shirts, and miscellaneous knickknacks predominate. Again, all of these items intentionally evoke Cajun ethnicity. They also display an ironic relationship with history, in which an idealized past is represented through contemporary media. An illuminating example of this ironic re-presentation may be found in the work of the popular artist Floyd Sonnier, whose images are ubiquitous at these festivals. Sonnier is a skillful draftsman, and a man old enough to remember Southwestern Louisiana in the decades before World War II. His paintings dwell on old Cajun barns, horse-drawn vehicles, musicians playing informally for friends and family under moss-hung oak trees, and humble old-style homes with outhouses. The rural imagery of these pictures portrays the lives of farmers and trappers, of people who live off the land and make their own entertainments.

As is the case with all artistic representations, the scenes in Sonnier's work are interpretations of the world. However, they are emotion-laden interpretations of a world that no longer exists. Even the humblest of homes do not have outhouses today and the musicians are professionals performing on stage, not playing informally on the porch under the moss. Sonnier's paintings are sold as prints, but they also take a variety of other formats. Booths will sell Sonnier images on T-shirts, coffee cups, plates, calendars, and virtually anything else that has a surface. Ordinary items of consumption are thus transformed into emblems of ethnic identity.

As iconography, Sonnier's art provides an interesting example of the commodification of history. Products sold at boutiques connect individuals to a version of history. It should be noted that ethnicity, although constructed, is not constructed ex nihilo. Sonnier can actually remember the scenes that he portrays. Similarly, the musicians draw on an indigenous musical tradition when musically inclined relatives and neighbors did indeed gather to play informally. The commodification of ethnicity does not involve inventing ethnic fictions so much as drawing on a deeply felt tradition and recasting this tradition in the form of reproducible, marketable products.

POST-INDUSTRIAL AMERICA AND THE COMMODIFICATION OF CAJUN ETHNICITY

In the overview of the changing socioeconomic context of Louisiana and Acadiana, we saw that the economy of "Cajun country" in Louisiana has become similar to the economy of other regions of contemporary America. The service sector provides the greatest proportion of jobs, although there is also a fairly large percentage of jobs in manufacturing, mining, and construction. Agriculture and related "traditional" activities do not employ many people. Cajun festivals are not inherited, primordial celebrations, but recently invented traditions, products of the contemporary socioeconomic setting. The concentration of Cajuns in blue-collar occupations appears to help maintain Cajun ethnicity by placing members of the group in common life situations and by promoting in-group social ties and in-group marriages. Nevertheless, the ways in which the ethnicity is expressed do not simply reflect the class situation of the group. On the one hand, ideas about the group draw heavily on an idealized agrarian past. On the other hand, these ideas tend to be expressed in ways dictated by contemporary consumer culture.

We have seen a complex relationship between ethnicity and festival attendance. Those who identify themselves as ethnic group members are more likely than others to participate in these events. However, the most self-consciously "authentic" ethnic display, the one that makes the greatest efforts to root itself in pastimes, crafts, and skills with the purest pedigrees of traditionalism, is the one that is most likely to appeal to outsiders, rather than insiders. Younger people, especially among those who identify themselves as Cajuns, are more likely to participate in festivals than older people. Younger people are also less likely than older people to be fluent in French, the single most important objective marker of this group.

In large part because the self-consciously ethnic Festivals Acadiens is set in Acadiana's urban center of Lafayette, festival attendants tend to be drawn more heavily from the urban-suburban region of Lafayette than from the more rural parishes. Although the majority of those in the area and at festivals are blue-collar workers or service workers, particularly among the Cajuns, people at the professional-managerial-technical level are proportionately the most likely to attend.

In looking at the actual occurrences of these festivals we have seen that they are concerned with the marketing of symbolically rich commodities in the context of the contemporary American market economy. Festivals are weekend events, not celebrations of harvests. They are organized as temporary shopping malls, with staged entertainments surrounded by boutiques. Still, although the form of the activities is that of the present-day cathedral of consumption, their content is historical nostalgia.

Why should ethnicity continue to exist, or even become more self-consciously emphasized, as linguistic and cultural markers weaken? Here, we should recall a central claim of ethnicity: ethnicity is based on claims of ancestry. Ancestry links one to an "authentic" past and provides one with an "authentic" identity precisely because it seems to be so deeply rooted. To the extent that individuals are socially identifiable as consumers, as people who are connected to one another through items of purchase, they lack the sense of having primordial ties and "authentic" identity. The answer to this dilemma may be to imbue commodities with the historical meaning, to make items of purchase reverberate with the significance of an idealized past. Indeed, this recent tack taken by Cajun activists and entrepreneurs on their heritage has been met with popular, commercial, and media success. It can be interpreted as an indication of the ability of Cajun ethnics to adapt to a changing socioeconomic environment. Thus Cajuns are not "selling off" their culture but rather accommodating it to a post-industrial, postmodern society.

A 22-year-old graduate student at a university in New Orleans, a native of Lafourche Parish, exemplified the accommodation of Cajun ethnicity to contemporary day-to-day life in his conversations with us:

> I guess it's the music that gives me a real sense of who I am and where I come from. My parents were Cajuns, but I don't think they ever talked about it that much. My grandparents spoke French and I wish I had learned it from them, but I didn't. I listen to Cajun music CDs, though, and I think, That's my culture and those are my people. For me, it's really the music more than anything else that keeps Cajun culture alive.

Buying compact discs and going to weekend festivals are hardly standard activities among those who live by hunting, trapping, and farming among the swamps and bayous. Still, the choice of products expresses a vital connection between modern people, who largely live by buying things in stores, and the hunters and trappers who preceded them.

Individuals increasingly participate in the contemporary economy as consumers, deriving social identities from choices of categories of products rather than from participation in social groups. Participation in the contemporary economy also means a disjunction between current socioeconomic position (as nine-to-five workers or oil-rig hands) and ideas about group membership derived from historical traditions. This disjunction tends to heighten ethnic awareness rather than diminish it: English-speaking grandchildren paradoxically have a greater attachment to ethnicity than their French-speaking grandparents, and the foreign-educated professor returns to Louisiana with a sense of his heritage that he never had as a child. The CD-purchasing student has a more acute sense of ethnic identity than parents who grew up in French-speaking households. Perceptions of historical tradition provide the substantive imagery of ethnicity, but this imagery must be reshaped into contemporary forms. To fit into a consumer economy, ethnicity must become a commodity.

The paradox of "commodified ethnicity" is that it can easily provide a vicarious sense of primordial identity even to nongroup members. Although Cajuns are more likely than non-Cajuns to attend festivals, the latter participate in large numbers. At Festivals Acadiens, the most self-consciously "authentic" ethnic event, the latter actually predominate. One woman, who moved to Louisiana from New York in the mid-1990s, exclaimed, "Oh, I go to all those Cajun festivals. I love the music and the food and those old-timey crafts. I think Cajun culture is just wonderful!"

A unique feature of Cajun ethnicity commodified is the involvement of insiders as entrepreneurs. If indeed Cajun individuals are hired by non-Cajun outfits as cooks, musicians, or customer service attendants, there is also significant involvement of Cajuns in the design, ownership, and management of places and events where ethnic culture is displayed or marketed. Statistical data by state and federal agencies do not allow us a detailed analysis of the connection between ancestry and business variables. Our evidence is thus largely anecdotal and much has been brought forth in this book. It suggests that Cajun musicians, chefs, artists, tour guides, performers, and interpreters of all kinds tend to be independent, involved in family-run businesses and work with local public entities in Southwestern Louisiana. They do not constitute a closed ethnic niche since they rely in part on the cooperation with nonethnic capital and entities such as record companies, banks, suppliers, private partners, and public bodies. Yet, as Cajuns have been taking an increasing role in shaping their identity, they also actively participate in its marketing on their own terms. The festival organizers, media producers, restaurant owners, writers, and artists we have met are not playing a role written in a multinational corporation's script, nor are they exploiting unsuspecting tourists by selling fake artifacts. As Cajun dancers and academics debated in the mid-1990s on the acceptibility of the jig as an idiom of Cajun culture, they helped create a form of ethnic cultural expression that was then displayed by groups of dancers performing in Cajun restaurants and festivals. The Cajun French Music Association has also set the requirement that songs and performances it considers for its annual Cajun music awards ceremony contain some French. More important, these actions by insiders set the boundaries, the features, and the conditions of acceptibility of items and behaviors both old and new in the current understanding of Cajunism. Among these criteria are economic considerations whose interplay with ethnic matters obey an arrangement in which power as well as profits are matters of negotiation. These comments by a Cajun activist resigning in 1992 from a committee to Vermilionville, a planned "living" Acadian history museum in Lafayette, illustrate the conflict between business and history, the elusiveness of authenticity, and the limits of insider power:

> I originally accepted to be a member of the Vermilionville Historical Steering Committee because I felt that Vermilionville had the potential of responding to a great need in the French-community of Louisiana. . . . If operated correctly this village could have been a useful tool in preserving the [Louisiana French] culture. However . . . instead of recognizing our culture'spiritual and historical values, the authorities or decision makers want to use our culture as a commodity, a way to make money. . . . The irony is . . . that it proves that the authorities have no faith in our culture's ability to "sell itself."

Vermilionville has been operating as a moderately successful commercial endeavor run by a public entity of Lafayette Parish, the heart of Acadiana. Buildings are modern replicas of antebellum architecture, a well-stocked gift shop is operated by attendants wearing traditional bonnets for an ethnic look and tennis shoes for comfort, and a blacksmith demonstrates his skills to paying visitors and schoolchildren on field trips. It sits near an Acadian culture center funded by the National Parks Service and competes with the Village Acadien across town, another tourist attraction run by a private association for the disabled.

Vicarious ethnicity may actually be the key to much of contemporary resurgent ethnicity. Commodified ethnicity can provide a sense of being connected to a meaningful past (albeit a somewhat weaker sense) to out-group members as well as in-group members. One need only reflect that the Native American renaissance in literature that has made best-selling authors of Native American writers such as Sherman Alexie could not have taken place if it had to depend on Native American readers alone. Similarly, African American identity is marketed as a commodity to both group members and nongroup members in television shows and music CDs. The upsurge in Cajun ethnicity means not only that younger people will increasingly claim membership in the group, but that the symbols of the group will increasingly be marketed by ethnics and nonethnics both to group members and to outsiders.

NOTES

1. John K. Galbraith, *The Affluent Society* (New York: New American Library, 1958).
2. Lawrence M. Friedman, *The Horizontal Society* (New Haven: Yale University Press, 1999).
3. R. Stephen Warner, "Work in Progress toward a New Paradigm for the Sociological Study of Religion in the United States," *American Journal of Sociology* 98 (1993):1044–1093.
4. Robert Bocock, *Consumption* (London: Routledge, 1993), 77. See also Roger Swagler, "Evolution and Application of the Term Consumerism: Themes and Variations," *Journal of Consumer Affairs* 28 (1994):347–361.
5. Pierre Bourdieu, *La distinction. Critique sociale du jugement* (Paris: Editions de Minuit, 1979).
6. See, for example, Miguel de Oliver, " 'Democratizing' Consumerism?: Coalescing Constructions of Subjugation in the Consumer Landscape," *Gender, Place, & Culture: A Journal of Feminist Geography* 4 (1997):211–234, George Ritzer, *Enchanting a Disenchanted World: Revolutionizing the Means of Consumption*, (Thousand Oaks, CA: Pine Forge Press, 1999).
7. Gill Crozier, "Empowering the Powerful: A Discussion of the Interrelation of Government Policies and Consumerism with Social Class Factors and the Impact of this Upon Parent Interventions in Their Children's Schooling," *British Journal of Sociology* 18 (1997):187–201.

8. Ulrick Beck, *Risk Society: Towards a New Modernity* (London: Sage 1991); Giddens 1992; Ulrick Beck, Anthony Giddens & Scott Lash, *Reflexive Modernization: Politics, Tradition and Aesthetics in the Modern Social Order* Cambridge: Polity Press, 1995).

9. De Oliver, " 'Democratizing' Consumerism?," 214

10. Ritzer, *Enchanting a Disenchanted World.*

11. Special Issue, "Symposium: Global Integration and the Commodification of Culture," *Ethnology* 39(2) (2000); Jan Loader, "Consumer Culture and the Commodification of Policing and Security," *Sociology* 33(2) (1999):373–392; Isa Blumi, "The Commodification of Otherness and the Ethnic Unit in the Balkans: How to Think about Albanians," *East European Politics and Society* 12(3) (1998):527–569; Michael Brown, "Can Culture Be Copyrighted?" *Current Anthropology* 39(2) (1998):193–222; see Steven Smith, "The Tourism Product," *Annals of Tourism Research* 21(3) (1994):582–595 for a systematic attempt at defining what such a product is, in this case tourist destinations.

12. References are numerous and deal with a great variety of society. Works by Pierre van den Berghe on Indians in Mexico and Central America (*The Quest for the Other: Ethnic Tourism in San Cristobal, Mexico*, Seattle: University of Washington Press, and "Marketing Mayas: Ethnic Tourism Promotion in Mexico," *Annals of Tourism Research* 22(3) (1995):568–588 are among van den Berghe's writings on the topic) represent a substantial and organized body. Peter Wade, "Working Culture: Making Cultural Identities in Cali, Columbia," *Current Anthropology* 40(4): 449–472 (1999) in Columbia; Rosalie Schwartz *Pleasure Island: Tourism and Temptation in Cuba* (Lincoln: University of Nebraska Press, 1997) in Cuba; Robert Wood "Touristic Ethnicity: A Brief Itinerary," *Ethnic and Racial Studies* 21(2) (1998):218–241; Tanya Korovkin "Commodity Production and Ethnic Culture: Otavalo, Northern Ecuador," *Economic Development and Cultural Change* 47(1) (1998):125–155 are recent valuable contributions.

13. Marjorie Esman, "The Celebration of Cajun Identity: Ethnic Unity and the Crawfish Festival" (Unpublished Ph.D. dissertation, Tulane University, 1981); Marjorie Esman, *Henderson, Louisiana: Cultural Adaptation in a Cajun Community* (New York: Holt, Rinehart and Winston, 1985).

14. Cécyle Trépanier. "La Louisiane française au seuil du XXème siècle: La commercialisation de la culture," in G. Bouchard (ed.), *La construction d'une culture, le Québec et l'Amérique française* (Sainte Foy: Presses de l'université Laval, 1993), 361–394.

15. Barry J. Ancelet, "Cultural Tourism in Cajun Country: Shotgun Wedding or Marriage Made in Heaven?" *Southern Folklore* 49(3) (1992):256–266.

16. Sara LeMenestrel, *La voie des Cadiens: Tourisme et identité en Louisiane* (Paris: Belin, 1999).

17. Esman, "The Celebration of Cajun Identity."

18. Barry J. Ancelet, Jay Edwards, & Glen Pitre, *Cajun Country* (Jackson: University Press of Mississippi, 1991), 228.

19. R.O. Fardon, *Counterworks. Managing the Diversity of Knowledge* (London: Routledge, 1995); Jeremy Boissevain, *Coping with Tourists. European Reactions to Mass Tourism* (Oxford: Berghahn, 1996); Barbara Kirshenblatt-Gimblett, *Destination Culture: Tourism, Museums and Heritage* (Berkeley: University of California Press,

1998); for an ongoing discussion, see journals such as *Annals of Tourism Research, Cultural Survival Quarterly*, and *Social Anthropology*.

20. Frederick L. Olmsted, *A Journey in the Seaboard Slave States.* 2 vols, (New York, 1856); R.L. Daniels, "The Acadians of Louisiana," *Scribner's Monthly* 19 (1879–1880):383–392; Charles Warner, "The Acadian Land," *Harper's New Monthly Magazine* 71 (1887):334–354; Hamilton Basso, "Bayou Country," *Holiday*, September 1949 (on file in Dupré Library, University of Louisiana at Lafayette).

21. Ancelet, Edwards & Pitre, *Cajun Country.*

22. See the findings of John Maines, "The Road to Mamou," American Demographics 10(5) (1988):45–47 on the market value of the Cajun label.

23. Page Gutierrez, *Cajun Foodways* (Jackson: University Press of Mississippi, 1992).

24. Cécyle Trépanier, *French Louisiana at the Threshold of the 21st Century*, Projet Louisiane, Monograph 2, (Quebec: Laval University, 1989).

25. Ancelet, Edwards & Pitre, *Cajun Country*, 137.

26. Gutierrez, *Cajun Foodways*, 115, 119.

27. Ancelet, Edwards & Pitre, *Cajun Country*, 146.

28. John Broven, *South to Louisiana: The Music of Cajun Bayous* (New Orleans: Pelican Press, 1983); Ann Savoy, *Cajun Music: A Reflection of a People*, vol.1 (Eunice, LA: Blue Heron Press, 1984); Ancelet, Edwards & Pitre, *Cajun Country.*

29. See Ritzer, *Enchanting a Disenchanted World*, on fairs and amusement parks as ancestors of Disney World.

30. Claire Puneky, "Fairs, Festivals Mark Rural Life of Louisiana," *Times Picayune* (New Orleans: 1961), October 16.

31. Puneky, "Fairs, Festivals Mark Rural Life," 1, 28.

32. These observations on the Washington Parish Fair are from the second author's personal experience.

33. LeMenestrel, *La voie des Cadiens.*

34. Jacques Henry, "The Louisiana French Movement: Actors and Actions in Social Change" in Albert Valdman (ed.), *French and Creole in Louisiana*, (New York: Plenum, 1997), 183–213.

35. Henry, "The Louisiana French Movement."

36. The decrease is probably because of a change in the reporting of events and manifestations by the Louisiana Office of tourism since it appears that some festivals in Acadiana are not listed. Other indications that ethnicity remains vibrant commercially are events by other groups such as the Black Heritage Festival, St. Patrick's Day, Calling of the Tribe powwow, and even an Irish/Italian festival in Lake Charles.

37. Barry J. Ancelet (ed), *Cris sur le Bayou: Naissance d'une poésie acadienne en Louisiane* (Montréal: Editions Intermèdes, 1980).

38. Louisiana Office of Tourism, *Louisiana Fairs and Festivals* (Baton Rouge: Louisiana Office of Tourism, 1998); Louisiana Office of Tourism, *Francofête 1999: Events and Attractions* (Baton Rouge: Louisiana Office of Tourism, 1999).

39. LeMenestrel, *La voie des Cadiens.*

40. Cited in LeMenestrel, *La voie des Cadiens*, 161.

41. Kara T. Bernard & Shane K. Bernard, *Encyclopedia of Cajun Culture*, www.cajunculture.com (1998).

42. In addition to Festivals Acadiens, festivals identified by respondents were the Cotton Festival, Crawfish Festival, Sugar Festival, Abbeville French Festival, Cajun

Fun Fest, Rice Festival, Frog Festival, Mardi Gras, Festival International de Louisiane, La Boucherie de Saint Martinville, Boudin Festival, Shrimp Petroleum Festival, New Orleans Jazz and Heritage Festival, Duck Festival, Zydeco Festival, Louisiana Folklore Festival, Strawberry Festival, Heritage Festival, Yambilee Festival, Alligator Festival, Cracklin Festival, Swine Festival, Cattle Festival, Catfish Festival, Boggie Bayou Festival, Cochon de Lait, Jour des Cajuns, and Bastille Day.

43. See Ritzer, *Enchanting a Disenchanted World*, p. 156 on the importance of the credit card for the "new means of consumption."

Conclusion: A Look at the Future

Throughout this book, we have seen two distinct but related issues: the structural basis of ethnicity and the perception of ethnicity. Members of an ethnic group have something in common that contributes to categorize them as a definable set. They are also people who believe that they share certain inherited cultural characteristics and who are believed by others to share these characteristics. In exploring the basis and the perception of Cajun ethnicity, we have pointed out the importance of the socioeconomic position of Cajuns in the past and in the present. Cajuns continue to occupy a specific niche in Louisiana society, but the society and the niche have been in the process of rapid change.

We have argued that Cajuns came into existence as the rural, French-speaking poor of Southwestern Louisiana. As people who were distinguishable by region, language, and economic class, they were the subject of stereotypical portrayals by outsiders. Over time, they came to accept and perpetuate these portrayals, although they tended to recast negative images in positive terms. The quaint pictures of farmers and trappers dancing to fiddle and accordion music under moss-hung oaks alongside the bayous became the commonly held visions of Cajun life.

As the Louisiana economy changed, we have argued, the agricultural and aquatic pursuits that gave rise to Cajun ethnicity rapidly ceased to be part of the social landscape. The structural basis of Cajun ethnicity did not disappear, though. Instead, the children, grandchildren, and great-grandchildren of the lower-income farmers became a regional working class. Although the French language declined in use and the people of Southwestern Louisiana became much more similar culturally to other Americans, Cajuns continued to hold something in common with one another: a disproportionate concentration in blue-collar positions. This arrangement placed them in the same sorts of jobs, and it helped to maintain social ties within the group. Despite the fact that they have assimilated culturally in many respects, Cajuns continue to have a surprisingly high level of endogamy. We have argued that this in-group marriage is a consequence of the tendency to marry within the region and within a socioeconomic status.

Continuity, then, has helped maintain this ethnic group as a group. They are no longer poor, French-speaking farmers, but they continue to hold a position in the social structure in common. Change, however, has also been important, and change has shaped the perception of Cajun ethnicity. They may be members of a regional working class, but the images that they hold of themselves and that others hold of them are based on idealized versions of the stereotypes formed in earlier years. The perception of ethnicity cannot be reduced to a simple reflection of the current situation of ethnic group members.

Cajuns continue to form a group, but the relationship of individuals to the group and to images of the group is increasingly problematic. Working-class Cajuns have a great deal in common with each other, but less and less in common with their own previous generations. Upwardly mobile Cajuns come from a group that continues to exist, but the ties of the upwardly mobile both to other group members and to previous generations have weakened.

People identify themselves as members of groups. This identification is most acute when the relationship between individuals and groups is most troubled. Cajuns continue to be a definable set of people, and the boundaries of this set are maintained by a dominant working-class socioeconomic status. Nevertheless, the structural basis of the ethnicity has been changing rapidly. The problem that faces group members, then, is to say just what it means to be a Cajun. To answer this question, they turn to ideas about tradition, images from the past that are self-consciously historical in character.

Those who cultivate the images of Cajun ethnicity most assiduously are those for whom identification with the group has become most difficult. The ethnic awakening of Southwestern Louisiana has taken place among all social classes because the changes in the economic context that we saw in Chapter 3 have posed questions of social identity for all. The changes have been greatest, though, for the minority of middle-class Cajuns who experience discontinuity with the past and disconnectedness with the blue-collar basis of present-day ethnicity. The majority of Cajuns proudly proclaim their heritage, but they do not pass French on to their children. The middle classes are those who struggle to maintain their French or to learn a French they never knew in childhood. The movement launched by the creation of the Council on the Development of French in Louisiana (CODOFIL) was and to this day largely remains a middle-class endeavor.

Expressions of Cajun ethnicity are not only stimulated by the changing socioeconomic environment, but also accommodate themselves to this environment. Ideas about the group may harken back to a rural past, but these ideas are packaged and sold in a modern, consumer economy. The festival celebrates ethnic heritage in a manner familiar to those for whom Wal-Mart and the mall are important features of life. Expressing "traditional" images of ethnicity as consumer products is a way of packaging views of the past in forms that fit present-day requirements. There tend to be more working-class Cajuns than middle-class Cajuns at festivals because this is largely a blue-collar ethnicity. However, the middle classes are proportionately much more likely to attend festivals and to buy ethnic products, just as they are more likely to take care in maintaining and cultivating the French language.

This contrast between ethnicity as objectively based on social class and ethnicity as a matter of self-consciousness and self-classification recalls Karl Marx's division of social class itself into two levels. According to Marx, the first, most basic level, is that of a distinguishable group of people who share objective material interests as a result of the role played by this group in the process of economic production. At this conceptual level, members of a given class may or may not be aware of their common interests or of their own existence as a class. Their commonality is inherent to their objective position. Marx termed this level the "Class-In-Itself," class as an objectively existing phenomenon.

The second level in Marx's categorization is that of conscious recognition of commonality. Here, a class may be defined as a distinguishable group of people, constituting a broad division of society, sharing material interests, who actually recognize and consciously act on those interests. Marx refers to a class that achieves this kind of self-awareness as a "Class-For-Itself."[1]

In distinguishing between the objective basis of Cajun ethnicity and the subjective awareness of it, we have discussed levels that may be thought of as Ethnicity-In-Itself and Ethnicity-For-Itself. However, although these levels are analogous to Marx's thinking about classes in some respects, there are also important differences. Marx's Class-For-Itself was one that had become aware of its own present-day existence and interests. In our self-conscious ethnicity, self-consciousness involves thinking about the past to meet the demands of the present.

Although there is a strong association between Cajun ethnicity and regional blue-collar status, Cajuns did not spring into existence as the working class of Southwestern Louisiana. Instead, they emerged over the course of history, and they owe their collective existence to historical development. Self-conscious ethnicity, then, does not simply reflect the current situation. Self-consciousness is an attempt to integrate ideas received from the past with experiences in the present. Ethnicity-In-Itself is a product both of common experiences in the present and ideas about a group built up over time. Ethnicity-For-Itself involves the effort to think about the experiences of the present in terms of inherited, historical ideas. The images of Southwestern Louisiana life expressed in media reports, paintings, songs, and jokes generally express nostalgic ideas about the past, rather than reflections of the present. Still, we have maintained that seeing the category of Cajun purely as a matter of symbolism is misleading for two reasons. First, the group continues to have an objective basis in American society. Second, by definition all symbols must stand for something. Although the stereotypes and portrayals of Cajun life do not directly reflect current realities, they are not empty; they do have referents. The self-conscious images of life along the bayous symbolize the gap between historically derived ideas of social existence and contemporary life situations.

Although we have been primarily concerned with exploring and explaining the paradox of Cajun ethnicity, we believe that our findings and our argument have broader relevance to the study of ethnic groups. In particular, we maintain that the ethnic revival or ethnic awakening in the United States since the 1970s should be seen as more than mere nostalgia. It is a part of a quest for social identity that has followed the enormous increase in socioeconomic and geographic mobility of the post–World War II period. Ethnic and racial occupational niches and residential settings have not disappeared, nor are they simply figments even to those who do not occupy them. There are still identifiable Italian and Irish neighborhoods in many cities, although their Italianness or Irishness may seem foreign to natives from Italy or Ireland. Despite an apparent decrease in discrimination against some of the most disadvantaged groups in America, African Americans, Puerto Ricans, and Mexicans continue to live in ethnic concentrations and to occupy statistically identifiable positions in the system of stratification. At the same time, the black and Hispanic middle classes have been growing steadily. Ethnic and racial groups are still social realities, but the connection of individuals to those social realities has become increasingly complicated and problematic. There is, then, a dialectic between the continuing structural basis of ethnicity and the problem of self-identification created by change in that basis. Most Italian Americans today do not live in Italian neighborhoods. However, both the existence of the neighborhood and the memory of an Italian American neighborhood serve as reference points for people seeking self-identification through communal membership. Clearly, there are enormous variations in the extent to which different ethnic or racial groups are based on objective positions in the social structure. Both regional ties and association with economic levels differ from one group to another. We would like to suggest, though, that ethnic differentiation and ethnic stratification have not only been historical building blocks of American society, but continue to be major facets of American life today. To understand the meaning of ethnic group membership for many Americans, we need to consider the portrayals of ethnicity that have emerged over the nation's history, the changing but still important part played by ethnicity in contemporary American life, the complicated connections to ancestral groups held by many Americans, and the adaptation of inherited ethnic portrayals to current situations to make sense out of contemporary life.

We propose that contemporary ethnicity in American society and in the larger Western Civilization (where the concept of ethnicity appeared and developed) remains a multilevel and complex phenomenon. Simple mechanistic explanations we have encountered in our exploration of Cajun ethnicity typically fail to deal adequately with this complexity. Cajun ethnicity does not exist today because of the mythical resilience of a cultural heritage to which people are primordially attached, as the popular Acadian activist discourse proclaims. It also cannot be reduced to a Marxist false consciousness spread over the masses by a capitalist few eager to maintain their domination over the dispossessed and the fooled. Finally, as we have repeatedly argued, Cajun ethnicity, for all its symbolism, is not a mere technique used by individuals to feel good about themselves by occasionally calling on their ancestors' roots and mothers' unique recipes. All these dimensions are indeed present in this and other ethnicities but in a set of intertwined dialectical relationships. Ethnicity is a product of historical facts and mythical reconstructions, changing objective socioeconomic positions and varying mental representations, and that of simplified symbols that represent a complex social reality. Each of these elements is related to the others, influencing their reality and perception, and in return being influenced by them.

THE FUTURE OF CAJUN ETHNICITY

Are Cajuns likely to disappear in the twenty-first century? Will French still be spoken in Louisiana two generations from now? Our answers to these questions are "no" and "in a sense, yes." Although attempts to predict the future are always risky, we are reasonably confident that Cajuns will still be around, in fact and in perception, for a long time. Geographic mobility into and out of Southwestern Louisiana is increasing, but the residents of the Acadian parishes do not seem to be scattering to other parts of the world. Throughout the new century, there will be people in this corner of America who have a sense of having long roots in the region; the more time passes, the longer these roots will grow. The socioeconomic mobility of individuals is also unlikely to dissipate the modern working-class core of Cajun ethnicity. The high rate of endogamy that we have pointed out and the noted tendency to pass on relative socioeconomic position over generations is likely to maintain ties among future Louisiana Cajuns.

If the structural basis of Cajun ethnicity is likely to remain intact for the foreseeable future, the perception and public presentation of it will almost undoubtedly grow. In 1999, the Lafayette Parish school board building presented a prominent display of pictures and posters drawn by the district's children. These were devoted to the Acadian exile from Canada and resettlement in Louisiana, a narrative that has become something of a regional patriotic epic myth. The fact that most of the schoolchildren who drew these pictures do not seem to have been Cajuns has not detracted from their willingness to accept the Acadian story as their collective, if not individual, mythology.

The fact that the Acadians have become the recognized ancestors of a geographic area, and not just the ancestors of their putative descendants in that area, has given the label "Cajun" a flexibility in application that enables it to extend beyond both its historical and contemporary socioeconomic bases. An inscription on one of the vaults in a mausoleum in suburban Lafayette reads, "Born a Texan, Died a Cajun." If most Southwestern Louisianians are not Cajuns in any strict sense, it is possible to become a fictive member of the group by residence. The area is Cajun country; therefore, the Cajun identity can in a sense be applied to all of those who live there and attach themselves to the regional epic. Thus, the sobriquet "Ragin' Cajuns" applies to all of the students at the University of Louisiana at Lafayette, regardless of actual ancestry. Cajun-as-regional-symbol supports Cajun-as-ancestry, since those who claim descent from the Canadian Acadian refugees stand for all of those in the area.

The only apparent opposition to adopting the Acadian epic as the central narrative of Southwestern Louisiana comes from some Louisianians of African background, who balk at having a white ethnic group as the symbol of the region. However, although some black students dislike the nickname, both black and white athletes compete as "Ragin' Cajuns" and both black and white spectators cheer the "Cajuns." In addition, black discomfort with a label that many take to exclude them has not undercut the status of Cajuns as regional representatives so much as it has led to the development of a racial parallel. "Creoles" (French-speaking people of mixed race or blacks) are increasingly celebrated as the black equivalent of Cajuns. Radio announcers who try to be inclusive refer to the local music as "Cajun and Creole music," and a number of Creole festivals have come into existence in recent years. Sometimes, then, Cajun-as-symbol refers to all Southwestern Louisianians. Sometimes the inhabitants are divided along racial lines with "Cajuns" standing for all whites and "Creoles" standing for all blacks, even though the majority of neither racial category can actually be identified with either ancestry by culture or family ties.

Cajuns, therefore, are likely to continue to remain as a group of people with a basis in the social structure of Southwestern Louisiana, and their status as regional symbols will encourage claims of identification with them. Claims of ethnic identification will also be encouraged, we believe, by growing numbers of individuals in the professions and in similar occupations who come from Cajun families. Some degree of detachment from their "roots" will intensify the interest of these upwardly mobile individuals in rediscovering those roots. The appeal of Cajun music, Cajun foods, and other local cultural expressions will become greater rather than diminish as the connections of members of the middle class with their history and their contemporary co-ethnics grow more complicated.

We have little doubt that the cultural expressions of ethnicity will take on more and more of the character of commodities. This is in part a consequence of the function of Cajuns as regional symbols. Those who manufacture and market products will seek to identify themselves with popular images of localism. It is also a result, though, of the fact that modern Louisiana is a part of the American society of mass consumption, in which people express themselves through their choices of goods. Unless there is a massive collapse of the national economy leading to far-reaching changes behavior, the "commodification" of life is likely to continue and increase. People will celebrate and proclaim their Cajun heritage by buying CDs (or the future equivalent), attending festivals, taking Cajun dance lessons, purchasing spices for their foods, or by memberships in hunting clubs that enable them to shoot for recreation on leased lands.

We also believe that the French language will survive in Louisiana, although in an attenuated and changing form. In Chapter 5, we observed that French language use is declining rapidly, even from the older living generations of the present to the younger ones. Even in the Acadian core and even in households in which there is at least one parent who speaks French, the overwhelming majority of minors in 1990 could not speak the language. Comparing households in which there was a parent who could speak French, we saw that Cajuns were actually less likely than others to pass on their ancestral language.

Despite these indicators, it is our view that some forms of French will probably be found in Louisiana for some time to come. The use of French is a central part of ideas about Cajun ethnicity, in the minds of group members and in the minds of others. As many Louisianians, especially in the middle classes, have become committed to rediscovering a French-based heritage, efforts to retain the language have grown. CODOFIL has made efforts to promote French language use, French-immersion programs have become established in many Louisiana schools, and individuals are making the effort to learn the language. All of this suggests that there will be Francophones in the state well into the twenty-first century. It also suggests, though, that Louisiana French will become more similar to standard French, as it is passed on through lessons, and that it will take on something of a museum quality. More and more, those who speak French will be those who learned it in school or whose parents taught it to them as a special, self-conscious goal. It will not be the product of isolation, and those who use it will use it from choice, not out of the need to communicate.

French is also likely to become even more closely associated with the artistic expression of Cajun ethnicity, particularly with the music that has become so closely associated with Southwestern Louisiana. In a recent book on French language use in Terrebonne and Lafourche parishes, Kevin J. Rottet finds that young people are less likely than their elders to use the language and less proficient in it. However, Rottet also finds that listening to French music on the radio and singing in French appear to be common among the youngest speakers. In fact, the youngest people in this sample are actually more likely than their elders to employ French in these musical contexts.[2] Given the importance of music and musical events as ways of expressing ethnicity in a consumer economy, we believe it is probable that Cajun French will survive in a special niche: it will be the language of Cajun music. Words and phrases from songs are likely to slip into everyday use, helping French maintain an attenuated existence in Louisiana.

Change, in language and in society, is inevitable. But as people experience changes, they also attempt to reach back into the past, to make the world knowable through inherited concepts and to define themselves in the present by reinterpreting history, not discarding it. The Louisiana Cajuns of tomorrow will assuredly be different from those of today and yesterday. Still, we think it is safe to say that they will be.

NOTES

1. For a succinct discussion of this distinction, readers may want to look at Joseph Lopreato & Lawerence Hazelrigg, *Class, Conflict and Mobility* (San Francisco: Chandler Pub. Co., 1972), pp. 24–29.
2. Kevin J. Rottet, *Language Shift in the Coastal Marshes of Louisiana* (New York: Peter Lang, 2001).

Bibliography

PRIMARY DATA SOURCES

Ancelet, Barry. 1996a. "On Coonass." Manuscript on file with author.

Ancelet, Barry. 1996b. "Ragin' Cajuns: What's in a Name?" Manuscript on file with author.

Anderson, Bob. 2001. "Farewell to a Legend," *Morning Advocate*, (Baton Rouge, LA), September 7.

Angers, Trent. 1990. *The Truth About the Cajuns.* Lafayette, LA: Acadian House Publishing.

Arceneaux, George. 1974. *Youth in Acadie: Reflections on Acadian Life and Culture in Southwest Louisiana.* Baton Rouge, LA: Claitor's Publishing Division.

Arceneaux, Jean. 1994. *Je suis Cadien.* Merrick, NY.

Archivo General de Indias, Papeles procedentes de Cuba, legajo 188C, folios 62–63, Seville, Spain.

Ardoin, Karrel. 1994. *Cajun Culture and Humour.* Mamou, LA.

Barde, Alexandre. 1861. *Histoire des Comités de vigilance aux Attakapas.* Saint Jean Baptiste, LA: Imprimerie du Meschacébé et de l'Avant-Coureur.

Bass, Shermakaye. 1998. "Cutting Loose in Cajun Country." *New York Times*, January 4.

Basso, Hamilton. 1949. "Bayou Country." *Holiday.* September (on file in the Vertical Files, Dupré Library, University of Louisiana at Lafayette).

Baudry des Lozières. 1802. *Voyage à la Louisiane et sur le continent de l'Amérique septentrionale fait dans les années 1794 à 1798.* Paris: Dentu.

Belisaire. 1998. "Les Cajuns, le pays Cajun." www.belisaire.fr.

Bernard, Antoine. 1936. *Le Drame Acadien.* Montréal: Les Clercs de Saint Viateur.

Bernard, Ryan. 1980. "The Cajuns." *Houston City Magazine* (October): 41–43, 109–113.

Bernard, Kara T. & Shane K. Bernard. 1998. *Encyclopedia of Cajun Culture.* www.cajunculture.com.

Berquin Duvallon, Pierre-Louis. 1803. *Vue de la colonie du Mississipi, ou des provinces de Louisiane et de Floride occidentale, en l'année 1802.* Paris: Imprimerie Expéditive.

Beulah. 1898. Letter to the editor in Mary Alice Fontenot & P.B. Freeland, 1976. *Acadian Parish, Louisiana. A History to 1900.* Vol. 1. Baton Rouge, LA: Claitor's Publishing Division.

Bilger, Burkhard. 1999. "Enter the Chicken: On the Bayou, Cockfighting Remains Undefeated," *Harper's Magazine* 298, March (1786) 48–57.

Biographical and Historical Memoirs of Louisiana. 1892. Chicago: Goodspeed Publishing.

Birmingham, Nan Tillson. 1988. "Cajuns, Crocs and Crayfish." *Town & Country* (May): 147–156.

Blanchet, Catherine Brookshire. 1970. "Louisiana French Folk Songs Among Children in Vermilion Parish, 1942–54." Unpublished Master's Thesis. Lafayette, University of Southwestern Louisiana.

Bolton, Herbert Eugene, ed. 1914. *Anastase de Mézières and the Louisiana-Texas Frontier 1768–1780.* 3 vols. Cleveland, OH: Arthur Clark Company.

Bossu, Jean Bernard. 1763. *Nouveaux voyages aux Indes occidentales.* Reprint, Paris: Aubier-Montaigne, 1980.

Bossu, Jean Bernard. 1777. *Nouveaux Voyages dans l'Amérique Septentrionale.* Amsterdam: Changuion.

Brackenridge, H.M. 1814. *Views of Louisiana.* Pittsburgh, PA: Cramer, Spear and Eichbaum.

Bradshaw, Jim. 1991. "Culture, not blood, defines today's Cajuns." *Sunday Advertiser* (Lafayette, LA), January 13.

Bragg, Rick. 1995. "A Cajun Tradition Won't Die Down," *New York Times*, December 24.

Bragg, Rick. 1996. "In Louisiana, Card Games Reveal the Cajun Spirit." *New York Times*, February 18.

Browne, Turner. 1977. *Louisiana Cajuns.* Baton Rouge: Louisiana State University Press.

Buckingham, James Silk. 1842. *The Slave States of America*, 2 vols. London: Fisher.

Burchfield, R.W. (ed.). *Oxford English Dictionary, A Supplement to.* 1972. Oxford: Clarendon Press.

Cable, George W. 1886. *The Creoles of Louisiana.* New York: Charles Scribner's Sons.

Cable, George W. 1888. *Bonaventure.* Reprint, New York: International Association of Newspapers and Authors, 1901.

"Cajun." 1996. *Microsoft Encarta Encyclopedia.* Funk & Wagnall Corporation.

"Cajun happy with status." (Letter to the editor by Beatrice Duhon Murphy) 1988. *Daily Advertiser* (Lafayette, LA), June 1.

"Cajuns of the net." 1998. www.geocities.com/BourbonStreet/2373/member.html.

Cassidy, Frederic G., ed. 1985. *Dictionary of American Regional English. Cambridge*: The Belknap Press of Harvard University Press.

Castille, Jeanne. 1983. *Moi, Jeanne Castille de Louisiane*. Paris: Lunot-Ascot Editeurs.

Castrillo, Shawn. "Free Speech Alley reflects racial frustration." 1992. (Lafayette, LA) *Vermilion* 88(29): October 23.

Chateaubriand, François René vicomte de. 1827. *Voyage en Amérique, en Italie, au Mont Blanc* in *Oeuvres Complètes*. Paris, 1929.

Chopin, Kate. 1894. *The Complete Works*. Edited by Per Seyersted. Baton Rouge: Louisiana State University Press, 1969.

" 'Coon Ass' bill passes: Haik says it's stupid." 1981 *Daily Iberian* (New Iberia, LA), July 12.

Craigie, William A. & James R. Hulbert, eds. 1938. *A Dictionary of American English*. Vol 1. Chicago: University of Chicago Press.

Daigle, Jules. 1984. *A Dictionary of the Cajun Language*. Ann Arbor, MI: Edwards Brothers.

Daigle, Pierre. 1972. *Tears, Love and Laughter*. S. Church Point, LA: Acadian, Pub. Enterprise.

Dana, Edmund. 1819. *Geographical Sketches of the Western Country*. Cincinnati: Locker, Reynolds & Co. Printers.

Daniels, Jonathan. 1938. *A Southerner Discovers the South*. New York: MacMillan.

Daniels, R.L. 1879. "The Acadians of Louisiana." *Scribner's Monthly* 19: 383–392.

Darby, William. 1816. *A Geographical Description of the State of Louisiana*. Philadelphia: John Melish.

Darby, William. 1818. *The Emigrant's Guide to the Western and South-Western States and Territories*. New York: Kirk and Mercein.

Dauphin, Gary. 1995. *Evangeline: A Study in Cajun Culture*, CD ROM sponsored by the Center for French and Francophone Studies (Louisiana State University), Fondation CODOFIL, National Data Products, and the Educational Technology Review Center (University State of Louisiana).

Davis, Rebecca H. 1887. "Here and There in the South V: In Attakapas." *Harper's New Monthly Magazine 75*: 913–925.

"Decay of Cajun culture causes many to lament." 1986. *Sunday Advertiser* (Lafayette, LA), October 5.

De La Houssaye, Sidonie. 1983 [1888]. *Pouponne et Balthazar*. Lafayette: The Center for Louisiana Studies.

De Leon, Edwin. 1875. "The Bayou Teche." *Eclectic Magazine* 84: 353–362.

Delery, Simone & Gladys Renshaw. 1932. *France d'Amérique*. Chicago: D.C. Heath and Company.

Denett, Daniel. 1876. *Louisiana As It Is*. New Orleans: "Eureka" Press.

Dennett, John. 1866. *The South As It Is 1865–1866*. Edited by Henry M. Christian. New York: Viking Press, 1965.

Dewailly, Gretchen. 1981. "T. Paul Robin—Last Real Cajun." *Sunday Advertiser* (Lafayette, LA), June 28.

Ditchy, Jay K., ed. 1932. *Les Acadiens louisianais et leur parler*. Paris: Librairie E. Droz.

Editorial. 1966. *Sunday Advertiser* (Lafayette: LA), December 4.

"Edwards under Fire for 'Coonass' Jibe." 1972. *States-Item* (New Orleans), October 24.

Fabre-Surveyer, Edouard. 1938. *Une journée française à Lafayette et autres récits de voyage*. Montréal.
Feibleman, Peter. 1973. *The Bayous—The American Wilderness*. New York: Time-Life Books.
Finerty, J.F. 1880. "Far South." *Chicago Times*. November (on file).
Fletcher, Joel. 1947. *The Acadians in Louisiana Today*. Lafayette: Southwestern Louisiana Institute.
Flint, Timothy. 1826. *Recollections of the Last Ten Years*. Boston: Cummings, Hilliard and Company.
Flint, Timothy. 1835. *Journal of the Rev. Timothy Flint from the Red River to the Ouachitta, or Washita, in Louisiana in 1835*. Alexandria, LA.
Foote, Ruth. 1997. "Farrakhan plan stirs label debate." *Morning Advocate* (Baton Rouge, LA), July 24.
Ford, Kenneth. 1984. "Cajuned-out." *Acadiana Profile* 11(5): 16.
Fortier, Alcée. 1894. *Louisiana Studies; Literature, Customs and Dialects; History and Education*. New Orleans: F.F. Hansell and Bro.
Gallassero, Hilda. 1970. "Myriad Descriptions Found for Cajuns of Louisiana." *Daily Advertiser* (Lafayette, LA), August 30.
Gallasserro, Hilda. 1981. "Are you a Cajun?" Lafayette, LA: *Acadiana Profile* 9(2): 2.
Geenen, Bernard. 1984. *Au Fil de la Louisiane*. Bruxelles: Les Editeurs d'Art Associés.
Gérin, Pierre & Pierre M. Gérin. 1982. *Marichette: Lettres Acadiennes 1895–1898. Sherbrooke*, Québec: Editions Naaman.
Goldman, David. 1996. "Cajun Country Sojourn." *Country Living* 19(9): 28(+).
Gould, Philip. 1980. *Les Cadiens d'Asteur—Today's Cajuns*. Lafayette, LA: Galerie Press.
Graves, Ralph. 1930. "Louisiana, Land of Perpetual Romance." *National Geographic* 57(4): 393–482.
Guidry, Richard. 1971. "Un Cajen en Guadeloupe." *Acadiana Profile* 3(1): 4.
Guidry, Ron. 1999. "A Cajun Man's Swamp Cruise." www.cajunman.com.1999.
Guirard, Greg. 1989. *Cajun Families of the Atchafalaya: Their Ways and Words*. Self-published.
Hallowell, Christopher. 1979. *People of the Bayou: Cajun Life in Lost America*. New York: E.P. Dutton.
Hamm, Bob. 1972. "What Is a Cajun?" Pamphlet on file with author.
Hansen, Harry, ed. 1971. *Louisiana A Guide to the State*. New York: Hastings House.
Harmon, J.J. 1989. "What is Authentic Cajun?" *Times of Acadiana* (Lafayette, LA), April 12.
Harmon, J.J. 1993. "What's in it for us?" *Times of Acadiana* (Lafayette, LA), August 13.
Historical Records Survey. 1940. *The Favrot Papers 1695–1769*. New Orleans, Louisiana State Museum.
Historical Records Survey. 1941. *The Favrot Papers 1769–1781 Volume 2*, New Orleans: Tulane University of Louisiana.
Hogsdon, Adam. 1824. *Letters from North America*. 2 vols. London.
Houser, Dave. 1998. "Bayous, Blues and Beignets." *Trailer Life* 58(2): 65(+).

Hudson, Marylin. 1969. *Acadiana Unlimited: A Tour of Southwest Louisiana.* Baton Rouge, LA: Claitor's Publishing Division.

Hutchins, Thomas. 1784. *An Historical Narrative and Topographical Description of Louisiana and West Florida.* Philadelphia: for the Author and Robert Aitken.

"Imitation Cajun." 1989 *Times of Acadiana* (Lafayette, LA), March 22.

"I've been called a Coonass just because I'm from Louisiana." 2001. Comment on www.nola.com/forums/cajun, July 19.

Jacobs, Howard. 1971. "Cajun Laugh-in." *Acadiana Profile* 3(2).

Jaray, Gabriel-Louis. 1937. "Le destin français en Louisiane." *France-Amérique*, Août: 153–158.

Johnston, Margaret Avery. 1893. *The Acadians in Story and Song.* New Orleans: F.F. Hansell and Bro. Publishers.

"Justin Wilson, 87, Cajun Chef and Humorist." 2001. *New York Times*, September 7.

Kane, Harnett. 1943. *The Bayous of Louisiana.* New York: Hampton Publishing.

Keating, Bern. 1966. "Cajunland: Louisiana French-speaking Coast," *National Geographic* 129(3): 352–391.

Ketchum, Richard. 1957. *The American Heritage Book of Great Historic Places.* New York: American Heritage Publishing.

Keyes, Frances Parkinson. 1950. *All This Is Louisiana.* New York: Harper & Brothers Publishers.

King, Edward. 1875. *The Southern States of North America: A Record of Journeys.* London: Blackie & Son.

Kneeland, Douglas. 1968. "Cajuns Seek French Culture Out of Mixed Past." *New York Times*, May 9: 49, 56.

LA Gazette de Louisiane. Vol. 3, 4 (Novembre 1990), 7 (Février 1991), Vol. 4, 1 (Août–Septembre 1993), 8(Janvier/Fevrier 1995). Lafayette, LA: Fondation CODOFIL.

Laborde, Erroll. "Quarter Cajun." 1986. New Orleans: *Gambit*, April 5–11.

Lanman, Charles. 1856. *Adventures in the Wilds of the United States and British American Provinces.* 2 vols. Philadelphia: J.W. Moore.

Lauvrière, Emile. 1931. "Pélerinage acadien et canadien en Louisiane." *France-Amérique.* Août–Septembre.

Lauvrière, Emile. 1940. *Histoire de la Louisiane Française.* Paris: G-P Maisonneuve.

LeBlanc, André. 1850. "Historical and Statistical Collections of Louisiana: The Parish of Assumption." *DeBow's Review* 9(3): 286–290.

LeBlanc, Dudley. 1932. *The True Story of the Acadians.* Lafayette, LA: D.J. LeBlanc.

Lockett, Samuel. 1871. *Second Annual Report of the Topographical Survey of Louisiana: Report of Superintendent for 1870.* Baton Rouge: Louisiana State University.

Lockett, Samuel. 1873. *Louisiana As It Is.* Edited by Lauren C. Post. Baton Rouge: Louisiana State University Press, 1969.

"Louisiana Battling Counterfeit Cajun." 1989. *New York Times*, March 18.

Louisiane. 1980. Lafayette, LA, 41 (December) (a newspaper published by Media-Louisiane).

Louisiane Française. 1978. Lafayette, LA. 11 (April 1), 12 (April 15), 13 (May 1), 15 (June 15), 16 (July 1) (a newspaper published by CODOFIL).

Martin, Désirée. 1877. *Les veillées d'une soeur ou le destin d'un brin de mousse.* La Nouvelle-Orléans: Imprimerie Cosmopolite.

Martineau, Alfred. 1937. "Les survivances françaises en Louisiane." *Revue d'histoire des colonies françaises.* 2ème trimestre: 113–124.

McMillan, James B. 1943. "Lexical Evidence from Charles Sealsfield." *American Speech* 18: 119.

Mereness, Newton D., ed. 1916. *Travels in the American Colonies.* New York: MacMillan.

Moses, Jennifer. 1998. "Bayou Country." *New York Times Magazine.* March 1: 53–64.

Mullener, Elizabeth. 1988. "A Cajun Journey." *Times Picayune* (New Orleans): August 14–18.

Nordhoff, Charles. 1876. *The Cotton States in the Spring and Summer of 1875.* Reprint, New York: Burt Franklin, 1965.

Noyes, J.O. 1868. "Cotton Planting at Port Hudson," *Putnam's Magazine* 2(7): 46–57.

Old Settler. 1888. Letter to the Editor in Mary Alice Fontenot & P.B. Freeland, 1976. *Acadian Parish, Louisiana. A History to 1900.* Vol. 1. Baton Rouge, LA: Claitor's Publishing Division.

Olivier, Robert. 1936. *Pierre of the Teche.* New Orleans: Pelican Publishing.

Olmsted, Frederick L. 1856. *A Journey in the Seaboard Slave States.* 2 vols. New York: Dix Edward and Co.

Pecot, Marguerite. 1932. "The 'Cajun.' " Master's Thesis. Baton Rouge: Louisiana State University.

Perrin, William Henry, ed. 1891. *Southwest Louisiana: Biographical and Historical.* New Orleans: Gulf Publishing Company. Reprint, Baton Rouge, LA: Claitor's Publishing Division, 1971.

Perrin du Lac, François Marie. 1805. *Voyage dans les 2 Louisianes.* Paris: Capelle et Renand.

Peytavin, John L. 1894. "Traité sur l'éducation au dix-neuvième siècle." *Comptes-Rendus de l'Athénée Louisianais.* 1 Novembre: 163–170.

Pierce, G.W. 1851. "Historical and Statistical Collections of Louisiana: Terrebonne." *De Bow's Review* 10 (December): 601–611.

Pittman, Philip. 1770. *The Present State of the European Settlements on the Mississippi.* Reprint, Gainesville: University of Florida Press, 1973.

Post, Lauren C. 1962. *Cajun Sketches.* Baton Rouge: Louisiana State University Press.

Poutchartrain, Blake (pseudonym). "New Orleans Know-It-All." 1988. *Gambit*, November 22.

Prentiss, S.S. 1855. *Memoir of S.S. Prentiss.* Edited by his Brother. New York: Charles Scribner.

Price, H.B. 1850. "Terrebonne Parish, Louisiana." *De Bow's Review* 8(February): 146–150.

Prichard, Walter, ed. 1938. "A Tourist Description of Louisiana in 1860." *Louisiana Historical Quarterly* 21(4).

Prichard, Walter, Fred Kniffen & Clair Brown, eds. 1945. "Southern Louisiana and Southern Alabama in 1819: Journal of James Leander Cathcart." *Louisiana Historical Quarterly* 28(3): 735–921.

Ralph, Julian. 1893. "Along the Bayou Teche." *Harper's New Monthly Magazine* 87: 870–884.

Ramsey, Carolyn. 1957. *Cajuns on the Bayou.* New York: Hastings House.

Reed, Revon. 1976. *Lâche pas la patate: Portrait des Acadiens de la Louisiane.* Montréal: Editions Parti pris.

Reed, Roy. 1976. "Cajuns resist the melting pot." *New York Times Magazine.* February 29.

"La région Cajun." 1998. www2.cajun.net.

Rhodes, Albert. 1873. "The Louisiana Creoles." *Galaxy* 16: 252–260.

Robert, Adolphe. 1940. *Mémorial.* Manchester, NH: L'Association Canado-Américaine.

Robin, C.C. 1807. *Voyage dans l'intérieur de la Louisiane, de la Floride occidentale et dans les îles de la Martinique et de Saint Domingue.* 3 vols. Paris: F. Buisson.

Rodrigue, Georges. 1976. *The Cajuns of Georges Rodrigue.* Birmingham, AL: Oxmoor House.

Roller, David C. & Robert W. Twyman. 1979. *The Encyclopedia of Southern History.* Baton Rouge: Louisiana State University Press.

Roman, Marguerite. 1924. "Les Acadiens au XXème siècle." *Comptes Rendus de l'Athénée Louisianais.* Mai: 12–23.

Rudloe, Jack & Anne Rudloe. 1979. "Louisiana's Atchafalaya: Trouble in Bayou Country." *National Geographic* 156(3): 376–97.

Rushton, William F. 1979. *The Cajuns: From Acadia to Louisiana.* New York: Farrar, Strauss & Giroux.

St. Martin, Thad. 1937. "Cajuns." *Yale Review* 26: 859–862.

Sancton, Thomas. 1991. "Why the Good Times Roll." *Time* 44 (November 4): 36.

Sauvalle, Paul Marc. 1891. *Louisiane-Mexique-Canada: Aventures Cosmopolites.* Montréal: Desaulniers et Leblanc.

Signal writer. 1888. Editorial in Mary Alice Fontenot & P.B. Freeland, eds. 1976. *Acadian Parish, Louisiana. A History to 1900.* Vol. 1. Baton Rouge, LA: Claitor's Publishing Division.

Simpich, Frederick. 1947. "Louisiana Trades with the World." *National Geographic* 92(6): 705–738.

Smith, Griffin Jr. 1990. "Cajun Still Loving Life." *National Geographic* 178: 41–65.

Smith-Thibodeaux, John (pseudonym). 1977. *Les francophones de Louisiane.* Paris: Editions Entente.

Sonnier, Floyd. 1982–1987. *Mes Acadiens-My Acadians: A Calendar.* Scott, LA: Floyd Sonnier.

Sothern, James & Jerry Charpantier. 1977. *Cajun Dictionary.* Houma, LA: Rachel Hebert.

Southern Pacific Lines. 1929. *Evangeline Country.* New Orleans: Southern Pacific Lines.

Sparks, W.H. 1882. *The Memories of Fifty Years.* 4th ed. Philadelphia: E. Claxton & Company.

Spell, Arden. 1956. *Life in Louisiana Cajun Country.* Asheville, NC.

Stephens, Edwin. 1933. "The Story of Acadian Education in Louisiana." Address to the Louisiana Historical Society. Reprint from *Louisiana Schools,* 19–24. Louisiana Room, Dupré Library, University of Louisiana at Lafayette.

Stiles, Beryl. 1977. *A Cajun's Persuasion: A Decade of Newspaper Columns in St Mary*. Detroit: Harlo.

Stoddard, Major Amos. 1812. *Sketches, Historical and Descriptive, of Louisiana*. Philadelphia: Published by Matthew Carey, A. Small printer.

Talland, Robert. 1957. *Evangeline and the Acadians*. Eau Claire, WI: E.M. Hale and Company.

Tassin, Myron. 1976. *Nous Sommes Acadiens/We Are Acadians*. Gretna, LA: Pelican Publishing.

Tauriac, Michel. 1980. *La Louisiane aujourd'hui*. Paris: les éditions j.a.

Thidodeaux, Ron. 2001. " 'Coonass' carries baggage some prefer to forget." *Times-Picayune* (New Orleans), July 17.

Trillin, Calvin. 1979. "U.S. Journal: Mamou, LA." *New Yorker* 55(8): 119–124.

Trillin, Calvin. 1995. "The Nutria Problem." *Atlantic Monthly* 275(2): 30(+).

Untel de Gravelles, Marc. 1979. "Mille Misères—Laissant le bon temps rouler en Louisiane." Projet Louisiane Monograph No. 5, Québec: Université Laval.

Uzee, Philip. 1986. "The Acadians." *Louisiana History* 27(3): 295–297.

Vogel, Théodore. 1978. "Lâche pas la patate!" *Partir* 40: 31(+).

Warner, Charles. 1887. "The Acadian Land." *Harper's New Monthly Magazine* 74: 334–354.

Waud, Alfred Rodolph. 1866. "Acadians in Louisiana." *Harpers' Weekly*, October 20, p. 670. Reprinted in Timothy Reilly, "Early Acadiana Through Anglo-American Eyes (Part 2)," *Attakapas Gazette* 1977 12(3):pp. 160–161.

Whatley, Randall & Harry Jannise. 1978. *Conversational Cajun French I*. Baton Rouge, LA: Chicot Press.

"Who are the Cajuns?" 2001. In "Culture at a Crossroads." *Times-Picayune* (New Orleans), July 15.

Wilson, Martha. 1954. "Cajun Country: Their Unchanged Eden. After Nearly 200 Years It's Beginning to Change." *Shreveport Times* (Shreveport, LA), July 15.

Writers Program. 1941. *Louisiana: A Guide to the State*. New York: Hastings House.

GENERAL REFERENCES

Alba, Richard. 1985. *Italian-Americans: Into the Twilight of Ethnicity*. Englewood Cliffs, NJ: Prentice-Hall.

Alba, Richard. 1986. "Interpreting the Parameters of Log-Linear Models." *Sociological Methods and Research* 16: 45–77.

Alba, Richard. 1990. *Ethnic Identity: The Transformation of White America*. New Haven: Yale University Press.

Alba, Richard & Reid M. Golden. 1986. "Patterns of Intermarriage in the United States." *Social Forces* 65(1): 202–223.

Allahar, Anton. 1994. "More Than an Oxymoron: Ethnicity and the Social Construction of Primordial Attachment." *Canadian Ethnic Studies* 26:18–34.

Allain, Mathé. 1978. "Twentieth-Century Acadians." In *The Cajuns: Essays on Their History and Culture*, edited by Glen Conrad, 129–141. Lafayette, Center for Louisiana Studies.

Allain, Mathé. 1989. " 'They Don't Even Talk Like Us': Cajun Violence in Film and Fiction," *Journal of Popular Culture* 23(1): 65–76.

Allard, Réal & Rodrigue Landry. 1986. "Subjective Ethnolinguistic Vitality Viewed as a Belief System." *Journal of Multilingual and Multicultural Development* 7: 1–12.

Allen, Walter R. & Joseph O. Jewell. 1996. "The Miseducation of Black America: Black Education since *An American Dilemma*." In *An American Dilemma Revisited: Race Relations in a Changing World*, edited by Obie Clayton, Jr. New York: Russell Sage Foundation, 169–190.

Ancelet, Barry. 1988. "A Perspective on Teaching the 'Problem Language' in Louisiana." *French Review* 61(3): 345–356.

Ancelet, Barry. 1990. "Cajuns in Film." Paper presented at the meeting of the American Association of Teachers of French, New Orleans, LA, July.

Ancelet, Barry. 1992. "Cultural Tourism in Cajun Country: Shotgun Wedding or Marriage Made in Heaven?" *Southern Folklore* 49(3): 256–266.

Ancelet, Barry. 1994a. "From Evangeline Hot Sauce to Cajun Ice: Signs of Ethnicity in South Louisiana." Paper presented at the meeting of the American Folkore Society, New Orleans, LA, October.

Ancelet, Barry. 1994b. *Cajun and Creole Folktales: The French Oral Tradition of South Louisiana*. New York: Garland.

Ancelet, Barry Jean, Jay Edwards, & Glen Pitre, eds. 1991. *Cajun Country*. Jackson: University Press of Mississippi.

Ancelet, Barry & Elemore Morgan. 1984. *The Makers of Cajun Music*. Austin, University of Texas Press.

Anderson, Benedict. 1983. *Imagined Communities: Reflections on the Origin and Spread of Nationalism*. London: Verso.

Appelbaum, Richard P. & William J. Chambliss. 1997. *Sociology*. 2nd ed. New York: Longman.

Arceneaux, Maureen. 1982. "Acadian to Cajun: Population, Family and Wealth in Southwest Louisiana, 1765–1854," Ph.D. Dissertation. Salt Lake City, UT: Brigham Young University.

Arendt, Hannah. 1951. *The Origins of Totalitarianism*. New York: Harcourt.

Arsenault, Bona 1965. *Histoire et généalogie des Acadiens*. Québec: Le Conseil de la Vie française en Amérique.

Bakalian, Anny. 1993. *Armenian-Americans: From Being to Feeling Armenian*. New Brunswick, NJ: Transaction Publishers.

Balibar, Ernest & Immanuel Wallerstein. 1988. *Race, nation, classe, les identités ambiguës*. Paris: La Découverte.

Bankston, Carl L. III. 1995. "Southeast Asians in Louisiana." In *A Refuge for All Ages: Immigration in Louisiana History*, edited by Carl Brasseaux, 661–677. Lafayette: Center for Louisiana Studies.

Bankston, Carl L. III. 1997. "Bayou Lotus: Theravada Buddhism in Southwestern Louisiana." *Sociological Spectrum* 17 (4): 453–472.

Bankston, Carl L. III & Stephen J. Caldas. 2001. *A Troubled Dream: The Promise and Failure of School Desegregation in Louisiana*. Nashville, TN: Vanderbilt University Press.

Bankston, Carl L. III & Stephen J. Caldas. 1998. "The American School Dilemma: Race and Scholastic Performance." *Sociological Quarterly* 38: 423–429.

Bankston, Carl L. III & Jacques Henry. 1998. "The Socioeconomic Position of the

Louisiana Creoles: An examination of Racial and Ethnic Stratification." *Social Thought and Research* 21: 253–277.

Barringer, Herbert, Robert W. Gardner & Michael J. Levin. 1993. *Asian and Pacific Islanders in the United States.* New York: Russell Sage Foundation.

Barry, David. 1989. "A French literary renaissance in Louisiana: Cultural Reflections." *Journal of Popular Culture* 23: 47–63.

Barth, Fredrick. 1969. *Ethnic Groups and Boundaries: The Social Organization of Culture Difference.* Boston: Little, Brown & Co.

Beck, Ulrick 1991. *Risk Society: Towards a New Modernity.* London: Sage.

Beck, Ulrick, Anthony Giddens, & Scott Lash. 1995. *Reflexive Modernization: Politics, Tradition and Aesthetics in the Modern Social Order.* Cambridge: Polity Press.

Bernard, Shane. 1996. *Swamp Pop: Cajun and Creole Rhythm and Blues*: Jackson: University Press of Mississippi.

Blalock, Hubert. 1967. *Toward a Theory of Minority Group Relations.* New York: Wiley.

Blauner, Robert. 1972. *Racial Oppression in America.* New York: Harper and Row.

Blumi, Isa. 1998. "The Commodification of Otherness and the Ethnic Unit in the Balkans: How to Think about Albanians." *East European Politics and Society* 12(3): 527–569.

Board of Regents. 1983. Report on the Commission on French as a Second Language. Baton Rouge, LA: Board of Regents.

Bocock, Robert. 1993. *Consumption.* London: Routledge.

Boissevain, Jeremy, ed. 1996. *Coping with Tourists. European Reactions to Mass Tourism.* Oxford: Berghahn.

Bonacich, Edna. 1972. "A Theory of Ethnic Antagonism: The Split Labor Market," *American Sociological Review* 37: 547–559.

Bond, George C. & Angela Gilliam, eds. 1997. *Social Construction of the Past: Representations as Power.* New York: Routledge.

Bourdieu, Pierre. 1972. *Outline of a Theory of Practice.* Reprint, Cambridge: Cambridge University Press, 1977.

Bourdieu, Pierre. 1979. *La distinction. Critique sociale du jugement.* Paris: Editions de Minuit.

Bourdieu, Pierre. 1982. *Ce que parler veut dire. L'économie des échanges linguistiques.* Paris: Fayard.

Brabant, Sarah. 1977. "The Acadian Family: Anachronism or Paradigm?" *Attakapas Gazette* 12(4): 201–208.

Brasseaux, Carl. 1978. "Acadian Education: From Cultural Isolation to Mainstream America." In *The Cajuns: Essays on their History and Culture*, edited by Glen Conrad, 212–224. Lafayette,: Center for Louisiana Studies.

Brasseaux, Carl. 1989. *In Search of Evangeline: Birth and Evolution of the Evangeline Myth.* Thibodaux, LA: Blue Heron Press.

Brasseaux, Carl. 1992. *Acadian to Cajun: Transformation of a People 1803–1877.* Jackson, University Press of Mississippi.

Brasseaux, Carl & Glenn Conrad. 1982. *A Selected Bibliography of Scholarly Literature on Colonial Louisiana and New France.* Lafayette, Center for Louisiana Studies.

Brasseaux, Carl, Keith Fontenot & Claude Oubre. 1994. *Creoles of Color in the Bayou Country.* Jackson, University Press of Mississippi.

Brasseaux, Carl, Emilio Fabrian Garcia & Jacqueline Voorhies, eds. 1989. *Quest for the Promised Land.* Lafayette, Center for Louisiana Studies.

Brassieur, Charles R. 1982. "The Modern Atchafalaya Culture: Results of the Ethnographic Survey." In *Archeology and Ethnology on the Edges of the Atchafalaya Basin, South Central Louisiana*, edited by Jon L. Gibson, 153–242. Lafayette, LA: Center for Archeological Studies.

Brink, Florence Roos. 1948. "Literary Travellers in Louisiana Between 1803 and 1860." *Louisiana Historical Quarterly* 31(2): 1–32.

Broven, John. 1983. *South to Louisiana: The Music of Cajun Bayous.* Gretna, LA: Pelican Publishing Company.

Brown, Becky. 1993. "The Social Consequences of Writing Louisiana French." *Language in Society* 22: 67–101.

Brown, Becky. 1997. "Development of a Louisiana French Norm." In *French and Creole in Louisiana*, edited by Albert Valdman, 215–235. New York: Plenum Press.

Brown, Michael. 1998. "Can Culture Be Copyrighted?" *Current Anthropology* 39(2): 93–222.

Bryk, Anthony S. & Stephen W. Raudenbush. 1992. *Hierarchical Linear Models: Applications and Data Analysis Methods.* Newbury Park, CA: Sage Publications.

Buss, David M. 1985. "Human Mate Selection." *American Scientist* 73: 47–51.

Buss, David M. & Michael Barnes. 1986. "Preferences in Human Mate Selection." *Journal of Personality and Social Psychology* 50: 559–570.

Clarke, Clifford. 1985. "Religion and Regional Culture. The Changing Pattern of Religious Affiliation in the Cajun Region of Southwest Louisiana." *Journal for the Scientific Study of Religion* 24(4): 384–395.

Clarke, Clifford. 1988. "Assimilationist Views of an Ethnic Region: The Cajun French Experience in Southwest Louisiana," *Social Science Quarterly* 62(2): 433–451.

Clifford, James & George Marcus, eds. 1986. *Writing Culture: The Poetics and Politics of Ethnography.* Berkeley: University of California Press.

Collard, Clyde. 1975. The Cajun Family: Adjustment to Modern Trends. In *The culture of Acadiana: Tradition and Change in South Louisiana*, edited by Steven DelSestro and Jon Gibson, 111–118. Lafayette: University of Southwestern Louisiana.

Condon, Sherri & Pamela Pittman. 1992. "Language Attitudes in Acadiana." In *Cajun Vernacular English: Informal English in French Louisiana, Louisiana English Journal*, edited by A.M. Scott, 56–72. Special Issue, Lafayette, University of Southwestern Louisiana.

Conrad, Glen, ed. 1978. *The Cajuns: Essays on Their History and Culture.* Lafayette: Center for Louisiana Studies.

Consulat Général de France. 1979. *La Question du Français en Louisiane.* La Nouvelle-Orléans: French Consulate.

Conzen, Kathleen, David Gerber, Ewa Morawaska, George Pozzetta & Rudolph Vecoli. 1992. "The Invention of Ethnicity: A Perspective from the U.S.A." *Journal of American Ethnic History* 12(1): 3–41.

Creté, Liliane. 1978. *La vie quotidienne en Louisiane 1815–1830.* Paris: Hachette.

David, Marc. 1996. Riziculture et Mardi Gras: l'organisation du travail et le carnaval rural dans la petite production marchande en Louisiane, mémoire de maitrise, Québec: Université Laval.

Debien, Gabriel. 1978. "The Acadians in Santo Domingo: 1764–1789." In *The Cajuns: Essays on their History and Culture*, edited by Glen Conrad, 21–96. Lafayette: Center for Louisiana Studies.

Debord, Guy. 1967. *La Société du spectacle.* Paris: éditions Champ Libre.

Debyser, Francis, Jan Lobelle, André Paquette, Robert Paris & Lawrence Richard. 1978. 1978 Evaluation of Louisiane Statewide CODOFIL French Program. Lafayette, LA.

de Heusch, Luc. 2000. "*L'ethnie.* The Vicissitudes of a Concept." *Social Anthropology* 8(2): 99–116.

DelSesto, Steven & Jon Gibson, eds. 1975. *The Culture of Acadiana: Tradition and Change in South Louisiana.* Lafayette: University of Southwestern Louisiana.

Dennis, David C. 1995. "The Image of Louisiana in America 1800 to 1890." Master's Thesis. Lafayette: University of Southwestern Louisiana.

De Oliver, Miguel. 1997. " 'Democratizing' Consumerism?: Coalescing Constructions of Subjugation in the Consumer Landscape." *Gender, Place, & Culture: A Journal of Feminist Geography* 4: 211–234.

Department of Education. 1974. CODOFIL French Program 1974–1975. Baton Rouge: Louisiana Department of Education.

De Vos, George & Lola Romanucci-Ross, eds. 1975. *Ethnic Identity: Continuities and Change.* Palo Alto, CA: Mayfield.

Domengeaux, James. 1986. "Native-Born Acadians and the Equality Ideal." *Louisiana Law Review* 46: 1151-1195.

Dominguez, Virginia. 1986. *White by Definition: Social Classification in Creole Louisiana.* New Brunswick, NJ: Rutgers University Press.

Dormon, James. 1983. *The people Called Cajuns: An Introduction to an Ethnohistory.* Lafayette: Center for Louisiana Studies.

Dormon, James. 1984. "Louisiana's Cajuns: A Case Study in Ethnic Group Revitalization." *Social Science Quarterly* 65: 1043–1057.

Dormon, James. 1992. "Louisiana 'Creoles of Color': Ethnicity, Marginality, and Identity." *Social Science Quarterly* 73: 615–626.

Dormon, James, ed. 1996. *Creoles of Color of the Gulf South.* Knoxville: University of Tennessee Press.

Dubois, Sylvie, W. Gautreau, H. Margot, M. Mélançon, & T. Veler. 1995. "The Quality of French Spoken in Louisiana: Linguistic Attitudes Towards the Varieties of French in Cajun Communities." *SECOL Review* 19(2): 126–150.

Dubois, Sylvie & Megan Mélançon. 1996. "Cajun is Dead: Long Live Cajun. Shifting from a Linguistic to a Cultural Community." *Journal of Sociolinguistics* 1(1): 63–93.

Dural, Carolyn. 1987. "Bibliographie des écrits louisianais français de 1900 jusqu'à nos jours." In *Les autres littératures d'expression française en Amérique du Nord*, edited by J. Tessier et P-L. Vaillancourt, 155–164. Ottawa.

Edwards, Jay. 1991. "Family Organization." In *Cajun Country*, edited by Barry Jean Ancelet, Jay Edwards, & Glen Pitre, 69–76. Jackson: University Press of Mississippi.

Edwards, Jay & Maida Bergeron. 1991. "Folk Medicine." In *Cajun Country*, edited by Barry Jean Ancelet, Jay Edwards & Glen Pitre. 95–100. Jackson: University Press of Mississippi.

Eriksen, Thomas H. 1993. *Ethnicity and Nationalism*. London: Pluto Press.

Esman, Marjorie. 1981. "The Celebration of Cajun Identity: Ethnic Unity and the Crawfish Festival." Ph.D. Dissertation. New Orleans: Tulane University.

Esman, Marjorie. 1985. *Henderson, Louisiana: Cultural Adaptation in a Cajun Community*. New York: Holt, Rinehart and Winston.

Esman, Marjorie. 1993. "About the Cajuns." *Mississippi Quarterly* 47(1): 113–125.

Estaville, Lawrence. 1986. "Mapping the Cajuns." *Southern Studies* 25(2): 163–171.

Estaville, Lawrence. 1990. "The Louisiana French Language in the Nineteenth Century." *Southeastern Geographer* 30(2): 107–120.

Ethnology. 2000. Symposium: "Global Integration and the Commodification of Culture." 39(2).

Ewen, Stuart. 1988. *All Consuming Images: The Politics of Style in Contemporary Culture*. New York: Basic Books.

Fanon, Franz. 1968. *Les damnés de la terre*. Paris: Maspéro.

Fardon, R.O., ed. 1995. *Counterworks. Managing the Diversity of Knowledge*. London: Routledge.

Featherstone, M., ed. 1990. *Global Culture*. London: Sage.

Fisheries Statistics and Economics Division, National Marine Fisheries Service. 1998. *Fisheries of the United States*. Silver Spring, MD: National Marine Fisheries Service.

Fishman, Joshua. 1966. *Language Loyalty in the United States*. The Hague: Mouton & Co.

Fishman, Joshua. 1977. "Language and Ethnicity." In *Language, Ethnicity and Intergroup Relations*, edited by H. Giles, 15–57. London: Academic Press.

Fishman, Joshua. 1985. "Am and Goy as Designations for Ethnicity in Selected Books of the Old Testament." In *The Rise and Fall of Ethnic Revival: Perspectives on Language and Ethnicity*, edited by Joshua Fishman et al., 15–38. Berlin: Mouton.

Fishman, Joshua. 1990. "What Is Reversing Language Shift (RLS) and How Can It Succeed?" *Journal of Multilingual and Multicultural Development* 11(1–2): 5–36.

Forêt, Michael. 1989. "A Cookbook View of Cajun Culture." *Journal of Popular Culture* 23(1): 23–36.

Forêt, Michael. 1992. "Acadian Versus Cajun: What's in a Name? An Essay Review." *Louisiana History* 33(4): 417–421.

Friedman, Lawrence M. 1999. *The Horizontal Society*. New Haven: Yale University Press.

Galbraith, John K. 1958. *The Affluent Society*. New York: New American Library.

Ganguly, Rajat & Ray Taras. 1998. *Understanding Ethnic Conflict: The International Dimension*. New York: Longman.

Gans, Herbert. 1979. "Symbolic Ethnicity: The Future of Ethnic Groups and Cultures in America." *Ethnic and Racial Studies* 2(1): 1–20.

Gans, Herbert. 1992. "Comment: Ethnic Invention and Acculturation, A Bumpy-Line Approach." *Journal of American Ethnic History* 12(1): 42–52.

Gans, Herbert. 1994. "Symbolic Ethnicity and Symbolic Religiosity: Towards a

Comparison of Ethnic and Religious Acculturation." *Ethnic and Racial Studies* 17(4): 577–592.
Gaudet, Marcia. 1989. "The Image of the Cajun in Literature." *Journal of Popular Culture* 23(1): 77–88.
Geana, Geoghita. 1997. "Ethnicity and Globalisation. Outline of a Complementarist Conceptualisation." *Social Anthropology* 5(2): 197–210.
Geertz, Clifford. 1973. *The Interpretation of Cultures.* New York: Basic Books.
Giddens, Anthony. 1992. *Modernity and Self-identity.* Cambridge: Polity Press.
Gilbert, William H. 1946. "Memorandum Concerning the Characteristics of the Larger Mixed-Blood Racial Islands of the Eastern United States." *Social Forces* 24(4): 439–440.
Gill, Crozier. 1997. "Empowering the Powerful: A Discussion of the Interrelation of Government Policies and Consumerism with Social Class Factors and the Impact of this Upon Parent Interventions in Their Children's Schooling." *British Journal of Sociology 18*: 187–201.
Gilmore, H.W. 1933. "Social Isolation of the French-Speaking People of Rural Louisiana." *Social Forces* 12: 78–84.
Girard, Maurice. 1991. "La survie passe par l'immersion." *Journal de Québec.* 15 avril.
Glazer, Nathan & Daniel Moynihan, eds. 1975. *Ethnicity, Theory and Experience.* Cambridge: Harvard University Press.
Gold, Gerald. 1978. *Cousin and the Gros Chiens: The Limits of Cajun Political Rhetoric.* Projet Louisiane 1, York University.
Gold, Gerald. 1979. *The Role of France, Quebec and Belgium in the Revival of French in Louisiana Schools.* Projet Louisiane Working Paper No. 7, Downsview, Ontario: York University.
Gordon, Milton. 1964. *Assimilation in American Life.* New York: Oxford University Press.
Gramling, Robert. 1989. "Concentrated Work Scheduling: Enabling and Constraining Effects." *Sociological Perspectives* 32: 47–64.
Gramling, Robert. 1996. *Oil on the Edge: Offshore Development, Conflict, Gridlock.* Albany: State University of New York Press.
Gramling, Robert & Sara Brabant, eds. 1984. *The Role of the Outer Continental Shelf Oil and Gas Activities in the Growth and Modification of Louisiana's Gulf Coast.* Washington, DC: U.S. Department of Commerce, National Oceanic and Atmospheric Administration.
Gramling, Robert & Sara Brabant. 1986. "Boomtowns and Offshore Energy Impact Assessment." *Sociological Perspectives* 27: 177–201.
Gramling, Robert, Craig Forsyth & Linda Mooney. 1986. "The Protestant Ethic and the Spirit of Cajunism." *Journal of Ethnic Studies* 15: 33–46.
Gramling, Robert & William Freudenburg. 1990. "A Closer Look at 'Local Control': Communities, commodities, and the Collapse of the Coast." *Rural Sociology* 55: 541–558.
Griolet, Patrick. 1986. *Cadjins et Créoles en Louisiane.* Paris: Payot.
Guillermou, Alain & Jeanne Ogée, eds. 1993. *En Lutte pour l'Avenir du Français.* Paris: Biennale de la langue française.
Gurr, Ted Robert. 1993. *Minorities at Risk.* Washington, DC: United States Institute of Peace.

Gutierrez, Page. 1992. *Cajun Foodways.* Jackson: University Press of Mississippi.

Hall, Gwendolyn Midlo. 1992. *Africans in Colonial Louisiana: The Development of Afro-Creole Culture in Louisiana in the Eighteenth Century.* Baton Rouge, Louisiana and State University Press.

Hall, John R. 1992. "The Capital(s) of Culture: a Nonholistic Approach to Status Situations, Class, Gender, and Ethnicity." In *Cultivating Differences: Symbolic Boundaries and the Making of Inequality*, edited by Michèle Lamont & Marcel Fournier, 257–288. Chicago: University of Chicago Press.

Hechter, Michael. 1975. *Internal Colonialism: The Celtic Fringe in British National Development, 1536–1966.* London: Routledge and Kegan Paul.

Henry, Jacques. 1982. "Le Mouvement Louisianais de Renouveau Francophone: Vers Une Nouvelle Identité Cadjine?" Ph.D dissertation. Paris: Université Paris V, René Descartes.

Henry, Jacques. 1986. "L'enseignement du français en Louisiana: L'effort continue. *Parlements et Francophonie* 60: 98–110.

Henry, Jacques. 1988. "Un statut pour les Cajuns." *France Amérique*, 23–29 juin and 30 juin–6 juillet.

Henry, Jacques. 1990. "Le français nouveau arrive?" *LA Gazette de Louisiane* 1(3): 1–5.

Henry, Jacques. 1997. "The Louisiana French Movement: Actors and Actions in Social Change." In *French and Creole in Louisiana*, edited by Albert Valdman, 183–213. New York: Plenum.

Henry, Jacques & Carl Bankston. 1998. "Propositions for a Structuralist Analysis of Creolism," *Current Anthropology* 39(4): 558–566.

Hilton, James L. & William von Hippel. 1996. "Stereotypes." *Annual Review of Psychology* 47: 237–272.

Hintze, James & Larbi Oukada. 1977. "The Lexical Item *Creole* in Louisiana." *Journal of the Linguistic Association of the Southwest* 2: 143–161.

Hirsch, Arnold & Joseph Logsdon, eds. 1992. *Creole New Orleans: Race and Americanization.* Baton Rouge: Louisiana State University Press.

Hobsbawm, Eric & T. Rager, eds. 1983. *The Invention of Tradition.* Cambridge: Cambridge University Press.

Horowitz, Donald. 1985. *Ethnic Group in Conflict.* Berkeley: University of California Press.

Hout, Michael & Joshua R. Goldstein. 1994. "How 4.5 Million Irish Immigrants Became 40 Million Irish Americans: Demographic and Subjective Aspects of the Ethnic Composition of White America." *American Sociological Review* 59(1): 64–82.

Huggs, Katrina. 1990. "The roots of the language." *The Times of Acadiana* (Lafayette, LA) October 10.

Isaacs, H.R. 1975. "Basic Group Identity: The Idols of the Tribe." In *Ethnicity, Theory and Experience*, edited by Nathan Glazer & Daniel Moynihan, 29–52. Cambridge: Harvard University Press.

Isajiw, Wsevolod. 1993. "Definitions of Ethnicity: New Approaches." *Ethnic Forum* 13(2)–14(1): 9–16.

Jenkins, Richard. 1994. "Rethinking Ethnicity: Identity, Categorization and Power." *Racial and Ethnic Studies* 17(2): 197–223.

Jones, Siâm. 1991. *The Archeology of Ethnicity: Constructing Identities in the Past and Present.* London: Routledge.

Jones, Stella. 1982. "The Impact of Acculturation on Cajun Husband/Wife Role/Perception and Values within the Family." Master's Thesis. Lafayette: University of Southwestern Louisiana.

Kammer, Edward. 1941. *Four Southwestern Louisiana Parishes.* Washington, DC: Catholic University of America Press.

Keefe, Susan Emley. 1992. "Ethnic Identity: The Domain of Perceptions of and Attachment to Ethnic Groups and Cultures." *Human Organization* 51(1): 35–43.

Kein, Sybil, ed. 2000. *Creole: The History and Legacy of Louisiana's Free People of Color.* Baton Rouge Louisiana State University Press.

Kennedy, Ruby Jo Reeves. 1946. "Single or Triple Melting Pot? Intermarriage Trends in New Haven, 1870–1940," *American Journal of Sociology* 49: 331–339.

Kirshenblatt-Gimblett, Barbara. 1998. *Destination Culture: Tourism, Museums and Heritage.* Berkeley: University of California Press.

Kitano, Harry H. 1988. "The Japanese American Family." In *Ethnic Families in America: Patterns and Variations*, edited by Charles H. Mindell, Robert W. Habenstein & Roosevelt Wright, Jr., 258–275. New York: Elsevier.

Kitano, Harry H., Wai-Tsang Yeung, Lynn Chai & Harry Hatanaka. 1984. "Asian American Interracial Marriage." *Journal of Marriage and the Family* 46: 179–190.

Kivisto, Peter. 1989. "The Attenuated Ethnicity of Contemporary Finnish-Americans." In *The Ethnic Enigma: The Salience of Ethnicity for European-Origin Groups*, edited by Peter Kivisto, 67–88. Philadelphia: Balch Institute.

Korovkin, Tanya. 1998. "Commodity Production and Ethnic Culture: Otavalo, Northern Ecuador." *Economic Development and Cultural Change* 47(1): 125–155.

Kosmin, Barry, Sidney Goldstein, Joseph Waksberg, Nava Lerer, Ariella Keysar, and Jeffrey Scheckner. 1991. *Highlights of the CJF 1990 National Jewish Population Survey.* New York: Council of Jewish Federations.

Labov, Theresa & Jerry A. Jacobs. 1986. "Intermarriage in Hawaii, 1950–1983." *Journal of Marriage and the Family* 48: 79–88.

Landry, Rodrigue & Réal Allard. 1991. "Can Schools Promote Additive Bilingualism in Minority Group Children?" In *Language, Culture and Cognition: A Collection of Studies in First and Second Language Acquisition*, edited by L. Malavé and G. Duquette 198–231. Clevedon, England: Multilingual Matters.

Landry, Rodrigue, Réal Allard & Jacques Henry. 1996. "French in South Louisiana: Towards Language Loss." *Journal of Multilingual and Multicultural Development* 17(5): 442–468.

Larouche, Alain. 1981. *Ethnicité pêche et pétrole: Les Cadjins du bayou Lafourche en Louisiane francophone.* Projet Louisiane, monographie 1, Toronto: York University.

Larouche, Alain. 1983. "Les Cadjins du Canal Yankee." In *Du continent perdu à l'archipel retrouvé: le Québec et l'Amérique Française*, edited by Dean Louder & Eric Waddell, 235–258. Québec: Les Presses de l'Université Laval.

LeMenestrel, Sara. 1999. *La voie des Cadiens: Tourisme et identité en Louisiane.* Paris: Belin.

Levin, Michael J. & Susan J. Lapham. 1993. "Ancestry Reporting in the 1990 Census: Towards the 2000 Census." Unpublished paper presented at the Annual Meetings of the Population Association of America, Cincinnati, OH, April 3–5.

Lieberson, Stanley. 1980. *A Piece of the Pie: Blacks and White Immigrants Since 1980.* Berkeley: University of California Press.

Lieberson, Stanley. 1981. *Language Diversity and Language Contact.* Stanford, CA: Stanford University Press.

Lieberson, Stanley & Mary Waters. 1988. *From Many Strands: Ethnic and Racial Groups in Contemporary America.* New York: Russell Sage Foundation.

Lieberson, Stanley & Mary Waters. 1993. "The Ethnic Responses of Whites: What Causes Their Instability, Simplification, and Inconsistency?" *Social Forces* 72(2): 421–450.

Loader, Jan. 1999. "Consumer Culture and the Commodification of Policing and Security." *Sociology* 33(2): 373–392.

Lopreato, Joseph & Lawrence Hazelrigg. 1972. *Class, Conflict and Mobility.* San Francisco: Chandler.

Lorenzen, David. 1999. "Who Invented Hinduism?" *Comparative Studies in Society and History* 41(4): 630–659.

Louisiana Office of Tourism. 1998. *Louisiana Fairs and Festivals.* Baton Rouge: Louisiana Office of Tourism.

Louisiana Office of Tourism. 1999. *Francofête 1999: Events and Attractions.* Baton Rouge: Louisiana Office of Tourism.

Marcantel, David. 1984. "Statut légal du français en Louisiane." *Parlements et Francophonie 54*: 34–43.

Massignon, Geneviève. 1962. *Les parlers français d'Acadie: Enquêtes linguistiques.* 2 vols. Paris: Honoré Champion.

Moerman, Michael. 1965. "Ethnic Identification in a Complex Civilization: Who Are the Lue?" *American Anthropologist* 67(5–1): 1215–1230.

Murphy, T.W. 1999. "From Racist Stereotype to Ethnic Identity: Instrumental Uses of Mormon Racial Doctrine." *Ethnohistory* 46(3): 451–480.

Myrdal, Gunnar, Richard Steiner & Arnold Rose. 1944. *An American Dilemma: The Negro Problem and Modern Democracy.* New York: Harper.

Nagel, Joane. 1986. "The Political Construction of Ethnicity." In Competitive Ethnic Relations, edited by Susan Olzak & Joane Nagel. New York: Academic Press.

Nagel, Joane. 1994. "Constructing Ethnicity: Recreating Ethnic Identity and Culture." *Social Problems* 41(1): 152–176.

Neumann, Ingrid. 1985. *Le Créole de Breaux Bridge, Louisiane: étude morphosyntaxique, textes, vocabulaire.* Hamburg: H. Buske.

Novak, Michael. 1971. *The Rise of Unmeltable Ethnics.* New York: Macmillan.

Oukada, Larbi. 1978. "The Territory and Population of French-speaking Louisiana." *Revue de Louisiane/Louisiana Review* 7(1): 5–34.

Paine, Jeffery. 1998. *Father India: How Encounters with an Ancient Culture Transformed the Modern West.* New York: HarperCollins.

Parenton, Vernon. 1938. "Notes on the Social Organization of a French Village in South Louisiana." *Social Forces* 17: 73–82.

Poirier, Pascal. 1953. *Glossaire acadien.* Moncton: Université St Joseph.

Portes, Alejandro & Ruben Rumbaut. 1990. *Immigrant America: A Portrait.* Berkeley: University of California Press.

Post, Lauren C. 1940. "Acadian Animal Caste in Southwest Louisiana: Some Sociological Observations." *Rural Sociology* 5(2): 183–191.

Poutignat, Philippe & Jocelyne Streiff-Fenart. 1995. *Théories de l'ethnicité.* Paris: PUF.

Puneky, Claire. 1961. "Fairs, festivals mark rural life of louisiana." *Times Picayune* (New Orleans) October 16.

Read, William. 1931. *Louisiana French.* Baton Rouge: Louisiana State University Press.

Reilly, Timothy. 1977–78. "Early Acadiana Through Anglo-American Eyes," *Attakapas Gazette* 12:1(1977): 3–20, 12:3(1977): 159–77, 12:4(1977): 185–94, 13:2(1978): 53–71.

Ritzer, George. 1999. *Enchanting a Disenchanted World: Revolutionizing the Means of Consumption.* Thousand Oaks, CA: Pine Forge Press.

Roosens, Eugeen. 1989. *Creating Ethnicity: The Process of Ethnogenesis.* Newbury Park, CA: Sage Publications.

Rottet, Kevin J. 2001. *Language Shift in the Coastal Marshes of Louisiana.* New York: Peter Lang.

Royce, Anya P. 1982. *Ethnic Identity, Strategies of Diversity.* Bloomington, IN: Indiana University Press.

Ruggles, Steven, Matthew Sobek et. al. 1997. *Integrated Public Use Microdata Series: Version 2.0.* Minneapolis: Historical Census Projects, University of Minnesota.

Said, Edward. 1979. *Orientalism.* New York: Random House.

Sandberg, Neil. 1974. *Jewish Life in Los Angeles.* Lanham, MD: University Press of America.

Savoy, Ann. 1984. *Cajun Music: A Reflection of a People.* Vol. 1. Eunice, LA: Blue Heron Press.

Schnapper, Dominique. 1991. *La France de l'intégration. Sociologie de la nation en 1990.* Paris: Gallimard.

Schneider, David. 1968. *American Kinship: A Cultural Account.* Englewood Cliffs, NJ: Prentice-Hall.

Schor, Judith B. 1998. *The Overspent American: Upscaling, Downshifting, and the New Consumer.* New York: Basic Books.

Schwartz, Rosalie. 1997. *Pleasure Island: Tourism and Temptation in Cuba.* Lincoln: University of Nebraska Press.

Seydlitz, Ruth & Shirley Laska. 1994. *Social and Economic Impact of Petroleum "Boom and Bust" Cycle*, New Orleans: U.S Department of the Interior, Minerals Management Service, Gulf of Mexico OCS Region.

Sharp, Lesley. 2000. "The Commodification of the Body and Its Parts." *Annual Review of Anthropology* 29: 287–328.

Smith, A.D. 1981. *The Ethnic Revival in The Modern World.* Cambridge: Cambridge University Press.

Smith, Steven. 1994. "The Tourism Product." *Annals of Tourism Research* 21(3): 582–595.

Smith, T. Lynn. 1934. "An Analysis of Rural Social Organization in Louisiana." *Journal of Farm Economics* 16(4): 680–688.

Smith, T. Lynn & Homer Hitt T. 1952. *The People of Louisiana.* Baton Rouge: Louisiana State University Press.

Smith, T. Lynn & Vernon Parenton. 1938. "Acculturation among the Louisiana French." *American Journal of Sociology* 44: 355–364.

Smith T. Lynn & Lauren C. Post. 1937. "The Country Butchery: A Co-operative Institution." *Rural Sociology* 2: 335–337.

Snipp, C. Matthew. 1989. *American Indians: The First of this Land.* New York: Russell Sage Foundation.

Ruggles, Steven, Matthew Sobek et al. 1997. *Integrated Public Use Microdata Series: Version 2.0.* Minneapolis: Historical Census Projects, University of Minnesota.

Sollors, Werner, ed. 1996. *Theories of Ethnicity: A Classical Reader.* New York: New York University Press.

Sowell, Thomas. 1981. *Ethnic America: A History.* New York: Basic Books.

Spradley, James. 1980. *Participant Observation.* Fort Worth, TX: Harcourt, Brace, Jovanovich.

State of Louisiana. 1981. *Official Journal of the Proceedings of the Senate of the State of Louisiana.* Vol. 4. Baton Rouge: State of Louisiana.

Steinberg, Stephen. 1981. *The Ethnic Myth: Race, Ethnicity and Class in America.* New York: Atheneum.

Steltenkamp, Michael F. 1993. *Black Elk: Holy Man of the Oglala.* Norman: University of Oklahoma Press.

Swagler, Roger. 1994. "Evolution and Application of the Term Consumerism: Themes and Variations." *Journal of Consumer Affairs* 28: 347–361.

Tentchoff, Dorice. 1975. "Cajun French and French Creole: Their Speakers and the Questions of Identities." In *The Culture of Acadiana: Tradition and Change in South Louisiana*, edited by Steven DelSesto & Jon Gibson. Lafayette: University of Southwestern Louisiana.

Tentchoff, Dorice. 1977. "Speech in a Louisiana Cajun Community." Ph.D. Dissertation. Case Western Reserve University, Cleveland, OH.

Thibaud, Pierre. 1979. "1972–1974: Deux années de coopération à Mamou (Louisiane)." In *The Role of France, Quebec and Belgium in the Revival of French in Louisiana Schools*, edited by Gerald Gold, 60–81. Projet Louisiane 7, York University.

Thompson, E.P. 1963. *The Making of the English Working Class.* Harmondworth: Penguin Books.

Thompson, Richard H. 1989. *Theories of Ethnicity: A Critical Appraisal.* Westport, CT: Greenwood Press.

Tinker, Edward Larocque. 1932. *Les écrits de langue française en Louisiane au XIXème siècle.* Paris: Honoré Champion.

Tinker, Edward Larocque. 1933. *Bibliography of the French Newspapers and Periodicals in Louisiana.* Worcester, MA: American Antiquarian Society.

Tregle, Joseph. 1992. "Creoles and Americans." In *Creole New Orleans: Race and Americanization*, edited by Arnold Hirsch & Joseph Logsdon, 131–185. Baton Rouge: Louisiana State University Press.

Trépanier, Cécyle. 1989. *French Louisiana at the Threshold of the 21st century.* Projet Louisiane, Monograph 2, Quebec: Laval University.

Trépanier, Cécyle. 1991. "The Cajunization of French Louisiana: Forging a Regional Identity." *Geographical Journal* 157(2): 161–171.

Trépanier, Cécyle. 1993. "La Louisiane française au seuil du XXème siècle: La commercialisation de la culture." In *La construction d'une culture, le Québec et l'Amérique française*, edited by G. Bouchard, 361–394. Sainte Foy: Presses de l'université Laval.

Trouillot, Michel-Ropl. 1991. "Anthropology and the Savage Slot: The Poetics and Politics of Otherness." In *Recapturing Anthropology: Working in the Present*, edited by Richard Fox, 17–44. Santa Fe, NM: School of American Research Press.

U.S. Bureau of the Census. 1932a. *Fifteenth Census of the United States—1930—Population. Vol. 3. Reports by States Alabama-Missouri.* Washington, DC: Bureau of the Census.

U.S. Bureau of the Census. 1932b. *Fifteenth Census of the United States—1930—Population. Vol. 4. Occupations by State.* Washington, DC: Bureau of the Census.

U.S. Bureau of the Census. 1943. *Sixteenth Census of the United States—1940. Characteristics of the Population. Vol. 2 Part 3. Louisiana-Michigan.* Washington, DC: Bureau of the Census.

U.S. Bureau of the Census. 1952. *Census of Population—1950. Vol 2. Characteristics of the Population, Part 18—Louisiana.* Washington, DC: Bureau of the Census.

U.S. Bureau of the Census. 1963. *Census of Population—1960. Vol 1. Characteristics of the Population, Part 20—Louisiana.* Washington, DC: Bureau of the Census.

U.S. Bureau of the Census. 1973. *Census of Population—1970. Vol 1. Characteristics of the Population, Part 20—Louisiana.* Washington, DC: Bureau of the Census.

U.S. Bureau of the Census. 1981. *Census of Population—1980. Vol 1. Characteristics of the Population, Part 20—Louisiana.* Washington, DC: Bureau of the Census.

U.S. Bureau of the Census. 1983. *Detailed Population Statistics—Louisiana.* Washington, DC: Bureau of the Census.

U.S. Bureau of the Census. 1992a. *1990 Census of Population. General Population Characteristics. United States.* Washington, DC: Bureau of the Census.

U.S. Bureau of the Census. 1992b. *Census of Population and Housing, 1990. Public Micro Use Data Samples (5%)* [Machine readable data files]. Washington, DC: Bureau of the Census.

U.S. Bureau of the Census. 1992c. *Census of Population and Housing—1990. Public Micro Use Data Samples. Technical Documentation.* Washington, DC: Bureau of the Census.

U.S. Bureau of the Census. 1993. *Census of Population—1990. Social and Economic Characteristics, Louisiana.* Washington, DC: Bureau of the Census.

Valdman, Albert, ed. 1997. *French and Creole in Louisiana.* New York and London: Plenum Press.

van den Berghe, Pierre. 1981. *The Ethnic Phenomenon.* New York: Elsevier

van den Berghe, Pierre. 1994. *The Quest for the Other: Ethnic Tourism in San Cristobal, Mexico.* Seattle: University of Washington Press.

van den Berghe, Pierre. 1995. "Marketing Mayas: Ethnic Tourism Promotion in Mexico." *Annals of Tourism Research* 22(3): 568–588.

van den Berghe, Pierre. 1997. "Rehabilitating Stereotypes." *Ethnic and Racial Studies* 20(1): 1–16.

Veltman, Calvin & Benoît Lacroix. 1987. *L'avenir du français aux Etats-Unis*. Québec: Editeur officiel du Québec.

Vickers, Scott B. 1998. *Native American Identities: From Stereotype to Archetype in Art and Literature*. Albuquerque: University of New Mexico Press.

Waddell, Eric. 1979. "French Louisiana: An Outpost of *L'Amérique française*, or Another Country and Another Culture?" Projet Louisiane, No. 4, Montréal.

Wade, Peter. 1999. "Working Culture: Making Cultural Identities in Cali, Columbia." *Current Anthropology* 40(4): 449–472.

Warner, R. Stephen. 1993. "Work in Progress toward a New Paradigm for the Sociological Study of Religion in the United States." *American Journal of Sociology* 98: 1044–1093.

Waters, Mary. 1990. *Ethnic Options: Choosing Identities in America*. Berkeley: University of California Press.

Weber, Max. 1922. *Economy and Society*. Vol. 1. Reprint, New York: Bedminster Press, 1968.

Wetsel, David. 1987. CODOFIL et la langue française en Louisiane: Cajun ou Standard?" In *Les Acadiens: Etat de la Recherche*, edited by J. Lapointe and A. Leclerc, 151–169. Québec: Conseil de la Vie Française en Amérique.

Willie, Charles V. 1979. *The Caste and Class Controversy*. Bayside, NY: General Hall.

Wilson, Kenneth & Alejandro Portes. 1980. "Immigrant Enclaves: An Analysis of the Labor Market Experiences of Cubans in Miami." *American Journal of Sociology* 86(2): 295–319.

Wilson, William Julius. 1978. *The Declining Significance of Race: Blacks and Changing American Institutions*. Chicago: University of Chicago Press.

Wood, Robert. 1998. "Touristic Ethnicity: A Brief Itinerary." *Ethnic and Racial Studies* 21(2): 218–241.

Yinger, J. Milton. 1994. *Ethnicity: Source of Strength? Source of Conflict?* Albany: State University of New York Press.

Zhou, Min & Carl Bankston III. 1992. "Variations in Economic Adaptation: The Case of Post-1965 Chinese. Korean and Vietnamese Immigrants." *National Journal of Sociology* 6(2): 105–140.

Zhou, Min & Carl Bankston III. 1995. "Asian-American Entrepreneurship: The Causes and Consequences." *National Journal of Sociology* 9(2): 1–36.

Zhou, Min & Carl Bankston III. 1998. *Growing Up American: How Vietnamese Children Adapt to Life in the United States*. New York: Russell Sage Foundation.

Index

About the Author

JACQUES M. HENRY is Associate Professor of Sociology at the University of Louisiana, Lafayette.

CARL L. BANKSTON III is Associate Professor of Sociology at Tulane University.

www.ingramcontent.com/pod-product-compliance
Ingram Content Group UK Ltd.
Pitfield, Milton Keynes, MK11 3LW, UK
UKHW041130071026
15587UKWH00009B/378

9 780275 978174